Beloved Dissident

EVE SMITH

db db db db db db db db db db db db db db db db db db

Beloved Dissident

EVE SMITH

(1904 - 1988)

Arthur Cathers

Drumadravy Books

db db db db db db db db db db db db db db Blyth Canada

To

EVE GREY SMITH

For friends, colleagues, readers & rabble-rousers. May we all learn from Eve's commitment, integrity, tenacity—and her great caring for the good Earth.

First paperback edition 1997

DRUMADRAVY BOOKS
BLYTH, ON, CANADA. N0M 1H0

Canadian Cataloguing in Publication Data

Cathers, Arthur V.

Beloved Dissident EVE SMITH

ISBN 0-920390-05-6 (pbk)

1 Smith, Eve 1904-1988 2 Politics—British Columbia
3 Co-operative Commonwealth Federation (CCF)—
New Democratic Party (NDP)—social democracy
4 Socialism—democratic socialism—*Socialist Fellowship*
5 Ecology—nature—wildlife
I Cathers, Arthur V. II Title

Text, cover design, back cover photo—**Drumadravy Books**
Photo page 180—Robert Dill
Photos pp 13, 48, 74—British Columbia Archives
Front cover, all other photos—John/Eve Smith collection
Printed & Bound in Canada

Contents:

Eve Smith never tired of this peaceful scene and beautiful view at the foot of the Smiths' small South Pender Island acreage. She worked consistently to preserve the integrity of the island's waterfront and beach areas and keep them open to all.

Preface: **Learning About Eve**

TOO FEW BOOKS CHART THE LIVES of exceptional Canadian women such as Eve Smith. Neither rich nor famous, she was a strong-willed political activist and educator, a naturalist, writer and self-educated ecologist. She was also a vital, personable and unforgettable woman.

I met Eve Smith at her BC Gulf Islands South Pender home in 1973. As a socio-economic policy consultant to the BC government, I was intrigued by her ideas and passionate advocacy as expressed in letters to the press and to government agencies. I arranged to visit and found her reading letters, clipping newspapers and sorting them into filing boxes at her feet.

I marvelled at the extent of Eve's activity and the scope of her interests, her research and contacts. She was then 69, looked about 55, and engaged in a steady flow of correspondence and information exchange on an astonishing variety of topics with interest groups, highly-placed international experts, officials and politicians in the US, UK and Canada.

Eve encouraged everyone to share her vision and her goal of a well informed and democratically-structured society, with each one of us *involved and active*, ever vigilant of the uncaring, profit-seeking enemy—the corporate world—and its sins against our ecosystems and against humanity.

After an afternoon and evening talking and debating non-stop with Eve Smith I understood that here was a person of rare courage and conviction. She did not—*could not*—give up, even after forty years of participation in so many issues—perhaps a few too many issues, given the limitations imposed by her poor health and any one individual's capacity to cope. Why this extraordinary degree of effort and dedication, I wondered.

"Any *responsible* person," she admonished, "simply *has* to be involved." That was the essence of Eve, the tough, forged-in-combat core that distinguished her from the part-timers, the dabblers in social change. She was steadfast, consistent—and *relentless.*

Eve was one of those rare characters who engaged in lifelong learning. She willed herself, despite restricting health difficulties, to keep hard at it. She was strong-minded, tough, sometimes even "a hard-boiled character," according to John Smith, the man who knew her best for over fifty years.

While some of her friends thought her lifelong faith in socialistic solutions was simplistic, Eve knew fairly precisely what she believed and expounded her well-researched views on many issues with dignity, honesty and unwavering conviction.

Eve was well equipped mentally and emotionally for her chosen activities and was not deterred one iota when opponents tried to publicly malign her—as a *rebel, radical, socialist* or *dissident.* She was all of that and she wore such epithets, intended as disparagements, as badges of honour.

She delighted in the Albert Einstein quote I sent her which I felt suited her situation: *"Great spirits have always encountered violent opposition from mediocre minds."*

She found it difficult to suffer gladly the lethargic. She scorned the bright but intellectually lazy who didn't work a fraction as hard as she did—and therefore didn't understand as much or use their talents as effectively or wisely.

I came to think of Eve as a sort of political horticulturist, sowing her many socio-ecological plots, germinating, sprouting and tending a host of hopeful, imaginative and positive pursuits amidst the well-composted soil of her South Pender Island base.

Eve worked hard to gather the potent seeds of accurate information and informed opinion in her reading and from the responses to her letters of enquiry. She was constantly dispersing that knowledge, always prodding and encouraging people, persistently cultivating her many pods of activism.

Selflessly, she shared her small victories, her "good news," her harvest of clippings—*always clippings*—her concern for the environment and her touching, special caring for wildlife, the pressured and "precious creatures" of the natural world.

For many of her innumerable contacts, she became *the* source of the most up-to-date information—"the latest gems"—which she had painstakingly extracted from knowledgeable people.

Most lastingly perhaps, she gave lovingly of her generous spirit to anyone engaged, however tentatively, in the struggles to protect and preserve the natural world which she never ceased to wonder at and which she loved with such rare and honest passion.

That was Eve Smith!

*

In her earlier years Eve Smith never hesitated to speak out, to jump into a leadership position. She would do so, said her partner, John Smith, "at the drop of a hat." Eve was never much concerned with "making a mark" for herself. She never sought election. She was amused to hear talk of "writing her up."

Eve worked with dedication to stiffen the resolve of political comrades through her CCF and socialist education activities from the 1930's to the mid-1950's, and later to advance the work of her many friends in the peace movement providing impetus to the crucial anti-nuclear, pro-peace struggles.

In her later years, she found, I believe, her best niche—and worked to jolt our TV-fogged collective consciousness to a better understanding of countless ecology-related concerns.

Eve's zestful, positive personality and vital work deeply affected a great many friends, correspondents, colleagues and scores of her readers who learned from and treasured her columns and articles. Certainly almost all who met her were touched, and many were inspired, by her uncommon caring and openness, the strength of her commitment and her great love for the good Earth.

Eve was, at once, courageous, provocative, supportive and energizing. While at times bitingly, impatiently critical of those who misused their authority (or their opportunities to give leadership to social change), Eve was better known to her friends as a cheerful, optimistic celebrant of life and hope.

She had a great sense of fun. On one visit I did some dishwashing while I thought she was resting. "Make certain you wash off the soap thoroughly!" her voice commanded from her bedroom. "You mean *every single tiny little bubble?*" I laughed. That was all it took to set her off—*hooting!*

Eve was a link between generations. Undoubtedly she gave heart to many new and younger friends—draft dodgers and military service deserters among them—who came to Pender Island seeking refuge, peace and meaning for their lives. She prodded, encouraged and inspired many of them to greater awareness.

I found Eve Smith to be a person of substance, of character, who had a breadth and depth to her vision and thinking that I had not previously encountered in BC.

A few years later, as publisher of *Northern Times,* a newsmagazine serving Northwest BC, I persuaded Eve to write an educational column. I was delighted then to become her editor. Eve's efforts to educate, and to prevent man-made ecological abuses that would further denude and befoul our fragile estate were almost always sure-footed, consistent and, I felt, quite heroic. She uniquely linked politics, ecology and activism.

I have quoted Eve's words when possible while providing my own and others' views of events, particularly concerning dictatorial 'socialist' régimes, the failures in Canada of social democracy, and the elusive potential of democratic socialism.

Too few such radical, dissident, trail-blazing Canadian women existed. Almost none received appropriate recognition. So I will be pleased if this book helps to rescue Eve Smith's story from the undeserved anonymity which has obscured some of the best of women's radical endeavour and experience in Canada.

Eve would be delighted if the few glimpses of her life that I have here pulled together helped to motivate younger readers to become more involved in the issues of today. She would surely tell us it is our duty, our obligation, our responsibility to do so.

Acknowledgements:

When I was asked to consider writing a book to include Eve Smith's story, her long-time partner John Smith provided reminiscences and the hospitality of his home and garden. I thank him for that and for access to some of Eve's squirrelled-away jumble of papers, correspondence and mid-1980's interviews. I acknowledge Rachel Epstein's extensive work in making and transcribing those audiotapes and the Canada Council for assisting her.

Visiting the University of BC Library's personal archival collections, I was pleased to discover and make excerpts from several files of historical materials donated by Eve and others.

I credit Pat Cathers, Mary Cox, Norman Epstein, Paul Petrie, John & Barbara Taylor and others for auspicating my Homeric labours over many hundreds of uncatalogued papers and scraps of documentation. I thank Norman Epstein for a helpful reading of a first draft of the manuscript, and other friends of Eve Smith for providing interviews and letters. I am grateful to Nova Scotia's Chester Educational Foundation for its interest and support.

— A.V. Cathers, Drumadravy, January, 1997

1 *Dissident, Activist, Naturalist*

EVE SMITH WAS MUCH MORE than the sum of her many activities. Her nature-bound early years on Samuel Island and her firmly held socialist views were key factors in her involvement throughout her life in the great issues of her time, including her efforts to preserve the natural world which was so central to her being. Her work to protect the environment began decades before it became the fashionable, or merely chic, thing to do.

Eve adopted socialist convictions at the age of 28 after surviving a debilitating four-year bout with TB in Tranquille Sanitorium near Kamloops, BC. It was the same year, 1932, as the CCF's founding conference. She became actively involved in the Co-operative Commonwealth Federation and by the 1950's she had become a dedicated socialist educator working within, but often at odds with, the CCF. This "movement" was the closest Canada came to developing a democratic, broadly-based and socialist political party.

Disappointed that the CCF had abandoned its initial flirtation with a Marxist brand of socialism, Eve persisted in fighting the party's slide into the "mixed economy" politics of the CCF's social democrats and their early adoption of a mild form of liberal, welfare state capitalism.

Eve became a leading activist in the short-lived Socialist Fellowship, helping to keep it alive after the CCF leadership had condemned its adherents for their membership in "this party within the party." She joined the Socialist Party of Canada for a time, but was much more at home in such groups as the small but influential *League for Total Disarmament* which she helped to form, and a number of other pro-peace, anti-nuclear, single-issue groups which she found more relevant to her direct action style of advocacy and involvement.

She was deeply involved in the peace movement, adamantly opposing Canada's participation in World War Two and the CCF's support for that war. She was among those who protested

US nuclear warheads coming to Canadian soil at the Comox air base on Vancouver Island and joined an anti-radiation hazards coalition. As well, she supported those who successfully opposed the fluoridation of municipal water supplies.

Eve Smith became a founding member of the BC branch of the *Voice of Women*. She played a leading role as an educator, lecturer and as the BC VOW's Ecology Committee Chair. She wrote countless, meticulously-researched letters, special articles and presentations to government commissions. Over the years, she addressed British Columbians eloquently and passionately on a great many social, political and ecological issues.

A dedicated naturalist and environmentalist, she was also an ardent proponent of saner forestry practices and became a militant defender of wildlife. She was a contemporary and friend of such well known figures as scientist-writer Rachel Carson, who wrote *Silent Spring* (the consciousness-raising shocker that put ecology on the public agenda in the 1950's), and a favourite book of Eve's, *The Edge of the Sea.* Eve also worked to popularize in BC the concerns of Beatrice Trum Hunter, author of *The Mirage of Safety* and many other exposés of governmental laxity in protecting our food.

Eve exchanged letters, information, books and encouragement with these and many other scientists and concerned consumer groups who fought against destructive herbicides, pesticides and hazardous food additives. Trum Hunter sent Eve a copy of her book *Gardening Without Poisons* inscribed: "To Eve, with best wishes for sane, successful gardening. With Love and appreciation, Beatrice." Eve was something of a champion writer of letters to the press and to government officials. She kept her growing list of contacts well informed.

But Eve Smith's story starts and ends on BC's beautiful Gulf Islands. Perhaps the best way to begin to understand the environmental influences that shaped Eve's life is to read from the personal record so carefully maintained by Eve's mother, Winifred Higgs Grey. She was a gentle woman and keen observer who kept a detailed memoir of her arrival and the first few years of her new life on those then becalmed, idyllic and pristine Gulf Islands.

2 *Her Mother's Diary — 1896*

AS TEENAGERS IN ENGLAND, Winifred Higgs and her sister Mabel wrote to and received lively replies from their brother, Leonard, who was joyously struggling to carve out a farm operation from the heavily-wooded wilderness of beautiful South Pender Island.

The acreage Leonard pre-empted was named "Kloshe Illahie" which was Chinook Indian for "good land." He had included a sketch of his log cabin in the bush and photographs of island beaches and himself with friends, and anecdotes of his new life in "the Canadian colony" in 1896.

Winifred and Mabel had never seen beaches like those with old trees, logs and roots strewn about, and were intrigued by their brother's stories of his own and his friends' pioneering activities. When Leonard suggested the sisters make a holiday trip to see this rugged country for themselves, they were enthralled by the idea. They set out in June, 1896.

In due course they arrived at New Westminster and were taken by Leonard to the wharf to board the old sternwheeler, the *Rithet,* for an exciting trip through the swirls and eddies of Plumper (now Active) Pass and down Navy Channel to Saturna Island.

Even at an early age, Winifred was an inveterate note taker. She would meet and later marry the Ralph Grey mentioned in these scene-setting extracts from her diary:

"As it was low tide, the boat could not tie up at the wharf, so several row boats put out in answer to a warning toot to take off passengers and baggage. Mabel and I clambered over the side to find ourselves in a small dinghy with Leonard and Harold Payne whose name was so familiar (from Leonard's correspondence). Arthur Drummond took our trunks. I spied a little canoe drawn up under the trees, and on the beach were Gerry Payne and his sister Polly who was spending the summer with Harold Payne.

8

"It was getting late so Harold Payne said quite casually he would put us up for the night and Mr Drummond would take us and our baggage down to 'the Kloshie' in the morning in the 'Plunger.'

"There were no special formalities, either in manners or dress, and no one seemed to expect any thanks. We were in a new world of strange and unexpected, though delightful, experiences. Gerry Payne rowed us around the point to Breezy Bay; we climbed the steep bank to see his pretty frame house standing about 200 yards back.

"Gerry was a bachelor living with his farm helper, but when he later showed us to a bedroom upstairs, we found the bed made, basin and jug of water, towels and every convenience, and were told to make ourselves at home. We were amazed!

"Mabel and I were up early, too excited to sleep, and Gerry had 'fixed' a good breakfast of bacon and eggs, coffee and toast, which we ate in wonderment at his capability. We helped to wash the dishes, a novelty for us; left our bedroom tidy, and set off for the wharf where Mr Drummond was ready with the 'Plunger.'

"In loading up, a cabin trunk toppled into the water but was quickly hauled out. A little accident like that only added to the thrill of everything. The sail was hoisted but of course we knew nothing then of there being a 'fair tide' or 'tacking with a light breeze.' Down to Blunden Island, through Blunden Channel, we then crossed Camp Bay, passed the Greenhill and Gowlland Point, soon to be familiar, and turned into the 'Kloshie' bay.

"We could see a little log cabin on the bank and there was Leonard's wife, Em, hurrying down the path, while Thomas and Bay jumped from log to log and over the rocks in bare feet. Tom was seven and Bay just three.

"In the afternoon, Lillie Spalding, Arthur's wife, turned up with Hetty, their eldest girl. The adjoining ranch was owned by Arthur Stanford, whom we had known as a boy in Bromley, Kent. His father was the well known publisher of Stanford and Company from whom Mabel and I got a chart of BC's coastal waters and islands before we came out.

"The death of young Perkins from drowning had lately cast a gloom over the islanders. He had been a general favourite and Leonard had written to us about him, amongst others. Gale of wind; inexperienced. Started off to sail in gumboots! Upturned boat found by searchers Gerry Payne, Harold Payne and Ralph Grey.

"Leonard had added a large bedroom to the Kloshie house so Mabel and I could unpack in comfort. When it was fine we took our blankets and slept against a log. It was such a thrill to look up at the stars and wake in the morning to see a humming bird whirring over the patchwork flowers on our coverlets!

"Em, the first white woman on South Pender, has a store-room with many pickle bottles. Em explained they were for preserving fruit for winter. Far in advance of anything of the kind in England.

"There was no forestry department in those days and forest fires raged unmolested, filling the air with smoke and ash for weeks and blotting out all view of the mountains and islands. That summer we had a good deal of rain which kept the fires in check."

"In the early morning of our second day, Leonard took me to the open window and pointed eastward. The smoke, which we had not realized was there, had lifted in the night and revealed the lovely islands—'casting down their golden crowns around the glassy sea.' Towering above them on the horizon the magnificent peak of Mount Baker raised its 11,000 feet high above the Coast Range and Cascade Mountains. A lump came in my throat and tears filled my eyes. It was unbelievably beautiful!

"Arthur Spalding and his family lived about two miles inland. There was no road of course, just a single-file rough trail through the forest. We passed a group of large glacial rocks and a monster known as the Big Rock. Over the hill we stumbled, over loose boulders and roots of trees, down into Arthur's valley, or flat, of fields and cultivated land divided by his snake fences, past his barn built by Arthur Spalding and Leonard Higgs, and then the climb to the house, a nice frame building covered with a vine and creepers.

"There we found Arthur, Lillie and her two younger sisters, Gertie and Aline Mackay, and three little girls, Hetty, Bessie and Bea, the latter about two years of age. They showed us around the place and their lovely flower garden with its fine display of polyanthus. Aline disappeared to make tea and jelly-cake. Mabel and I were astonished that a girl of sixteen could make a cake at a moment's notice.

"Arthur and Lillie Spalding were terrific workers. Arthur ploughed with a yoke of oxen—great clumsy brutes. Lillie kept the three little girls so tidy and clean and their long hair curled. One evening she went down to the flat and shot a deer that had been devouring their crops. Arthur grew wheat for his chickens and used a flail on the barn floor to thresh the grain from the chaff. Of course they longed for a boy and in '99 Herbert arrived, after Mabel and I had returned from England to live here.

"All the islanders raised sheep and lambs to be shipped and sold in Victoria. It was quite a trip for those on Pender to row them up to Saturna to be put on the steamer; the sheep, calves and pigs had their legs tied together.

"Stanford's cow broke her leg wandering among the logs and had to be shot. He got out his wash boiler and he cut up Bossy-cow into convenient pieces and boiled her down till she made meat essence, like Oxo cubes. This he cut into squares, wrapped them in grease paper and sold to his grocer in Victoria.

"Leonard showed us the 'field' at the back of the house. It was his pride because it had involved a lot of heavy clearing, sawing down immense trees and burning the brush. 'Where is it?' we asked, looking around among huge, blackened stumps four or five feet high, with some grass in between, and stepping over the occasional log. 'Why . . . here! *This* is the field.' We had expected acres of lush meadow land, as in England!

"Ralph Grey was away, up the Fraser River fishing. He left Billy Trueworthy to look after his sheep. Most of the ranchers had sheep turned out on the range to fend for themselves, but every now and then they had to be rounded up for ear-marking the lambs. Billy was a master at this job and no one could touch him. He could run for hours, up and down hill, through the woods, till he miraculously got a band of sheep into a corral—with the help of his little mongrel dog. He never seemed to tire.

"From the Kloshie we saw steamers of all kinds plying their trades, an occasional four-masted schooner from Australia with her sails set if there was breeze enough, and the big ocean liners which passed majestically down the strait, glittering white on the blue water.

"The beach was an endless source of interest. Mabel and I often went beachcombing with the Kloshie children. You never knew what you might find, from a canoe to a bundle of stair-car-pet or a crate of lanterns. If you wanted lumber for a pigpen or rabbit hutch, you hunted along the beach and would be sure to find what you needed.

"Mabel and I settled down to absorb island life including picnics, hunting and camping parties. We had never rowed a boat but Leonard put us alone in a little boat to follow the rest across Saturna Channel and past Seagull Islets. We laughed and groaned by turns and made it to Fiddlers Cove, about six miles, for our first row. Another day we rowed to Skipjack Island, the home of thousands upon thousands of gulls. One could hardly put a foot down without treading on an egg or baby bird, they were so wonderfully camouflaged.

"The portage at the head of Bedwell Harbour, Pender Island, was a sort of halfway meeting place for Saturna and South Pender folk. On a picnic outing there the first thing we saw, on running up the bank from the beach, was two dead bucks, their horns interlocked, both entangled in a fisherman's net which had been strung out over posts to dry.

"On an expedition up Jackass Mountain, a sudden wind got up that soon amounted to a gale. We walked single file as trees were beginning to fall in every direction. We counted sixty-nine trees down between Bedwell and the Kloshie.

"South Pender had no wharf and no steamer called. People sailed or rowed. The nearest store and post office was at Saturna wharf, a three mile pull, almost invariably against a head tide.

"One day the men were talking about what chances one had of surviving an upset from a boat in rapids. Mr Warburton Pike, a most reticent man, casually remarked he had 'always found it best to cling onto a sack of flour as it floated a longer time. A sack of sugar soon soaked and sank quickly.' He was evidently speaking from personal experience, though no one had known these things to happen to him.

"A feeling had been gradually consolidating in our minds—Mabel's and mine—that life in England was going to be very tame after this experience, even allowing for the fact that everyone had been in holiday mood. In fact, the seed was sown the day we arrived and had gradually been growing. We would make a home on the islands. We began to make plans and to choose a site for a little house which Leonard said he would have built for us to be ready when we came back the following spring.

"On the other side of Greenhill there was a dear little bay with fairly good beach for a boat and fine garden soil, a grand view of Mount Baker and only about seven minutes' walk from the Kloshie. There we bought five acres and Leonard drew up plans for a house which was to cost $500.

"Reluctantly, out came our cabin trunks, now half empty of the clothes and oddments we had brought for Em Higgs and the children. Into these trunks now went huge clam shells, sea urchins, purple starfish, eagles' feathers, arrowheads, stone hammers, a snake's skin, beaded mocassins, deer's antlers, seagulls' eggs and a very precious puffin's egg—all of which made the Custom's House officers stare when we got home to England. We bid a fond farewell and Leonard went with us to Victoria. As we passed South Pender the next day on the *Rithet* we could see, standing out on the bluff in front of the Kloshie, Em and the children waving towels tied to sticks."

*

Winifred and Mabel returned the next year, 1897, to settle first at *Blue Tarpon* near the Kloshie. It wasn't long, however, before Winifred married Ralph Grey, known in those days as "Archie" (after his initials R.G.). Mabel had a new home built, the *Loggia,* and lived there for a few years before marrying Martin Grainger in June 1908, at Mayne Island, and moving to Esquimalt on Vancouver Island.

Ralph Grey had left his home in Northumberland, England, at thirteen to ship out as a trainee seaman on H.M.S. *Conway*. At fifteen he served as a midshipman in the merchant service on the sailing ship *Multiades.* In the following few years he and his family suffered the enormous loss of three of his older sisters to TB. No wonder, thought Winifred, Ralph so often seemed introspective.

With others from the Gulf Islands, Ralph headed north to the rush for gold in 1898. Nothing panned out for him there—only the thrill of participating in that physically challenging, if romantic, adventure. In '99, R.G. joined a survey party heading for northern BC's Stikine River country. The plan was to plot a rail line for projected mines in the area but nothing came of it.

Winifred and Ralph were wed July 7, 1900, at Harold Payne's place on Saturna Island. A practical man, Ralph had cut hay the day before and it needed turning. Their wedding day was spent making hay while the sun shone—gloriously.

By all accounts, Ralph Grey was a gentle-mannered, well-read man of socialist inclinations. Indeed, he had written occasionally for UK publications about his working class life and travels. He thoroughly enjoyed his outdoor life and the hard work of making a living by farming his Samuel Island homestead.

He and Winifred were able to joke about Ralph's often quiet if not sombre demeanor. "When he looked tragic," said his wife, "I would say, 'Archie, don't be grumpy!' " Then they would laugh.

Ralph did strike some visitors as unusually quiet, almost morose. Friends who knew them well, however, insisted he was a steady, well-contented man who loved his married life on Samuel Island with Winifred and delighted in their two daughters, Contie and Evie. But the loss of three siblings and later his mother to TB had left a deep, sobering mark on the man's psyche.

Ralph and Winifred Grey built a fine family home on Samuel Island. It was solid, well designed, comfortable and boasted an elegant fireplace. In time, Ralph Grey added two bedrooms, a bathroom and a verandah.

Evie Grey had revelled in the natural, wooded, family-farm environment of Samuel Island where living far from friends and neighbours did not seem at all unusual. When the family moved to Esquimalt, Evie started school and became a spirited youngster with a keen interest in athletics. She would rush home to ride a horse and delighted in just roaming about the countryside with her sister Contie and their friends.

3 *Beginnings: On Samuel Island*

EVE WAS FORTUNATE IN HER PARENTS and in the idyllic, rustic setting where they chose to live. Her mother and father were intelligent, even-tempered people. Their home, Samuel Island, where Eve spent her first six years—after her birth in 1904 at the home of a Victoria midwife— seemed to her some sort of magical fantasy land. It was a small, beautiful island wedged between Mayne and Saturna islands, but a huge playground for a child, where Evie could explore almost endlessly and thrill to the wonders of nature's flora and fauna.

Ralph Grey and a friend, George Rutherford, had purchased Samuel Island from a man named Flanagan. George soon moved on to South Africa and Ralph was then able to buy his share.

Winifred Higgs Grey and Ralph Grey, and then their children, Constance and Evelyn, were virtually the only full time inhabitants homesteading on Samuel Island throughout Evie's early years there. There were several Japanese settlers, including Nakamura and his wife Cormi, and another man named Yamaoka, who helped Ralph on the farm, but they would move to work in the Fraser River area in the fishing season.

Ralph had a team of oxen known as "Kimping-Dush" to the children, but Ralph had named the team Kipling and Thrush. He used them for ploughing and gathering hay which he cut by hand with a scythe.

One fine day in Eve's memory, her father came home precariously balancing in his rowboat a tiny donkey he had bought from the Bradley-Dynes family who ran the post office on Saturna Island. The family called her *Alice Pretty Girl* but young Evie had trouble with her c's and r's so the donkey became *Alli Pitty Girl.*

The girls adored *Pitty Girl* and would ride her together. When she'd had enough of them she would simply pitch them forward over her head so they would tumble harmlessly off, preferably into a ditch. More than a pet, the donkey was used by Eve's father for chores such as hauling wood.

Her father, said Eve, "must have been the original non-chauvinist male. He was almost too diffident; he was always so helpful. He had lived alone for some years and was used to baking bread and doing his laundry. Mother said she was quite surprised after she got married and her husband continued doing things around the house, even darning his own socks."

When the girls were babies, it was their mother who helped the father to wash the diapers. Eve recalled that her mother had been mainly in charge of a terrific garden of vegetables, fruit and flowers and "she was very good at outdoor things."

The Grey family had the run, more or less, of the entire island. A few Indians would arrive, stay for a while, and move on. When he was to marry, Ralph invited people from the neighbouring islands to help him with a house-building bee. He cleared a good portion of the smaller end of Samuel Island which was perhaps 500 acres in total, made hay and ran a few cows. They also had a vegetable garden and bartered their produce for the other required staples. That was the way things were done in the early 1900's. People just pitched in, knowing that when they needed assistance themselves, it was usually available.

Young Evie and Contie (who was also known for some time as "Birdie") were brought up in a nurturing home—the family working closely together in a natural environment. No doubt Eve's fond memories of that happy, gulf island lifestyle prompted her return many years later to the islands, to make her permanent home on South Pender. But being relatively alone on Samuel Island was just a natural state of affairs for little Evie. There seemed nothing peculiar or unusual about it.

There were other children in their lives, but getting together was no easy matter. The only way to get around was by boat. They would have to row over to the other islands occasionally to see their friends. On Saturna there were the Gerald Payne and Harold Payne families, each with four children, all within a few years of each other, and the Payne children would pay return visits to the Greys' home on Samuel from time to time.

The Greys had relatives on North Pender and others on South Pender. The latter were the Spaldings who had started a big farm in the valley. Eve's family would simply row over to Little Bay, as they then called it, and walk to the farm. The girls would play with the children there and get to ride in an honest-to-goodness horse-'n-buggy.

On Saturna Island there were just two or three families at that time and a bachelor or two who farmed. There were a few more on Mayne Island. One book suggests most of these people were so-called remittance men, some of them relatively wealthy ne'er-do-wells who had trouble conforming to a restrictive life in England. Their families encouraged them in their great adventure in the New World by providing them with travel money and income support while they established themselves, or failed to do so, somewhere in the colonies. Certainly many of them carved out a good life—some even making a fortune in forestry or mining—in the colonial wilderness.

Others had a less dramatic, perhaps less exaggerated, story. These were people of strictly limited private means, or none, who farmed because they yearned for a peaceful, pastoral lifestyle, or simply because they loved farming.

As far as Eve knew, her father had no private funds other than the money he had invested in their house. Eve's mother received a small income, for a time, from England. But their home was no mere shack-in-the-bush. It was a comfortable, solid, well-designed, well-finished home boasting even an elegant fireplace. Ralph soon added two bedrooms, a bathroom, and a verandah.

As a child, Eve enjoyed corresponding with her paternal grandfather, but her mother's parents were deceased before Winifred married Ralph. After a brief return to England, Winifred and Mabel settled on the Gulf Islands, having set their goals to find good men and live happy lives. Eve's early life was blessed with two special men: her gentle father, and her brilliant, caring uncle, Martin Grainger.

Ralph served for a time as a Justice of the Peace in 1894. Then, fresh from his luckless trip to the Klondike, he set hard to work clearing a portion of the south end of his new property, Samuel Island.

The Indians who moved from place to place on the islands were of lifelong interest to Eve Grey Smith. "Wherever you see the beaches and the banks," said Eve, "you'll see middens where the Indians camped and cooked and ate their food, very often shellfish. You could find arrowheads, spearheads and a sort of mortar and pestle where they ground their maize. They made beautiful baskets and all sorts of things out of deerhide.

"The Indians certainly didn't have our white concept of land ownership. They'd live here in the summer and then paddle away in their big, beautifully-hewn cedar canoes to some more sheltered place for the winter.

"My Dad worked the land on Samuel Island. He didn't dislodge either the Indians or the Japanese who lived in a few shacks, part of the year, on the north end of Samuel.

"There is still one reserve on South Pender Island, a point off to the left of Bedwell, and it's the most beautiful spot on the island. There's a trail and people go out there for picnics. There are reservations on the other islands as well. But they took the land away from the Indians and then gave them these bits of reservations and said: you can live on these few acres."

For years Eve retained a broken spearhead and would speculate for visitors that the notches on either side were simply ornamentation or perhaps represented a number of animals or people killed.

Eve's aunt Lilly, who married her great uncle, a Spalding, was part Indian. "When the first white men came there were far more Indian women than white women, so many of the men lived with or married Indians and had children with them. I do not remember anyone mistreating or talking down to an Indian until much later in life.

"The Indians used to come to Saturna Island to get arbutus knees. This is where the branch grows out of the trunk of an arbutus tree and it makes a very strong support for the inside of a canoe."

Eve describes her sister Contie as "very bright and a born leader. She was two years older and I just followed along happily in her footsteps. It didn't worry me a bit that she got a lot of attention. We got on extremely well as long as we were on the island.

"Mother used to have some help with us and with the house when we were little. Our helper was quite poor and came from some little English city, perhaps straight from a crowded slum area, and she couldn't get used to the isolation of the islands. In those days of course you did all your laundry by hand. If you wanted to wash clothes or have a bath, you heated the water on the stove and poured it into a tub. Mother did much of the outside work, so our helper would care for us kids for two or three hours a day. She liked to take us for walks and let us know what was going on with the plants and birds.

"She was a very interested student herself. At low tide she would take us out onto the beaches and the reefs and show us the clams at one level and the mussel shells at another. You could look at the rocks and see the strata, as it were, where different things lived.

"Mother and Dad never had a lot of money. Mother would make some of our clothes but most of them were second hand. I was quite excited when a bundle of used clothes would arrive from England; they were all new to me."

Evie and Contie would wear long woollen underwear. Their normal habit was overalls but when they wore skirts on occasion, particularly if they faced wintry weather in the boat, their mother would get them into layers of woollen, flannel and cotton petticoats, an embroidered petticoat, and only then the dress and long, black woollen stockings.

It was a memorable event for Evie when her sister first wore beige stockings made of Lisle silk. A friend immediately informed the family that this was certainly improper! Eve comments: "It was known if you were seen in the streets wearing beige stockings that you were a prostitute, especially since skirts were getting shorter. But later beige stockings came very much into fashion and I don't know what prostitutes then did to identify themselves."

It was always a special occasion, as well, when books arrived.

"The books we read, or had read to us, were an important aspect of our lives. Mother read to us every night before bed. She read aloud all the Beatrix Potter books, teeny books with absolutely adorable illustrations."

They had many books about animals, and the fact that they had farm animals themselves and wild deer, birds, seals and whales all around them gave young Evie a very early appreciation and love for animals and a deep respect for them.

"We couldn't find our cat one day and went all over the island looking for it. It had been caught in a trap and that was my first experience of how awful traps are. So we brought our pussycat home and nursed and looked after her.

"Dad was torn because there were quite a lot of mink on the island and they would get into the henhouse; they could chew right through the wire. I'm certain Dad hated doing it himself but he did set traps sometimes.

"We also had a barn cat named *Bicky*. One morning early when Dad and I went down to milk the cow (I was about five), *Bicky* brought her dead baby and laid it at Dad's feet for him to revive. I'm sure that's being anthropomorphic, but that's how it seemed. She was much too old to have kittens. She had one and it was dead. How I wept! We comforted her as best we could."

Ralph kept the heifers to fatten for a few months and then sold them. He would butcher an occasional sheep, calf, pig or deer, but Eve could not remember her father ever slaughtering an animal himself. "I guess Dad was about as good to animals as anyone could be, but in the winter he would shoot a deer for food. He never hunted for fun but there were people on the islands who did. We did some fishing and occasionally at low tide we would get a big crab and dig for clams. But in my childhood there were no oysters on the islands, certainly not on the outer islands."

When Eve's father cleared the land, the cut trees provided a ready supply of logs for their stove, "a proper, big old cast-iron cook stove," their source of heat and hot water. Ralph also built a smoke house where he cured bacon and ham. "And there were wild mushrooms. Oh the beautiful meadow mushrooms! I can remember us going out with three sizes of special wire baskets and we'd each pick these big, pink, luscious mushrooms."

The Greys retrieved driftwood to burn from the beaches. They used cedar for their fence rails because it would outlast fir or balsam or alder. The snake rail fences they built needed neither posts nor nails. They "made do" with whatever materials were at hand.

Eve recalled that she and Contie would even sometimes make their own toys from bits and pieces of driftwood found on the beach. They learned, as well, to make their own play houses "with several rooms in the corners of the snake fences," using boards that had drifted ashore.

In this near-to-natural environment, Eve easily adopted a respectful attitude to the land, the trees and shrubbery and the wildlife and farm animals that surrounded her, and the practice of conserving and reusing materials that stayed with her for life.

4 *Esquimalt: Student and Athlete*

WHEN EVIE GREY WAS SIX, her family moved to Esquimalt where her father had bought two acres of land. They hadn't wanted to move but the kids were ready now for school, and Evie's mother had developed some heart problems and Ralph wanted them to be closer to medical help.

Perhaps a degree too much of isolation and the need that Winifred always felt to be close to her sister Mabel also played a part in the decision to move. Mabel had lived nearby for a time on Samuel Island before heading back to England and marrying Martin Allerdale Grainger.

For the move to land next door to the Graingers in Esquimalt, the Greys hired a tug to pull their scow on which they packed their worldly goods and chattels—including a *cow!*

When the scow-with-a-cow was being unloaded at Esquimalt, Evie and Contie, accustomed to playing in irrigation ditches on Samuel Island, soon found an exciting new place to play. But Evie's mother was appalled to find they had dammed up one of the nearby open sewers and were happily getting down and dirty, so to speak, in the effluent.

About that time a few people contracted diphtheria which was attributed to such open sewers. Eventually the effluent was piped out to the open sea, a practice that continues even now. Years later, most of the beaches on southern Vancouver Island were posted as unfit for bathing.

The Greys lived in tents while a carpenter helped Ralph build their home. He hastened to add an outdoor privy such as they were used to on the smaller island. The girls made friends with a boy next door, Randal Matthews, and he remained a friend for many years. He taught them to stand on their hands and Evie was an apt pupil. The three spent much of their time roaming and exploring the countryside, an activity that Eve always enjoyed.

The girls first attended two private schools and later a public school. Evie was terribly shy about meeting people. Even with school friends she was shy until later in life, partly, she thought, because she had been brought up very differently and because she was somewhat in the shadow of Contie "who was very bright, clever and witty."

Eve remembered that Miss Barton of St. Margaret's private school had terrible difficulty getting good teachers and keeping them during the First World War. All sorts of war work was available which provided somewhat better pay. Eve, nevertheless, enjoyed school and did well in her subjects but she was particularly accomplished in athletics, as was her sister. Contie teamed up with Marge Leaming who was BC badminton champion and they soon became the BC doubles champions.

Contie, a typical teenager, wanted the latest clothes and fashions and was, Eve recalled, "a frightful trial to my mother" who made most of the children's clothes. "Contie started going out with boys much younger than I did. I wasn't much interested in boys as boyfriends; I was interested in playing with boys and running and jumping and climbing trees. Whenever I could I went off horseback riding." Both girls were friendly with another boy in the neighbourhood who was more or less Contie's boyfriend until she went off to England in her late teens.

The Greys' relations in England were somewhat better off financially, and offered to bear the costs of Contie attending finishing school there. This fateful decision was to set the Grey girls on very different life-tracks.

Evie's family had kept that cow from Samuel Island, and some chickens. Her mother and her Aunt Mabel, next door, added ducks and geese to their collective production. People were urged to produce as much as possible so surplus food could be shipped overseas to support the war effort.

Eve remembered a gander called *Murray;* his mate was *Miss Bishop*. Once a year they had twelve eggs and twelve babies which were then sold. Evie and Contie made rabbit hutches and big backyard runs for the rabbits. They kept the older ones as pets and tearfully sold the younger ones as food.

The girls did not get on nearly so well in their new home. They argued a lot and sometimes fiercely. Contie had gone to school first and made friends while Evie was left to herself much of the time. They would often spat at the breakfast table and their mother would have to separate them and send Contie off to school ahead of Evie so they wouldn't fight along the street. But Contie would wait around a corner for her sister and off they'd go to school together quite happily, united against the other girls, the "common enemy."

Evie, in her turn, became involved and very adept in sports. She delighted in riding her horse until her family could no longer afford to feed him. As Eve recalls: "It cost a lot to buy hay and at one point we just couldn't manage it. A friend of ours on Saturna Island offered to take him and just turn him loose on a large acreage of land. In the summer holidays I used to go over and see him. His name was *Meatface*. I would just go to the gate and call him, and wherever he was he'd hear me and come galloping over to me and I'd have a ride.

"Later I heard that he had died because it had been a very dry summer and this man had gone and nobody had thought that the horse wouldn't have water. His creek had dried up and his fence was too strong for him to break down and he just died from lack of water. That was a terrible heartbreak for me. I just thought it was so dreadful that he should die and probably be thinking I should be there giving him water."

There had been a warm friendship as well as a vague family connection between the Greys and Miss Barton and her two friends, the Miss Fenwicks. The three had started St. Margaret's school. But it seems that everyone in those years had a tale of woe. Eve explains the disaster that befell these three educators:

"The *Iroquois* sailed from Sidney around the Gulf Islands three days a week carrying passengers, freight and mail. One day Miss Barton and the Fenwicks were setting out on a trip around the islands and they were on the dock at Sidney waiting with the other passengers. But several people warned them not to go on board because the gulf waters were too rough.

"The story has it that Captain Sears scoffed at that suggestion. He said it was perfectly all right and to come ahead and board the ship. Most of them apparently did, and perhaps just a mile or so out, within sight of Sidney, the boat capsized.

"The *Iroquois* was built with an extra deck that it apparently should not have had, making it top heavy. It also had loose lumber piled aboard and in the storm the lumber slipped across the deck. The two Fenwicks, along with a number of others, were drowned.

"Miss Barton was thrown against a hot radiator and burned her hands very badly and was possibly knocked unconscious. Several boats dashed out to rescue some of the passengers, including the captain, but Miss Barton was not among them. She was found on the beach afterwards and a man gave her artificial respiration for a long, long time until finally she started breathing again and was all right.

"When we heard about it we brought Miss Barton to my aunt's house to stay until she was completely recovered. One scene in Miss Barton's bedroom I remember well. When she was washed ashore her long hair had become incredibly matted—like a kelp bed—so my aunt Mabel didn't attempt to comb it out until her friend was much better.

"Then one day my aunt asked me to get a book for Miss Barton to look at, to take her mind off the combing procedure. So I brought along this most marvellous atlas we had that was in *bas relief*. The mountains were raised on each page and you could see the rivers between the mountain ranges and the valleys and so on. I had never seen an atlas like it, so Miss Barton and I became absorbed in it while my aunt carefully combed out her hair. She had been so badly burned—on the palms of both hands—that it was a long time before she could do much of anything. In fact, I turned the pages and pointed out the features of the atlas. After that we became very close friends."

St. Margaret's, compared with some of the other private schools, was quite a simple place, almost austere. There were wooden buildings with desks and chairs, nothing fancy. But there was a big gymnasium with a ceiling as high as the building. It was here that Evie's athleticism began to shine.

There were three big ropes, two or three inches wide, and the girls would swarm up these ropes. But Evie had a special trick and she was the only girl in the school who could do it, or dared to do it. She would work her way up two ropes to the very top, twist her ankles around the ropes and then slide quickly to the gym floor—upside down! Eve describes the scene:

"Every year, sometime in December, we'd have a gym display at the school with marches and all sorts of athletic stunts with the apparatus, the pommel horse and so on, and I used to do this business of coming down the rope head first. It used to amuse me so much because to me it was so simple and of course it brought

Evie Grey, lean and fit at 17 (in 1921), enjoyed practising athletics at the beach. Here she does a Swedish Drill she learned from a favourite fitness instructor at "St. Maggie's" private school.

A fine athlete in her teenage years, she won several awards in both private and public school competitions in diving and track and field events, including the trophy she holds here.

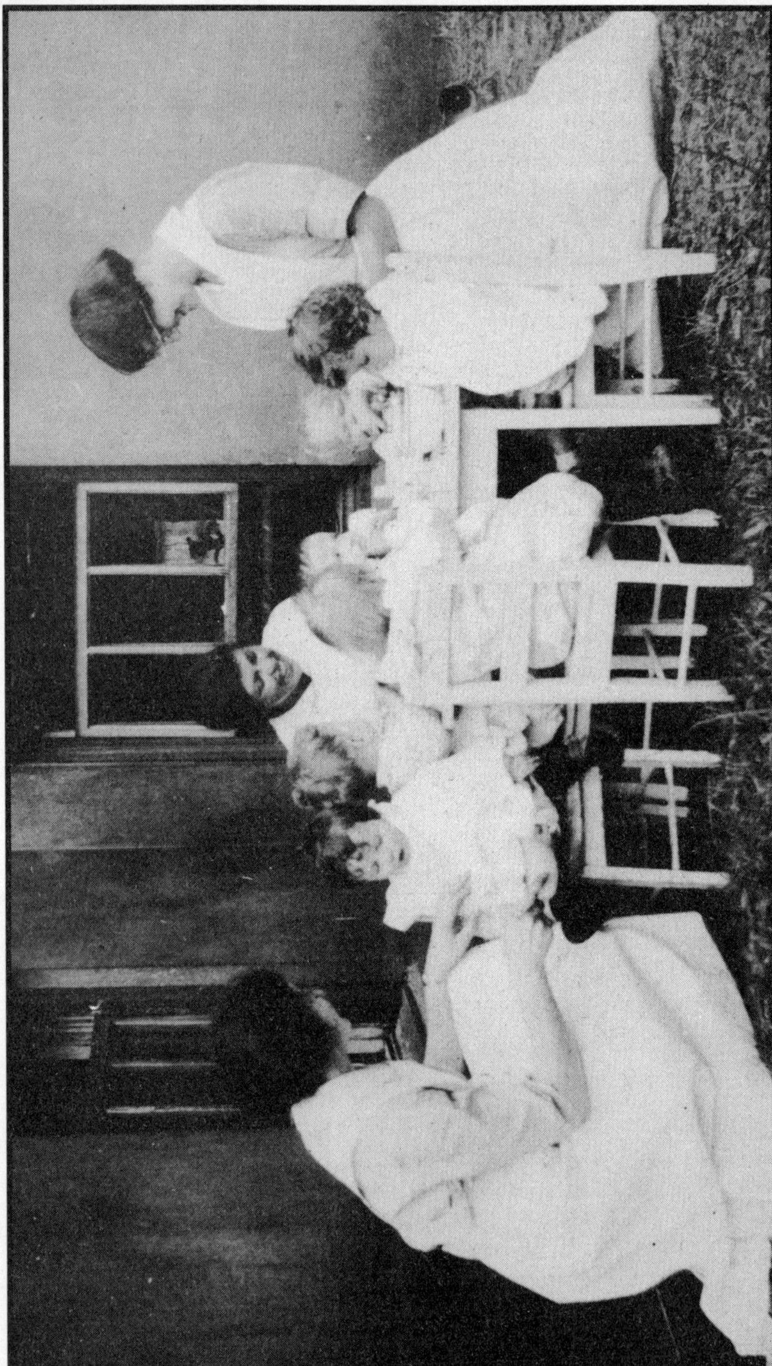

In 1922, Eve took a six months' training program in caring for infants at Vancouver's **Infants Hospital.** *Eve, centre, takes special delight in feeding time for the babies. At left, fellow trainee* **Frances Price.** **Elspeth Bickle,** *at right, became Eve's life-long friend.*

down the house. The audience—all the dear, loving parents, you know—would clap like mad and tell me how marvellous it was, and it was nothing. They used to say to me, 'you're lucky you didn't smash your head!' But I just knew when to stop." Indeed!

On another occasion that Eve remembered with amusement, the boarding house beside the school caught fire. Miss Barton was in the school house with a class when a small child came into the room, very sedately walked up to the director's desk and in a quiet, respectful tone said, "Miss Barton, the boarding house is on fire," just as though she were reporting some minor incident.

Poor Miss Barton: between teacher shortages because of the war, almost drowning, burning her hands, and her boarding school fire, she seems to have had quite a difficult time of it. But clearly, she had a soft spot for Evie.

At one point the Greys could no longer afford the private school fees and Evie attended Lampson Street Public School for two years. Evie returned to "St. Maggie's," however, when Miss Barton proposed to Winifred that her athletic young daughter could attend and no fees would be charged.

"A terrific sports teacher," at the school, a Miss Cotsworth, lost her fiancé during the war. "I remember the day she got the news. She was called into the office and came out looking like absolute death. She went tearing up the stairs three or four at a time with tears streaming down her cheeks and afterwards we were told about it. She was a marvellous teacher who taught us Swedish Drill, a very energetic type of drill—exercising and jumping around—and basketball, netball, grass hockey and tennis."

Despite St. Margaret's lack of facilities, Evie found it to be "fairly snobbish. People who thought they were a little better than others sent their girls and a few of them *did* put on airs."

These were the children of doctors, lawyers and other professionals or of military officers stationed at nearby bases. But there were also a number of students whose parents were off working in the Orient or India, and some of those pupils lost their parents in a Japanese earthquake during the First World War.

During those war years much of what Evie learned came to her from books. Ralph and Winifred were great readers and made sure their children had a good grounding in the children's classics, including the Greek myths such as *Jason and the Golden Fleece*. (One of their boats was called the *Argo*.) Books were prized possessions and the children looked forward with much anticipation and excitement to Christmas and birthdays when they were almost certain to receive special books.

Eve read everything of Dickens, Jack London's *Call of The Wild,* and all of Canadian naturalist Ernest Thompson Seton's books about animals, including *Wild Animals I have Known, Lives of the Hunted,* and *Wild Animals at Home,* all beautifully illustrated by the author.

Of course Evie was particularly interested in books about the Yukon Gold Rush because her father had been among those hardy souls who struggled up the Chilco Pass in 1898. Ralph Grey kept a diary of that adventure and some of his articles appeared in the U.K. publication *The Spectator.* He also wrote a regular column about his travels and jobs in BC, calling himself *The Wayfarer.* Eve notes that her family "also read the *National Geographic,* the *Illustrated London News* and a great variety of books, good, bad and indifferent."

Eve remembers picking books from among the library bookshelves in the sitting room at home and questioning her father about them. He was usually reticent to give his opinions about the books, preferring that his children drew their own conclusions.

Eve recalled that at twelve or so she plunged into the two volumes of *The Workers* and claimed it gave her "quite an idea of the working class." She also recalled reading at fifteen about a woman on the east coast of the US who had plenty of money but decided to wear old clothes and to leave everything behind her, just take a little suitcase with old clothes on her travels across the continents so she could see what it was like to be poor.

"I remember the story so well because this woman picked up whatever jobs she could, working in the most awful circumstances and living in abject poverty, and she could have written home for money at any moment but didn't. *The Workers* gave me another view of what it was like to be in the real downtrodden, exploited working class." Through the years her father, particularly, "had gathered a terrific library," Eve recalled, "including many fine poetry, philosophy and history volumes." Eve inherited some of her father's books and many of them are carefully inscribed with his notes, comments and queries, a practice she adopted.

Ralph Grey first became involved politically as a Home Rule proponent while working in Ireland with his father. For whatever reasons, "Archie" Grey seems to have confided little to anyone about these early years working in Ireland or his youth in Northumberland. Later, he became a member of the Socialist Party of British Columbia before getting married. Still later, he joined the Co-operative Commonwealth Federation led by J.S. Woodsworth, and took great pride in Eve's active role in the CCF.

"Dad had a number of terrible jobs during the war," Eve said, including work at the Yarrow Shipyards. He was patriotic and supported the war and even got into the army for a couple of years, but he did so more for the compensation received rather than the strange job he was given: operating the searchlights at Esquimalt Harbour. These searchlight batteries had been built right into the rock and were intended to light up the Juan de Fuca Strait toward Cape Flattery and illuminate any encroaching ships or submarines.

"It was so ridiculous; they hadn't got a gun that could shoot more than a couple of yards, and British Columbia had one tiny submarine that wouldn't even submerge!" That was Eve's later view of Canada's west coast defence posture through much of the First World War. She was only ten when the war started.

Ralph also worked for brief periods in low-level forestry office jobs but, although he was a studious man who could write well, he had no interest in or particular facility for office work.

His brother-in-law, Martin Grainger, was then busily drafting new and comprehensive forestry policy and regulations for the newly created Forest Branch. Both men wanted to avoid any suggestion of nepotism but Grainger no doubt informed Ralph about jobs coming up, assisting him to that extent. Ralph missed life on Samuel. Winifred was happy again to be close to her sister.

"Really, our lives were fairly calm," observed Eve. "We went to Esquimalt in 1910 and we left in 1918. Those were my school years. I never did anything very brilliant. I used to come out near the top of my class but I never was a scholastic genius.

"Mother and father were incredibly shy. They didn't ever talk about sex, for example. When I started to menstruate I didn't know a thing about it. When I asked mother about it she said, 'Oh well, that's just quite natural.' She just quietly reassured me. Commercial sanitary pads were then an unaffordable novelty, so you just made your own pads with towelling or some such material and wore an elastic around your waist.

"Mother just said: 'You see, this is how babies are made; you stop menstruating when you're pregnant.' Being the tomboy, harum-scarum type that I was, I was late in becoming curious about sexuality. On the other hand, having been brought up with lambs and calves and so on, I just accepted things as they came."

Ten when the First World War started, Eve remembered "there was a lot of patriotism and much war work going on." Once a week the girls would go to a neighbour's house and sit around rolling bandages and knitting socks for some unknown soldier-recipient.

"We'd put our name and address in them and we'd get letters back thanking us. I kept up a correspondence with three men and I met one of them once. He was married, came back to Victoria, and my mother took me to see him and his wife one day. They lived in a tiny, tiny little cottage in a neighbourhood where all the families were very poor. And I thought, this is what happens to a man who gives four years of his life fighting for King and Country and Democracy.

"When soldiers came home from the war, people in Victoria organized reception committees. My mother and I went down once to observe the scene at the CPR wharf where a ship was arriving, and it would be funny if it hadn't been so tragic. There were these three ladies who were the reception committee. Just six soldiers came off that particular boat, three of them on crutches and others with their arms in slings or heads bandaged. I'll never forget these ladies standing there shouting 'Hoo-ray, Hoo-ray, Hoo-ray,' and these soldiers drowning in embarrassment. It was pathetic."

So there was much about war, and people's attitudes concerning war, that bothered Eve as a youngster and she continued to be troubled, much later, by what she considered the stupidity of national leaders in the events leading to World War II. She would point, accusingly, to the corporate greed of industrialists and underscore the culpability of the politicians who, for reasons Eve thought totally unrelated to the precious lives of young Canadians, had the power to conscript them and send them off to be killed—and they did so, she felt, without remorse.

5 *Caregiver, Nurse in Training*

INCLUDED IN WINIFRED'S NOTES, kept in a scribbler and later transferred to her "remembrance book," was this early indication of a career path for young Evie Grey:

Overheard (Contie at 6, talking with a young friend.)

Small girl, aged 6: "When my sister grows up, she's going to be a nurse."

Second small girl, not yet 6: "What are you going to be when you grow up, married?"

First girl, with decision: "No! I'm going to be a lady!"

The next day, Contie produced, for her friend, the future nurse—her sister Evie, aged 4!

Whether the child of four had already set her mind on nursing, caring for children was the teen-aged Evie's first form of gainful employment. Before the family left Esquimalt, Eve would take occasional jobs looking after the children of friends and neighbours or doing housework on Saturday mornings for sixty cents an hour.

Her family lived in one of the poorer middle-class neighbourhoods and Eve was sure she was the only one from that area going to a private school. She often received high praise and commendation from the parents of her charges. This was the case with her first such job in Vancouver where she looked after the baby of a woman who was about to have another child, a homebirth.

Her family moved to Vancouver after the war mainly because Eve's aunt and uncle had moved. Martin Grainger had become secretary of the Alberni Pacific Lumber Company and then had gone into business on his own. Eve's mother, Winifred, and her sister Mabel, more or less inseparable most of their lives, again seized the opportunity to be close to each other.

The Grey family lived first in three rooms upstairs in a private house in the Dunbar area, then moved to a rented house on 16th Avenue just off MacDonald. Eve recalls the area was just being built up with bungalows but on the east side of MacDonald "there was the most lovely swamp with little trails running through it, and you often saw pheasants and lots of birds there among the scrub bushes. Between MacDonald and Arbutus there were acres of lovely swamp—just beautiful land—and when it wasn't too wet, there were trails you could take winding through the bushes."

Eve quickly realized her inadequacies in coping with children, especially with sick kids, so she signed on for six months' training at the Infants' Hospital, a separate hospital for sick children up to two years of age. She wanted the training to acquire greater confidence, authority and responsibility—and this was typical of Eve.

"There were some children's specialists who came to look after the babies there, including the famous Dr. Kinsmen. The Kinsmen Clubs and foundation were named after him. And I made another lifelong friend, Elspeth Buckell, who later married Bill Atkinson and had a daughter, Patricia."

The nurses at the hospital were in training from Vancouver General and there was a graduate head nurse in charge of each floor. The Infants Hospital was subsequently disbanded but the training Eve took there, along with the girl she had known best in Esquimalt, was considered "a very good experience, quite practical training."

"I remember some of the babies were so terribly ill with pneumonia. We had a super-heated steam room with steam from kettles so they didn't have to use up their strength keeping their bodies warm. They used to just gasp for breath. It was just dreadful to see these babies so sick when there was so little you could do for them."

Eve then took a job in Cranbrook looking after a child, Nancy Miles, who had infantile paralysis, known now as polio. The child's mother had written to the hospital and asked for a nurse. "My friend, Elspeth Atkinson, wanted to charge $60 a month but Mrs Miles thought that was too much. I went for $40 a month which seemed a fortune in those days.

"It was live-in with everything found. I had my nurse's uniform and they did my laundry. The money was completely mine since I had no expenses; they even paid my fare to Cranbrook and I lived in their home.

"The child was nine years old and paralyzed from the waist

down along with her left arm, so that her head and her right arm were not paralyzed. Her chest and abdominal workings were O.K. and nothing was wrong with her digestion. While I was there a Dr Green, an extraordinarily good doctor and a very fine fellow, taught me how to give Nancy certain kinds of exercises. They put rings hanging from the ceiling and she would put her arm in the ring and twist it around, and then I would do massage. She also had a little electrical massager which ran on a battery (you wet a sponge on this little buzzer thing) and I would massage up and down her arms and legs.

"She had this paralysis just a few months before I knew her and they had a graduate nurse for a while but I was a good deal cheaper and perfectly good enough. Her mother would give her about two hours of schooling every morning and she and I used to do some French together and we would read to each other. After lunch we would both have a rest and then I would take her out, bundling her up in a little hand sleigh and just haul her around town. Well, she was just the most popular person in town; everyone just adored Nancy Miles.

"Everyone said hello and gave her things and we would get in free to the Saturday afternoon show. She had two sisters who were also very friendly. Their father was a dentist and they also had a live-in maid who had her meals with me in the kitchen. They just wanted to be a family on their own, you see. My mother was sort of insulted by this, me eating with the maid, but why not? We got on fine together.

"I slept in Nancy's room because sometimes she needed help in the night. I also had a teeny room upstairs where I could rest in the daytime. It had been the master bedroom dressing room—about the size of a couch.

"I didn't make friends with any boys and didn't go out much except when a few of their friends would ask me out occasionally during the eight months I was there. My main recreation was riding. The doctor would loan me his horse whenever I wanted to ride which I sometimes did in the afternoon, or I would go skating or off for walks in the country with other girls I met.

"We would just head out of town a little way sometimes and make our own ski run. I borrowed the skiis and I had never skiied before or since, but I loved it. I had no trouble, you see, because I had bicycled and roller-skated so I had the necessary balance. I remember shooting between the trees. You know, it was just heaps of fun!

"The doctor's gardener used to take us out sometimes with a sleigh and team of horses. When the snow went off, the doctor's wife and this fellow took Nancy and me and taught me how to drive. Those old Fords, those 'Tin Lizzies,' were accelerated by hand with a lever on the steering wheel and you changed gears just by the pressure of your foot. But I never did have a driver's licence, not until I got a car of my own in the 1940's.

"But the interesting thing about Nancy was her swimming. The doctor arranged with the manager of the swimming pool for a time when nobody else was there in the morning. I would swim on my back holding her up under her arms and get her to move her legs and arms as much as she possibly could. In that way she got some use of her legs and her left arm and she soon managed to swim. Before I left she was able to swim across the pool on her own. She couldn't walk and couldn't stand up but she had braces made for her later which made her mobile.

"Nancy was a terrific person. I met her one day at a theatre in Vancouver and she was pulling herself up the stairs by the railing and she had these awful braces around her waist and down her legs and when she sat down she would have to undo a hinge at the knee.

"It was just about this time that an Australian nurse started the therapeutic practice of paralyzed people swimming. She really promoted the idea of putting people into the water just when this doctor in Cranbrook had started it with Nancy. And swimming then became a regular part of the treatment for infantile paralysis.

"Mrs Miles was a very positive person and they had taken their child's frightful tragedy in their stride. She never let Nancy feel sorry for herself; they just treated her as normally as possible. There wasn't a great fuss made over her. She was just one of the family and got around the house in her wheelchair. I would carry her upstairs to the bath every day and she would come down by herself just sitting on the stairway with her right hand on the railing, letting herself down stair by stair. Her mother told me I was better than the older nurse they had because I enjoyed doing things with Nancy, just as two companions. I wasn't the boss or the nurse so we got on very well indeed. Mrs Miles took a maternal interest in me—and it was only the second job I had."

Eve left to go home for a holiday and because her mother was ill in hospital after a hysterectomy. "In those days this was a fairly major operation and it took up to a year to recover from it." The doctors had also diagnosed an edema of the brain which caused Winifred to lose her power of speech sometimes. Eve had to write to Mrs Miles and tell her, regretfully, that she couldn't go back—but they corresponded for years.

Later, Nancy attended classes at UBC. "There was always someone who would volunteer to carry her books, so she'd be on her braces and crutches and just go galloping off. She graduated and must have been the first woman in BC to call sports on radio. She went back to Cranbrook and reported sports, play-by-play, as they were happening."

Eve's mother had been living for a time with Mabel in Kensington Place and Mabel paid for the services of a night nurse. Eve went every day to see Winifred and help look after her. "My aunt was getting on in life herself and I'm sure it wore her down to have an invalid in the house, and a nurse and me under foot as well, even though it was a large apartment. She put my mother into a nursing home in Kerrisdale, but I wasn't happy about her being there. The doctor said she might live two years, or maybe just two months, so we decided to bring her home to our small, four-room house.

"She came in an ambulance. Brought up the stairs on a stretcher she said, 'Oh, this is a home; how nice to be in a home!' It was one of the last complete thoughts she expressed. It was heavenly spring weather, and every day I would bring her fresh flowers from the garden and she would sit in a chair looking out the window. She loved porridge and cream and she would say, 'Oh, cream!' She wasn't able to read.

"Mother did require a lot of nursing care at that point. I had to keep turning her and bathing her. My husband Don, or his brother John if he was there, would lift her onto her bedpan and she would look up so sweetly and say, 'thank you,' rather like a duchess thanking her butler for handing her a cup of tea on a silver tray. They were both very good to her. Don came home one day with a bag of donuts and she took one and thanked him sweetly. She was capable of saying only a few words.

"It was a strange illness that I've never seen in anyone else. She had gradually lost her capacities to walk or eat or anything else. She would go into one of those comas and slowly lose the ability to talk. She would forget words and slur her speech. I found that I could comprehend her long after other people could not; even if I could understand only a few words, I could figure out what she intended. Then she'd just go into a complete coma, the longest lasting for weeks. With her in that condition I couldn't possibly handle her at home so she was in hospital three or four times.

"I have always treated people who are unconscious or who have had strokes as though they know what's going on. You'll sometimes see doctors and nurses talking in front of a patient when that patient's unconscious. Well, I think that it's essential to talk so that whatever you say you wouldn't mind them hearing. And I still feel quite strongly about personal contact. You hold their hand or you stroke their arm and let them know that you are there even if they seem to be quite unconscious.

"I remember once, years later, when my aunt was ill at home in her own flat after my uncle died. I was looking after her. If I heard her moving in bed I'd get up and go in and just sit on her bed and let her know I was there, or I'd wash her face or something. She told me quite a while afterward that she was sure I'd saved her life just by being there and letting her know I cared by taking her hand and washing her face. She knew, even when she was practically unconscious, that somebody was there, that there was some human contact."

Eve's loving care was required for three long years of her mother's illness. "Just when you thought that you couldn't comfort her and that her brain was going, she would gradually come out of it. This was very hard on Dad. He felt terrible about Mother but he didn't put it into words very much and I think I could have been of more comfort to him but I was concentrating on Mother."

Then Winifred made a quite remarkable recovery, so much so that Eve was able, finally, to enter nursing at Vancouver General Hospital. Her mother had a relapse later and the illness started all over again.

But once again she recovered and was amazingly well for years; she did the cooking, read lots of books, even wrote a little; they went for long walks and she was again quite involved and interested in life." For years it was an on-again, off-again, series of illnesses with Eve willingly, caringly involved with her mother and rejoicing with her and her father at each recovery. But the final, prolonged illness no doubt also took its toll on Eve.

When her mother died, said Eve, "We were all just so grateful that she hadn't lingered on any longer. She was 79 and during her final illness she suffered very little mentally. It had been much worse during her first illness, for example, in the 1920's. It had been a real horror, just agony. She had terrible hallucinations and I would sit with her for hours trying to explain things to her."

Through it all, Eve's determination to make herself useful and helpful to others—an approach to life perhaps set in her consciousness as early as four—had kept her on course to train as a nurse.

But she had not expected this to be a time for romance.

Eve entered her nurse's training at Vancouver General Hospital. Her parents pleaded to have her kept out of the TB wards. Perversely, the training staff soon put her to work with the very worst tubercular cases in the hospital basement where Eve soon contracted TB.

Eve and Ralph Grey enjoyed a strong daughter-father relationship.

6 *First Love, Hawaii, Tranquille*

UNEXPECTEDLY, LOVE WALKED IN. Eve soon became formally engaged to a man who had come to Canada to review our timber operations.

She met Ronald MacEwan at her Aunt Mabel's home when the young Scot was working and studying the lumber industry under the tutelage of her uncle, Martin Grainger. But Ronald would go off into the woods for weeks at a time to examine logging practices from scratch. His father, still in Scotland, was involved in the timber game and had sent his son to scout Canadian methods.

"Ronald wasn't earning any money, not that that worried me in the slightest. But we were soon very much in love; we became conventionally engaged. We used to climb Grouse and Hollyburn mountains. We'd take the bus from the little ferry that used to go from Vancouver over to Ambleside and you could get down to the beach in different places. That was where he actually proposed to me, on the beach in West Vancouver. An *official* proposal!

"He was very reserved and shy, but one of the nicest people I ever knew in my life. I had taken sandwiches and he remarked on how clever that was, to think of making sandwiches—but that was part of my life because I often used to go on picnics. Then I did what I've done all my life. Whenever I saw water, I would go into it, so I took off my shoes and stockings and rolled up my skirt and went paddling in the water. When it was almost time to take the bus back he asked if I would marry him. I said, 'Well, we do get on very well, don't we?'

"What interests me now looking back on it is that I was brought up in many ways just to be natural, without inhibitions or false ideas of sex. It was rather like religion in our family, a non thing, not discussed. But as soon as I realized that we were in love, I became quite affectionate; I think I'm naturally that way. So when we got onto the bus I took his hand and led him right to the back where we were alone and I put my arm around him and he put his around me and I have an idea that he was slightly embarrassed.

"I'm told that Scottish men are quite shy and reserved. Anyway, in those days you wouldn't just fling yourselves at each other. There wasn't any instant sex when I got engaged to him. Whenever he was back in town from his field work he would come to see me and, when I could get time away from my training, we spent time together.

"On one occasion when I was off duty and in my bedroom, the call came to my floor to say that I had a visitor. Of course I knew who it was and I went flying down the stairs past one of my friends who said, 'Don't scream!' because I had a habit of screaming with excitement. Ronald was in the big rotunda and I threw myself into his arms. We used to have lovely times. If I had an hour or two off duty we'd visit people or we'd walk up Little Mountain and walk around the woods there at the reservoir.

"Then he had to go back to Scotland. His father called him home and later sent him to Siberia to study the timber business there. This was after the Russian Revolution and the people he worked with lived in the former czar's summer hunting lodge which they had commandeered. He used to write wonderful, long letters about this and sent a postcard photograph of this lodge which looked more like a palace than a lodge. He had to walk miles to mail a letter and I got a letter every week."

When Ronald announced his intention to return to Scotland, Eve had wanted to chuck her training and go with him. "I didn't care a scrap that he was broke; you know when you have training as a nurse you can always do something. And I didn't care anyway. He wanted me to go with him but I dutifully gave in to my family's suggestion—we were more prone to do that in those days—that I finish my nurse's training and have that behind me."

The choice to take the training was made with the support and encouragement of her parents and despite the forebodings of her father who had lost his mother and three sisters to TB in England.

Eve was influenced by the six months' taste of nursing education at Infants Hospital which had affirmed her developing sense of caring and humanity. (Her rebellious cry of outrage against the inhumanity of her country's social system that would abandon hundreds of thousands of the poor and unemployed to their own devices was yet to come.)

The training staff had given apparent lip service to her parents' plea to keep Eve off the TB floor during her training but, perversely, had put her to work nursing people with advanced TB in the basement ward. That was a shocking environment for sick people and their nurses, indeed much worse than the TB wing where at least some cursory precautions were then taken.

"There were people with gonorrhea, people with advanced cancer and TB, drunks and drug addicts. It was down below the surface of the ground with windows facing onto an enclosed concrete area, so it was dark and poorly ventilated. One woman drug addict had marks all over her arms from injecting cocaine. She also had TB and used to cough and spit and wipe the spittle with her hand on the wall. We would wash it off with antiseptic and wash her, up to six times a day."

While in training, Eve's health suddenly broke down. She developed what her doctor called "pleurisy with effusion" and he had to insert a needle between her ribs into the pleural cavity to drain off the fluid. She was only twenty-three and had previously enjoyed the robust good health of a fine young athlete.

Eve was scheduled to complete her training the following year, 1928, but it was not to be. She was granted a leave of absence of six months from training. Then, for some unclear reason, but probably related to the fact that her mother, Winifred, had travelled to Hawaii in 1908 to recuperate from a health problem, it was thought that moving Eve to Hawaii's climate would be good for her. Eve later felt this was probably a terrible mistake.

With her sister Contie and her mother, Eve travelled second class to Hawaii aboard the *Niagara* and was sick all the way. She went immediately to hospital and was properly diagnosed there for the first time.

"The doctor said to me, 'Did anyone tell you that you have TB?' So I asked which lung it was and he said, '*both* lungs!' I asked what was going to happen and he told me I'd be in bed at least a year. I was in bed *four* years."

After a couple of weeks in hospital in Honolulu, Eve was moved. "They took me in a funny old truck, bumping up and down on a mattress on a wooden contraption, to the Leahi

Hospital, a TB sanitorium on Diamond Head. There was an awful lot of TB among the native Hawaiians. (White sailors had brought TB, gonorrhea, syphilis and alcohol to the native people.)

"First I was in a room with a lot of other people, then moved to this corner room in the main building. There were no windows or doors, but just openings. The doctor used to come in one opening and nip out another. There was no sort of privacy, even for sitting on a bedpan—not that it worried me.

"I was there for three months and it was lovely. The trees and vegetation were so beautiful with hibiscus and night-blooming cyrius. There were chamelions and lizards crawling up the walls. I loved them. My sister had married and was pregnant, so returned to Canada to have her baby while Mother stayed with me. We wrote back and forth to poor Dad but it was a difficult time for him."

Indeed, it must have been a terrifying period for Ralph Grey. Having lost five of his immediate family to the TB scourge, he now feared for the life of his beloved Evie. He wrote this thoughtful letter to her while she was in the sanitorium at Honolulu:

To Evie, my darling little girl:

I am often thinking of you. I try to find little items in the papers, comic or otherwise, that may interest or amuse you, but my thoughts for you go deeper. I think of the great fight that you are making, consciously or unconsciously, for self-control and self mastery. It is the greatest fight one can make and is demanded of us in many different circumstances and situations, and in none perhaps more difficult than yours. Whether I mention it or not, or how much or little you may realize it, you have to go thro' with it. It is the law of nature and life, and carries its consequences for us for good or ill according to the manner in which we face it, but there is no doubt that those who come thro' the trial, as I am sure you will do by virtue of your natural character, are the better and the stronger and more fitted for the responsibilities of life.

"It is hard that one like you, young, hopeful and with a good and honourable life behind you, should be called on to face such an exceptional emergency. There is more in life than is on the surface. There is an inner life, with which our best thoughts and efforts are concerned, and, whatever theories we may have about it, the essential thing is to face it with an open mind and honest endeavour and make the best of it as members of the human brotherhood, units of social life. My object in writing this is not to depress your mind with dark thoughts and the sense of insuperable difficulties, but to cheer and encourage you with the thought that there is good in the things of evil aspect and a hopeful element in our dark human problems. We are in touch with the good that pervades the universe, as well as the evil, and can work with and for it. I have little doubt that you will fight your battle and find your way better than I can tell you, but a little human sympathy and fellow feeling is sometimes acceptable and your old father longs to be in touch with you and help you. —Dad

*

"The nurses were of mixed Japanese, Chinese, Hawaiian parentage. They were very good and I liked them very much. I don't think they were as meticulously trained as at the Vancouver General Hospital. They were of every colour and hue; all sorts of people went to live in Honolulu. *Harpa haute,* half-white."

Dr. Strong, the TB specialist at VGH who had misdiagnosed Eve's illness, sent several cables to the doctor at the Honolulu San instructing that Eve be shipped home. Eve's doctor kept cabling back to say she wasn't well enough, but after three months he felt she could tolerate the voyage home.

"The people of Hawaii have this charming custom of putting leis around your neck—lovely wreaths of flowers. Well, I think every nurse in the place put flowers on me! Some of them were of paper and just beautifully made. I had some of them hanging in my room for a very long time."

Eve must have looked terribly ill, but managed, as almost always, to retain her sense of humour.

"As I was wheeled off the boat after the voyage from Hawaii to Vancouver I heard a child say, 'Mother, is it a deader?'

"I was put into bunk 13 in the railcar and I was told that it was seldom rented out because of people's fear of bad luck. Luckily, I wasn't the least bit superstitious, but it did strike me as funny, when I was so sick and on my way to the sanitorium, to be put into bunk 13!"

*

The Tranquille Sanitorium, near Kamloops, seemed to Eve to be a very well run institution. TB at that time was rampant. Many nurses were getting it because precautions were either nonexistent or not effective in the hospitals. There were *fifteen* other nurses at Tranquille Sanitorium when Eve was admitted.

The lack of appropriate protective measures in the TB wards, and hospitals generally, became a major public scandal! The public health authorities finally tightened up considerably on precautions.

Eve was met by an ambulance and taken to the women's building. There was also a men's building and little cabins which patients were transferred to when they were well enough to get up and walk around. They had their own laundry, kitchen and dining room and their own farm which produced quite a lot of the vegetables, fruit and bacon consumed by the patients. "Actually," said Eve, "the food was good."

"One of the jokes was that we used to be served bacon and it was usually too salty to eat so we mostly left it on our plates. So I wrote a piece for the monthly *Tranquillian* magazine which published articles to teach us about TB. My article was some nonsense about this bacon going into the slop buckets from our plates and back into the pigs and we'd soon get it back as bacon again—and they published it.

"We were expected to learn something about TB and how to take care of ourselves. We took our own temperatures, for example, and reported them. We had breakfast brought to us on a tray, except for patients who were well enough to get up and walk to the dining room. If you were up for one meal a day, you dressed, ate in the dining room and then undressed and went back to bed. The same if you were up for two meals a day. Between times you were in bed. About 10 a.m. we had a complete hour of rest with no reading and no talking. The rest of the time you could read or write. After lunch we would rest from 1 to 3 p.m. The patients who were called 'strict bed' just didn't get out of bed at all. That was my category for quite a long time, strict bed. The system was based on gradual change as you gained strength. Later, when I was allowed to get up to the toilet once a day, that was a big deal!

"In those days there were no drugs. The treatment was good food and rest. But an awful lot of people died. You feel frightfully weak and tired. It's an effort to hold a book to read. If you have pleurisy you have a lot of pain but my pleurisy was cured. I never had much of a cough, but shortness of breath made everything an effort. We'd have another rest period after supper for an hour and a half and then you could have a visitor.

"I think my mother managed to come up once but much of

that time she was ill. My Dad came a couple of times and I occasionally saw a friend going through that part of the country but you would go for months without seeing anyone other than the people in the san. We could listen to radio on headphones. We listened to Lux Radio Theatre and the Philadelphia Symphony once a week and the CBC carried a good music program every morning."

Eve also had much treasured time for reading. Her interest in many topics was stimulated or reawakened by the librarian at Tranquille, an older man and ex-patient who had one collapsed lung. He used to go around all the buildings with a wheeled cart full of books and he would sit and talk with Eve and often suggested books for her. She read the plays of George Bernard Shaw and the stories of John Galsworthy.

"I read Upton Sinclair's *Oil,* all about the oil rackets, and *The Jungle* which is about the Chicago stockyards and meat-packing plants, books exposing the exploitation of the working class, their terrible working conditions and the profiteering and cheating and cupidity of the private owners of industry. He exposed the ghastly unhealthy conditions in this very centre of the meat-packing industry in the U.S. One significant reaction at that time was people were horrified to think that they were eating this unclean meat."

Being at Tranquille, Eve lost touch with many of her old friends from Victoria but she did make a number of new friends in the san, including several of the nurses. Eve had one room-mate who painted a little but was quite obsessive about art. She bought all the books on art that she could lay her hands on. She was a good friend of Eve's for years after Tranquille and did much to stimulate Eve's budding interest in art and artists.

Eve tended to be philosophically positive—remarkably so—about whatever might happen to her. She maintained her gentle sense of humour along with a basically cheery personality and optimistic view of life. Being isolated tended not to upset her very much. But patients who had frequent visitors from nearby Kamloops, so busy and talking so much about their activities, were constantly reminded of their disabilities.

Eve and her friends used to put on little playlets on the stage in the big hall and people would come from Kamloops occasionally to entertain with a play or music, and then they started showing movies once a week. People would play cards and other games and listen to a quiz show over the radio and have their answers collected and the scores reported.

With her mother ill, her sister away in England, and her father sometimes unwell and working hard to make ends meet, she had few visits from her immediate family. It was all the more important then for Eve to receive this letter from her loving father—prophetic in accurately describing Eve as a later generation would perceive her: "brave, true-hearted, loyal."

Sept. 14 - 1931

My Dear Little Girl:

I have a sort of idea that my end may be pretty near at hand, and I want, before I pop off, to send you my love.

How inadequate such a message is to tell you all I think of you, of all the longings in my heart for you, my wishes for your welfare and happiness, and my deep regrets that my continual hope and desire to see more of you before I go, seems forever to be frustrated.

However, there is no good whining; one has to submit to fate. I have great satisfaction in believing that, whatever lies before you, you will always be the same brave, true-hearted and loyal woman that you have always been, and that, whatever your place in life may be, you will fulfill it nobly.

I cannot tell you how much you have been and are to me, one real good in my life. Goodbye — if it is to be so — my darling.

Dad

*

Eve was blessed to have such a caring father, and he did not, in fact, "pop off" until 1943, twelve years later.

But Eve had another correspondent, her "Uncle Monnie" Grainger, whose humorous, encouraging and cheering letters delighted her. They were written from the Graingers' cabin near Princeton. Evie had spent a happy summer holiday travelling through that rugged, mountainous area on horseback.

Her beloved Uncle Monnie had been her guide.

'Ralph Grey must have been the original non-chauvinist male,' said Eve of her father. 'He was almost too diffident. He had lived alone for some years and was used to baking and doing his laundry. It was Mother who helped my Father with the diapers.'

Eve Grey's uncle "Monnie" who, as ***Martin Allerdale Grainger,*** *wrote the novel* **Woodsmen of the West** *and sent a stream of cheering, encouraging letters to his niece, Evie, at Tranquille San.*

7 *Uncle Monnie's Cool Mind*

EVE TREASURED THE LETTERS from her uncle, Martin Allerdale Grainger: "Mart" to his friends, "Monnie" to his family. Eve's Aunt Mabel had also picked up a label. Among their closer associates, Martin and Mabel were known as "Mart" and "Dart."

Martin, as M. Allerdale Grainger, had authored that wonderful little book *Woodsmen of the West* in 1908, a novel clearly derived from acute observation during his time as a logger on the BC coast. It was reprinted in 1964 and again in 1983 and is a delightfully written look at turn-of-the-century forestry.

George Woodcock described the book as "the only BC novel of true originality and character, a fine autobiographical tale (full of documentary meat and outspoken for its time) about logging communities and camps on the coast and their muscle-bound and booze-befuddled inhabitants."

Martin Grainger, at one point, got himself stranded in northern BC's Cassiar country. He was sufficiently rugged, physically, to survive work as a back-packer in country considered too difficult for horses. He also learned about river boats by working on them.

Rejected by recruiters for the South African War, he was undeterred and decided to go anyway. He entrained to New York from BC, worked his passage on a horse transport, and then enlisted in the less choosey Lord Roberts Horse. He found time to try his hand at writing, including a column, *Life at the Front,* for an English paper.

Somewhere along the line, Grainger badly injured the arches of his feet, supposedly "by running beside his horse." Whether trying to make life easier for himself, or for his horse, the source does not make clear. He suffered great agony from the injury so the irrepressible Grainger became celebrated for wearing colourful mocassins on his tormented feet, and particularly for sporting them when he was presented to His Majesty, King George V.

He bounced from the war to stints of mathematics and jujitsu teaching in London, then returned to BC to engage in placer mining in Cassiar country and other places. Then, on Pender Island, he met Evie's future aunt, Mabel Higgs, then visiting her brother, Leonard Higgs, at his Gulf Island farmstead. Martin followed Mabel to England, convinced her to marry him, and only then quickly wrote *Woodsmen of the West* to earn his passage back to BC.

The suggestion that his wife travelled first class while he returned in steerage smacks of myth-making, but his novel was hailed as "authentic in every aspect" and is far more interesting therefore than the many, more romanticized, versions of that period by other writers, including Ralph Connor.

Eve's uncle, with a typically light and whimsical touch, dedicated his book *"To my creditors, affectionately."*

Grainger, of course, was not primarily a writer, but could have made a living at it, no doubt, if he had so chosen. Eventually, after several years picking up valuable experience in forestry, the independent-minded and perceptive forester was chosen to replace someone on a commission charged with bringing order to the largely chaotic, unregulated, graft-ridden forest industry.

As Secretary of a Royal Commission on Forestry, Grainger threw his considerable intelligence and energy into the work, pointedly outlining many of the problems and providing at least partial solutions. The final report recommended major changes and much stricter government control of forestry practices, formerly riddled with favouritism to political cronies, over-staking, overlapping leases and corruption. The many positive changes which were adopted in the province's first Forestry Act, passed in 1912, were largely attributed to Grainger.

Of course, a man who wore mocassins everywhere, even to tea at Buckingham Palace, was bound to add to his reputation as something of a character and humourist. But he was obviously a man with a serious, businesslike side to him. He returned to government as Chief Forester in 1916 to push ahead with further changes, but by 1919 felt he had had enough of government and returned to the role of private entrepreneur.

By the time Eve was confined to Tranquille, Grainger was manager of a private forest company. It was to seek refuge from this heavy load of business concerns that he began what soon became an habitual weekend practice of packing a bag and exploring on horseback. He probed his way regularly through the mountain wilderness of what he later described in his notes as "Arcadia." His passion for communing with the land and starscapes took him to the rugged country of the present-day Manning Park between Hope and Princeton.

He enjoyed himself immensely, jotting down his thoughts and feelings at great length, sending them to friends and relatives, including his niece, Evie. This is a typical passage:

"The stars came out bigger and more brilliant than when seen from lower country. I sat in my shirtsleeves brooding over space and stars and dark looming stupendous mountains, with a lump in my throat at the magnificence of it all. All I remembered of the agitated city life 100 miles away and far below shrivelled to pinpoint size. That is one reason why I make these mountain trips: it cools one's mind."

*

It was often while riding back on the train to Vancouver, that Grainger composed his cheery, finely-detailed letters. Here are excerpts from a few of the lengthy and encouraging letters (now housed in BC's public archives) to Eve Grey, his convalescing niece at Tranquille:

May 22, 1928

Dear Evie:

When I was crippled in 1914, the bottom fell out of my world. Month after month, those feet of mine were just wrecks. 1914 became '15, then came '16, '17—you remember how it was. Many a time, to a person devoted to physical activity and then already in his forties, it seemed like The Finish. Looking back now it is of course quite clear that such lugubrious ideas were a mistake. In any smash-up of that kind there are usually the makings of a new world—a bit smaller than the old one maybe but fine and dandy all the same. When you see MacMillan careering over mountain sides to photograph wild goat, or Andrews doing three men's work in charge of the largest logging camp in BC, you can see that lying up with T.B. for some months (tedious, wearisome, boresome as it inevitably is) does not shut off a vigorous future from those people who really go after it. Even lying up can become a sort of indoor sport after a person gets the big idea and the technique of how to do it. After ten months of it once, as a small boy, I remember being quite sorry to leave a hospital, rather like the leper attendant I may have told you about who, when our steamer was passing Leper Island (that unholy, bare, windswept sandspit with its gaunt buildings, at the entrance of Cape Town Bay), turned to me and said, "Well, there's the dear old place" and giggled happily.

You will be back on the Skyline, like MacMillan, in a year or so. Maybe you will have to live a lot on horseback, among mountains, so meanwhile I will keep you posted as to what is going on up there. Remember this too, that people like you and Dart and myself, and other good friends we know, who have stuck to regular exercise for years, have a tremendous pull in battling against illness. Their 500 billion cells have innate healthiness.

*

On the new big motor ferry *Princess Elaine* I breakfasted Friday morning . . .I had been over to Alberni the day before with VanDusen and his manager from Japan to discuss Jap squares and other delicatessen of the lumber business, such as the quantity of lumber per gang hour that Alberni stevedores stow into vessels (which averages 10.8, VanDusen says, instead of something else that he would like).

After breakfast we ruined two hours of bright sunshine, blue sea and airy, green islands and white distant mountains, by inhaling each other's cigars in earnest discussion as to whether or no Alberni should join the new selling company the sawmills are forming. Nine-thirty saw us erupt into the office, shattering Miss Browning's day thereafter with incessant jangling phone and buzzer calls; four phones going full blast; callers to be seen and callers butchered by trusted Dragons guarding us; all the fussomalorums you grin at when you visit our little fairy grotto . . . (this busy office); there were alarums between H.R. MacMillan and the sawmill folk about the selling company with which I somehow became mixed up; there was this and there was that—every kind of rush—till at 6:40 I bolted for home in a taxi and your father watched me grab a meal while we telephoned Dr Strong and drafted a cable to your Honolulu doctor in reply to one about you that had come mixed with our business cables earlier in the day. At 7:05 your Aunt phoned for a taxi; we piled in bundles of camp stuff; porters at the station ran with these bundles; the starting gong rang; we settled breathlessly in our seats on the Kettle Valley train just as 7:30 struck.

*

The stars were bright as I turned over in the new, doublepocket feather quilt, certainly the warmest thing I have ever slept in. A few minutes later, as it were, dawn filled the sky, then mist hung motionless on the alfalfa fields, budding leaves on trees above my bed were still. Profound peace—just a tiny murmur on the creek and cawing of distant crows waiting to grab turkey chicks over at Alf's place further down the flat. Four a.m. and breakfast time. How delightfully easy to roll out already dressed, shove on moccasins, take a handful of dead leaves and twigs to start a campfire, hang a billy to boil and prop up bread to toast. Ten calendar minutes to hot coffee and delicate cold-boiled rice taken plain, warming oneself crouched on the ground before the blaze, like a tramp. A good, new-born day with hectic yesterday and its worries blotted out and horses across the creek whinnying.

*

Then Dixie. Bert tells me the first time they ever saddled her was on a wild morning years ago when they had sheep on the high summits late in the Autumn. It started snowing heavily and for a desperate hour or two there was doubt whether the sheep could be driven down before the snow would bog them. The horses were loaded anyhow, in a hurry, shooed down the trail for home and then forgotten. Hours after, when the sheep had been saved, Bert caught up to Dixie waddling contentedly along the trail with saddle and clumsy pack underneath her tummy. Think of the fireworks you and I have seen when saddles slipped that way!

*

The first furniture in our shack was a sack of oats, and this made a great hit with the horses, who probably have not eaten oats a dozen times in their lives. The sight of me half a mile away stirs their thoughts at once. There is a little corral among the big trees just behind our shack and the boys leave horses there whenever Dart and I are expected from Vancouver. The shack is fine: 24' x 12' inside, with a side veranda 10' x12' where saddles hang on walls with pack bags, hobbles, cinch ropes and every sort of camp stuff. Chipmunks flip in and out and steal our oats; bluebirds are nesting a few feet away. Dart sleeps in the cretonned-alcove portion of the shack; the rest is living-room, with a five-dollar, sheet-iron cooking stove in tender memory of Klondike days. The stove, all the same, will knock spots off any heavy metal affair there is—for speed of cooking. It goes red hot in a whiff of time. A woman likes an indoor stove; for me the tramp's fire outside with pots suspended by wire hooks from a cross stick between two uprights.

*

Did you know that George, that wild-haired, red-faced bachelor of fifty, had once been engaged? It appears he had some lingering doubts, but the lady had him roped until they went one day to Wolf Creek. She was a good horsewoman and rode one of George's best. When they started to come home she stuck in spurs and beat George back to Princeton by four miles over a hard road. George realized that a woman who would treat a horse like that was no wife for him. . .This weekend Dart and I are going gypsying with our saddle horses and one pack-horse. We will camp on the high range.

Yours ever, Monnie

*

June 10, 1928

Dear Evie:

Two-forty-five in the afternoon and the telephone is ringing merrily like a kettle on the hob, but Miss Browning and I are going to try to get off something to remind you of the horse country that you will be back to in due course, in spite of interruptions.

*

The train had not yet whistled away up at Jura when the little Ford roared its way up the steep hill to Belfort Station yesterday afternoon. Dart and Constance had come up to see me off, as well as George and Bert driving the car, so we sat in front of the little shed and looked over the beautiful rolling country below us with the Three Brothers, still splotched with snow, in the far distance. Everything is green this year after Summer rains, and indescribably beautiful. When you walk or ride around, you are constantly getting little shocks from the beauty of the flowers, the contours of the hills, the little creeks, deer and what not.

*

As we sat there George, after taking a nap like some large animal, underneath a nearby tree, began to talk about bears. Years ago when he was young he remembered an old Indian telling him (with convincing detail) how there came one Winter a spell of terribly cold weather, something much worse than anything the old Indian had known. He was camped, could not keep warm and got scared as evening came on, so he went up the hills to a place that he knew of where there was a bear den and crawled in among the bears. He said they stirred and grunted a little in their sleep from time to time but did not wake up or take notice of him. When morning came he started for home.

*

George said you could tell a young bear's Winter home from an old one's. Young bears would just scoop out a hole underneath a root or a log, but the old ones, learning every year by experience, would make themselves much more comfortable. They would pack in lots of dry grass and leaves and make themselves a nice nest. Sometimes when there would be untimely rains in the early Spring, some of the bears' dens would get wet and you would see them out looking for new quarters. He had sometimes poked a stick down into a black bear's den and got them to come out. In fact in mild weather they did not seem to be so dead asleep but would not stir when it was really cold.

*

Talk about horse intelligence—when I opened an eye next morning, Dixie, watching me, nickered at once. Then as I made no move towards the canvas nosebag that she uses, she reached forward, picked up a canvas pad which keeps the pack box away from Edna's ribs, and threw the pad at me. Still I did not move, so she got a canvas girth and threw it towards me. There were plenty of oats, so the hints worked.

*

Dart and Constance have been spending ten days at our shack in that lovely grove of trees just across the little creek from Bert's ranch house. There are always a raft of children around Mrs. Thomas, her own and others who come and go indefinitely. . . They are the most united family we have ever met, so kind and considerate of each other, never the least hint of ill-temper or dispute . . . Of course it is what the tidy would call a hugger-mugger. Dogs worry sitting ducks until their frenzied quackings bring Dart or Constance running from across the creek; cabbage plantings wither because somebody has forgotten to turn the water on; the Ford goes to town without the tub of cream that should be shipped to Grand Forks; the Skyline camping equipment is a mere heap.

It was not until we were viewing that wide country from the high summit of the Elephant some hours later that I remembered leaving all the breakfast food spread out on the grass beside my tent and I remember Phyllis Thomas has a new large puppy dog. There was no dog seen that day, nor one large cake, one brown loaf, one pitcher milk, one-half pot porridge, one-half pound butter in aluminum screw-top tin, also missing. One dog sleeping it off somewhere.

You would like the birds that are nesting near our shack door—birds of dazzling bright blue; and the little baby grouse that George's marvellous sight alone could distinguish from the surrounding ground; and those beautiful mule deer standing close by at graze, then gliding away in their effortless bounding movement . . .

So I left that heavenly country yesterday evening, snoozing all the way in the train, and here Miss Browning has had her afternoon wrecked while we get these notes to you—there goes the phone . . . .

Ever your affectionate uncle.

*

Who wouldn't have loved to receive such wonderfully descriptive letters from a man so enamoured of mother nature and so obviously concerned and affectionate? To the lonely young woman laid up in an isolated sanitorium with TB and unable to have regular visits from her family, the letters were a delight.

The busy forestry company executive set aside his basket of important mail and flagged "urgent" cables from foreign buyers to scribble pages of detailed notes and pass them to his harassed secretary who would drop everything, type and post them.

What did the loyal Miss Browning think of this boss of hers who apparently cared more about the morale and well-being of his niece in the Tranquille sanitorium than about all the logs on the west coast? She probably adored him. So too, of course, did Evie.

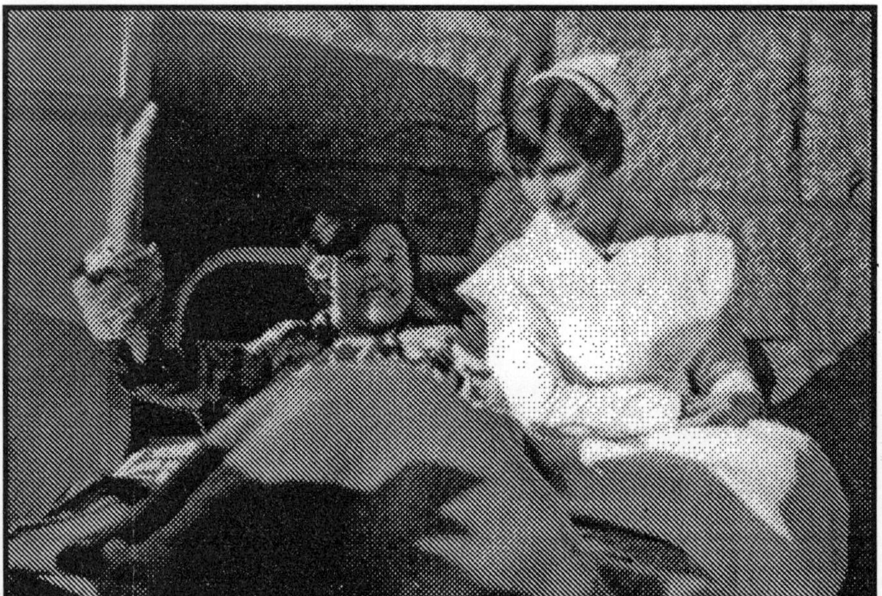

The Tranquille nurses marvelled at Eve Grey's spirit and good cheer. Eve entertained fellow patients and the staff with her funny story about the patients' leftover bacon being returned as feed to the pigs for recycling.

8 *Out of Bed and Into Politics*

AS EVE GAINED STRENGTH and began to feel better, her thoughts turned to leaving Tranquille and to how she might somehow make a new life for herself. Nevertheless, it came as a bit of a shock when she was told by the doctors at the san that there was nothing further they could do for her and she should leave.

In later years she wondered if her release had been precipitated or expedited because she began to show some interest in politics. She had listened carefully to several political speakers including CCFer Ernie Winch and George Williams, a socialist railwayman from nearby Kamloops.

She had taken her first tentative political step by distributing the CCF literature which the speakers left with her to the several patient areas and "even to the san office —missionary style!"

*

Meantime, the absentee love of her life, Ronald MacEwan, was studying forestry in Russia. "I guess this was selfish of me but I wanted him to come back. I had no idea how long I'd be lying in bed, or what the future held for my health, although I was always optimistic. His father naturally wanted him, as his eldest son and heir, to be close to home.

"But after my first year in the san I really wasn't any better, so I got my mother to write to him and call off our engagement. I think I reasoned it would be easier just to carry on, to try to get better and to rest without that preying on my mind. And it did seem pretty awful that he should be tied down to somebody who was going to be ill for years."

In those days TB was considered a dreadful thing. Many people just didn't get better, were more or less invalids the rest of their lives, or died.

These possibilities were no doubt weighing on Ronald MacEwan's mind and it would have been in keeping with Eve's great generosity of spirit to free her betrothed from his commitment.

"My mother made it very definite that I was at the end of my tether, that I couldn't stand the suspense and that it would be easier for me to break it off. But it was a major tragedy for both of us because we were very fond of each other. I don't know what happened to him. We had a very brief reply and I never heard from him again."

No doubt Eve thought often, as we all do, of what might have been. What if her relationship had been allowed to develop without this unexpected turnaround in her health status? But life has a way of involving us, entangling us and sometimes rescuing us, or at least moving us quickly away from our perceived tragedies. The new entanglement for Eve Smith was her concern for the well-being of her fellow British Columbians, and the answers she thought she was finding—in politics.

*

While Eve was in the san, working class people across Canada were enduring the soul-wrenching unemployment, poverty and personal trauma of the Depression. As a consequence, the drive toward developing a home-grown socialist movement was gathering momentum.

Groups of left-wing politicos, progressive farmers and trade unionists, university lecturers and an eclectic group of socialist intellectuals had been having periodic meetings during those very same years, 1928-32, that Eve was confined at Tranquille.

Many of these thinking people were content, initially, with efforts to increase communication and socialist political education between and among these left-leaning groups, and to create "a movement towards socialism." Others were more intent, some even hell-bent, on moving quickly towards organizing the early founding of a new, broadly based political party to contest provincial and federal elections in a drive for political power.

That dichotomy, indeed, presaged the ongoing conflict within the growing socialist movement and within the new, federated alliance of groups and individuals working towards a "co-operative commonwealth," whatever hopeful message those imprecise words might convey to oppressed Canadians.

There were the deadly serious students and advocates of social change, the Marxian theorists and planners, who intended, or thought they did, to replace the capitalist system with a fully planned socialist society where the evils of joblessness and poverty amidst plenty would be eliminated by organizing the economy to priorize and meet human needs—and not for profitability.

But, inevitably, even among those who paid lip service to promoting "socialism," there were the politically ambitious, the job-seekers, the lawyers who found their involvement good for business, the social democrats, so certain they could manipulate the capitalist system *better* than the bona fide capitalists had run it, that is with professed concern for the interests of "the poor, the needy, the disadvantaged."

Later on, there was much less discussion of "Democratic Socialism" and rather more talk of an ill-defined "social democracy" including a fudged and confusing message about a "mixed economy," a version of capitalism, if you will, with a slightly more humane approach than the unbridled version. With the flush of early, if limited, CCF electoral success, the political junkies swarmed aboard—those who simply enjoyed the excitement, the challenge, and the material rewards of chasing after electoral power and of "building a competitive political machine."

The "convinced socialist" contingent rarely represented more than 20 to 30 percent of the amalgam of forces within the CCF in BC, and less elsewhere, but they were determined to "keep the party on track" to the cherished, if enduringly elusive, goals of a socialist society.

The "social democrats," always in control of the CCF's party machinery, cared little for political education, cared even less for socialist terminology and rhetoric, and earnestly set to work signing up members and campaigning to win seats in provincial legislatures and the federal parliament.

The objective of the party, defined as a "Co-operative Commonwealth," was a concept sufficiently broad, and broadly interpreted, to be adapted to whatever policies social democrats might from time to time advocate. For those few, however, who took the trouble to wade through the eight pages of the party's 1933 statement of principles and policies—the later much-maligned *Regina Manifesto*—the intention to socialize a controlling portion of Canada's key economic sectors was abundantly clear.

Certainly George Williams had no difficulty outlining the shape of a future Canadian socialist society. He set it all out for Eve and other members of his audience at Tranquille in a two-hour, no-holds-barred lecture linking the ownership of resources and the means of production, the drive for great wealth by Canada's then relatively few major capitalists, to predictable results: poverty, inequity and unemployment.

Williams spoke in more than abundant detail to the small group and Eve listened carefully. While much of her earlier reading had been suggestive of the conclusions now drawn so meticulously by Williams, no other person had previously spelled out for her such a comprehensive socio-economic analysis. She was intrigued and decided to participate and to learn more.

For Eve Smith, that exposition by George Williams was a defining moment and distinct turning point, "a complete eye-opener," as she put it. "I had never really thought much about wages and profits, production for use and to meet human need, and people selling their labour power and so on.

"We were well into the Depression then and I began to understand why we had such poverty in the midst of plenty; that a few people controlled Canada's resources and production facilities; that they employed you only if they needed you to produce commodities, and if they didn't pay you enough wages you couldn't buy that production and so production would slow down or stop. The classic capitalist business cycle. In some ways it's as simple as that!"

As soon as Eve got to Kamloops she found her friend, who had been at Tranquille, living at a little rooming house in a single room with a gas plate and a shared bathroom for $10. a month. Eve applied for relief and rented a similar room in the same building. Eve's new friend and her boyfriend were CCFers and took Eve along to party meetings in Kamloops.

Eve found that some of the people on relief had a feeling of shame or disgrace about accepting government assistance. She obviously did not share their concerns.

"I think relief payment, or welfare, is an insult; it becomes necessary when the capitalist system cannot provide decent jobs for people; you certainly shouldn't have to feel grateful for it.

"Anyway, I said to the welfare official that I wasn't long out of Tranquille and wasn't yet well enough to work and there wasn't any work anyway. He immediately said, "Certainly, of course, $12.60 a month." But I paid $10. a month for a room. How was I expected to live? Then I received 60 cents extra for milk from the Red Cross because I had TB!

"But I was very lucky. My aunt and uncle, who had a little money, gave me $25. a month which was eventually paid back to them after some years. I did other things to earn a little money, knitting for example. I knit socks and things for anyone who wanted something knit.

"But I was really getting deep into the CCF. It wasn't long before I just spent my life in the CCF.

"In the Kamloops CCF club there were quite a number of old Socialist Party of Canada men along with a few newcomers like myself. It was a railroad junction town for both the CN and CPR with railwaymen moving east and west. They would get off the trains and stay overnight in Kamloops and go out again the next day. There were men working on the roads, the engineers, conductors, linemen and all the rest of them. So I got to know quite a few railway people, and they were nearly all CCF.

"There were big machine shops down by the railroads where repairs were done on the trains and I think George Williams worked in one of those.

"Kamloops had a big CCF club with well over one hundred members and it was considered one of the most active in BC. We had classes at least once a week in economics, socialist philosophy, history and dialectics. Every Sunday evening we had an open forum with an outside speaker or one of our local people. We also had public speaking classes for the younger members and some of us would speak up at our regular open forums.

"We would hear an address for forty minutes and then there would be questions from the audience and anyone could come up to the front and say what they thought. It was a very democratic procedure in those days.

"There was a lot of good debate so we learned a great deal. In our socialist classes we read and studied and took our books home. There was a real ferment of interest in political knowledge and political action. I made some excellent friends then and kept in touch with many of them for years afterwards.

"One of them was Gerald Van who later went to Vancouver and then to Africa for 15 years. His letters were simply terrific. He understood so well what Kipling called *the white man's burden* in Africa. It is an old story of Europeans invading new worlds and exploiting the people and their resources for the financial gain of a few people back home.

"Well, all of this was a tremendous experience for me, something totally new for me. So far as party politics goes, I hadn't been involved before I went to Tranquille and before joining the CCF. Like most other people, I knew there were Conservatives and Liberals and that was just about all I knew. But I had read those Upton Sinclair books and they had made quite an impression. So did other events such as farmers ploughing their wheat under because they couldn't sell it at a profit. Food was actually being destroyed during the Depression! That's what *really* set me on the road towards the CCF.

"One of the first federal work camps was just on the outskirts of Kamloops. The government had a policy of putting these work camps way out in the country so the men weren't seen or heard much by the people in town. Out of sight, out of mind. The men did forestry work and different things at ridiculously low wages. But these 'jobs' were for single men."

In June, 1933, the Department of National Defence brought the BC road camps into a national relief camp program. It was designed by Major-General A.H.L. McNaughton in response to federal politicians' fears of insurrection by unemployed men roaming the country in groups.

Although down and out, these men were not beaten. In April, 1935, they walked out of their camps, en masse, converged on Vancouver and demanded more humane treatment and support, especially from Ottawa.

The reply from Canada's untroubled Tory Prime Minister R.B. Bennett? He told BC officials: "I won't be their wet-nurse!" The men, now organized in their Relief Camp Workers Union, held numerous marches, rallies and parades, one of them to Stanley Park where they sang the *Internationale* and demanded action to deal with their unemployment, homelessness, their terrible hunger and hopelessness.

But it was only when scores of them were "tin-canning" on downtown streets, and some of the men made a foray into the Hudson's Bay department store, that the police were called in to protect The Bay and its merchandise and Vancouver Mayor McGeer then read the Riot Act, on cue, but to no great effect.

Finally, the men decided to board CPR freight trains to take their case to Ottawa, but not before occupying the Vancouver Public Library, and demanding and getting money for food. The

CCF Unemployed Conference, along with other support groups, helped "the boys," as they were called, to prepare for their long trek to see their very own representatives within the hallowed halls of *their* House of Commoners.

Until 1934, people were obliged to line up to take their relief allowances in the form of flour, beans, sugar and butter. Then they were issued vouchers, scrip, to exchange for food, other goods and services. The centre of BC activity on behalf of the unemployed was in Vancouver. Eve worked with others in Kamloops, doing what they could to support the men and their families. But it was a grim task.

"There was another place where sick men were taken and I went and visited there a few times with other people in the CCF. It was a dreadful, desolate place. Thirty or forty men in one big ward with a toilet at one end of the room and the whole place smelled of stale urine. They were just huddled there. Forgotten men.

"It was a pretty bad era if you were poor. For a very long time there was no help, no sort of government assistance. People wanted to understand why there was poverty and unemployment and desperation and the CCF speakers, the good ones like George Williams, could explain that the basis of the economic system was solely profit, production for profit and not for human needs. And when you analyzed everything that was going on, profit and greed certainly superseded everything else.

"Profit was more important than your health, or supplying people with food or other things they really needed, and Williams gave a Marxian analysis. Today almost nobody knows what Marxism means, or socialism. Those words now mean a hundred different things to a hundred different people.

"We had an old store that was turned into a club house with one of the unemployed men living at the back and we paid rent by taking up collections. He had a little stove and whenever we had a public meeting we always served coffee and we'd all contribute sandwiches and charged ten or fifteen cents.

"Our whole attitude was that sure, women were oppressed. But so were men. We wanted to liberate *everyone,* not just women. Women, in any case, were not going to be liberated until men were liberated, until we were *all* liberated from the exploitation by private ownership.

"It was nearly always the women who cut the sandwiches.

But the men *did* serve the coffee! There was also *one* man, Stan Brooks, who made sandwiches—and they were *delicious!*"

Eve was surprised to find that many of the local CCF members, and not just visiting speakers, were well educated and cultured people. "They knew an awful lot about socialist philosophy but many other things as well: anthropology, archeology, history, poety, art. If you went into their homes you just found this out. Some of the best-educated people who never had more than three or four years of formal schooling had learned by living, working, reading and listening to other people. We used to have terrific discussions. As for me, well, I felt I was really just beginning to learn.

"I was among the youngest of the women involved, and in those days I looked younger than I was. Some of the oldtimers were thrilled that a young woman should be so interested, so they encouraged me for all they were worth. I wanted the practice so I used to get up and speak quite often.

"Gerald Van and two or three other young men were very keen and went to all the classes and we studied dialectics, the skills involved in critical enquiry or testing the truth of a theory through discussion and debate. And the Hegelian Theory of Idealism, Fueurbach's idea of gross materialism synthesized by Marx. I was particularly attracted to Dietzgen's ideas. We used to discuss these things so seriously! But since I still had TB and wasn't strong, I couldn't go out to meetings every night by any means. So I didn't get nearly so involved as some of these young men such as Gerald Van.

"It was interesting that some of the women didn't like to speak in front of their husbands, but I encouraged them to get up and speak. Then one of the women who was among the most active, formed a women's committee. We used to meet in the afternoons and talk and debate CCF policy and socialism and there were a few of us who made a study of Dietzgen and Hegel and dialectics and so on.

"I didn't really agree with the idea of having a separate women's group. When were women going to learn to talk in front of men, I insisted, if they just don't go and do it?"

In one of the few times on record when the CCF systematically grappled with the onerous tasks of researching and planning what it would do if one day called upon to govern, the BC CCF in

1935 set up a Planning Commission as a matter of urgency. Indeed, many CCFers were certain they would win the next election and were at pains to be prepared with a comprehensive program of action.

To begin with, they had no data and little internal CCF expertise. They began by getting their hands on all available financial statistics from the provincial and federal governments. They set out to learn in detail about the BC economy in its many facets: forestry, mining, agriculture, fishing, and to draft plans to present to the public for the coming campaign.

Later, the CCF provincial leader, Harold Winch, took a draft policy paper to an Ottawa conference with the *League for Socialist Reconstruction* and received a detailed critique of the plans from such CCF luminaries as Professor Frank Scott of McGill University. Winch was intent on winning and determined to be ready.

There was no money, initially, for the Planning Commission but Dr Telford financed some of its early work through his remarkably successful *Challenge Radio Fund*. He made regular appeals for funding to which people responded generously.

Matt Glenday, a radical labour organizer and political agitator who later became a close friend and correspondent of Eve's, took over the chairmanship of the Commission in the fall of 1935 and set to work.

Glenday set up eight departments, Forestry, Finance, Labour, Construction, Agriculture, Fisheries, Public Release and Policy & Tactics, the latter chaired by Harold Winch. Glenday's appeal in the *CCF Bulletin* was straightforward:

"Any ideas as to the method of setting up a new socialist order will be welcomed. Write us your suggestions." He then circulated a questionnaire to party members seeking their ideas and soliciting any technical expertise that might be available as he sought to flesh out plans for BC's first socialist government.

Glenday's program, most of which was eagerly lifted from the New Zealand Labour government's legislation, was considered "outlandlishly radical" by many of his more conservative CCF colleagues.

That perception was overcome, in time, as virtually all of Glenday's program was implemented by future "old-party" governments who considered it nothing less than enlightened self interest. Their interests, of course, included hanging on to power, stealing the thunder and platform of the CCF (those "Liberals in a hurry" as future Liberal prime minister Louis St. Laurent would describe them), and avoiding civil unrest.

But in 1935, some sections of the BC CCF thought it was "outrageously socialistic" to demand unemployment insurance, a legalized minimum wage, health insurance, guaranteed farm produce prices, pensions, control of credit and setting up a national bank. As was usual, the social democrats were uncertain what they stood for, afraid to "take sides," and terrified about losing electoral support.

The Bank of Canada was nationalized by the Liberals in 1938, just three years later. Much of this "overly ambitious program" became law. But not, however, Matt's program for the "complete socialization of industry."

This was far too radical for such CCFers as Angus and Grace MacInnis who had become champions of the "mixed economy" after they had taken the obligatory tour of Sweden to observe social democratic capitalism in action.

Matt Glenday's Planning Commission also advocated "as a priority" the takeover of BC's forest companies, certain that the province could thus provide jobs and wages for its unemployed as well as huge revenues to build BC's economic infrastructure and support its social programs.

It was a rare moment in the Co-operative Commonwealth's troubled history when a provincial CCF party had the courage to spell out a clear, unambiguous economic policy supporting the interests of the working class, along with at least the beginnings of a defined strategy to effect radical change in the social and economic status of the unemployed, and the people living amidst the poverty and social chaos perpetuated by the economic system supported by Liberals, Conservatives and their corporate allies.

The BC CCF, always keen to find new recruits, had even taken an active interest in the youth of the province and had begun a fairly serious effort to educate them politically.

But *political* schools? And in the *summer*?

9 *"Salute Your Bride, Mr Smith!"*

CCF SUMMER SCHOOL spawned a number of romantic liaisons, including that of Don Smith and Eve Grey. Starting from the earliest days of the BC section of the Co-operative Commonwealth Federation, regular summer schools were held by the party at various camps and farms throughout BC.

The first was at Fisherman's Cove in West Vancouver. They promoted socializing among the members to enhance solidarity, political education (of particular interest to Eve Grey) and leadership development designed to strengthen party organization in the local constituencies and, of course, in the elections.

In 1934, a man named Hedley, one of the few men of means who joined the CCF, owned a large property on Saltspring Island and made it available for a CCF summer school. Party members, visiting speakers and party staff would take the ferry from Swartz Bay and be met with a car ride to the school site. Another location was near Fulford Harbour on Pender Island where a local farmer allowed the use of a huge field. Still another was on Gabriola Island looking out onto the shore and lighthouse.

Benches would be set up for meetings in a barn, any available building or in the open air and people often slept in tents. Students, including groups of CCYM members (Co-operative Commonwealth Youth Movement), attended from many parts of BC, some from across Canada.

Speakers were paid travel expenses only and would lead debates on many aspects of party policy, current events and international affairs. Occasionally they planned and participated in political demonstrations, against unemployment, for example, or the beggarly levels of government relief.

Eve attended lectures, took part in debates and practised public speaking. In time, with her firm convictions and strong speaking voice, she became an accomplished, compelling speaker and a formidable debater.

One lecturer, George Weaver, was among the more eloquent

socialist writers, critics and lecturers. Eve agreed with his socialist critique of society and the economy and became a convincing speaker herself in defining socialism in what she felt were its pure, simple and achievable terms—just as she did in this quote, over fifty years later:

"Socialism means the public or common or social ownership of the people's resources and of the means of production, instead of private ownership; production for the purpose of serving human needs instead of for profit."

Eve could spell out her vision of a socialist society without hesitation and without the slightest doubt in her mind as to its practicality in both the short and longer term. She would often hammer away at the goal of a socialist economic framework and might even tackle explanations of such audience-challenging concepts as the eventual "withering away" of the state. Eve would sometimes delve into the specifics of socialist socio-economic planning via publicly-owned corporations, control of the banking system and people-driven monetary and fiscal policies. She had the conviction, dynamism and down-to-earth language that could reach an audience.

But Eve touched her audience most directly with people-related examples of the capitalist system gone awry. She found it particularly appalling that food production could be ploughed under, dumped or burned as it sometimes was in the Depression years when overproduction could not be profitably marketed.

Eve enjoyed the variety of socialist views presented at the summer camps but there was one man among them, younger than most, whose speeches particularly impressed Eve. "Whether it was world problems or aspects of Canadian society, so many of our difficulties centred on greed and excess profits. Don Smith showed clearly how, when you analyse what's going on in the world, the buying and selling, our social policy, education, everything—it would all come back to that word profit."

Eve would say many years later that "Don, in my opinion, went backwards and abandoned many of his earlier views. But at that time, there was a big controversy about Robert Connell, the first leader of the British Columbia CCF. He was a fine man, a reverend even, but he was pretty much a right-winger. The issue was whether or not he should remain as leader and I took an active part in that debate."

Connell was a decent man but no advocate for socialism. Indeed, he found it difficult to comprehend socialist thinking, much less espouse it or lead it —a not uncommon failing among CCF/NDP leaders. Eve was resting on the grass when Don found her and joined her in discussion. After sharing a number of views they soon found themselves in agreement that Connell, the former nature columnist, should be asked to step down—"and that's how we became friendly," Eve chuckled, "as the man said in the poem."

Robert Connell was ousted from the party but immediately formed one of his own, the short-lived Social Constructives. It was symptomatic of the sharp divides that separated various factions in the BC CCF that Connell was able to take three CCF MLAs with him, plus Bill Pritchard, the owner-editor of "the CCF's paper." *The Commonwealth*, it seems, was not the common property of the CCF members.

Matt Glenday stepped in and used his international contacts to somehow secure funding to start a successor, but this time party-owned, newspaper, *The Federationist*. Shortly thereafter, Eve found herself writing political articles, commentaries and book reviews for the new paper at the request of BC Member of Parliament Ernie Winch who was in charge of the political education committee. Don Smith also wrote articles regularly for the new paper. Eve and Don became close friends of the hard-driving union organizer and leftist political promoter Matt Glenday.

Don Smith had a fine talent for writing and soon became editor of the CCF's newspaper in BC. The couple developed a warm, respectful friendship.

Don and his younger brother John were immersed in the day-to-day political issues: who was running for what position, both within the party and for public office—including seats in the provincial legislature and municipal councils. Eve preferred to focus more intently on the philosophical aspects and principles of socialism and continued to study socialist writers.

Shortly after Eve and Don started seeing each other, Eve met Mildred Osterhout socially and discovered that Mildred, a social worker and disciple of Gandhi, had been going out with Don. "I felt badly about it and thought maybe I had stepped into her shoes without knowing it—which I suppose I had. But Don didn't treat women badly. He was one of the least male chauvinist men I ever met. We liked to attend meetings and share a public platform and I just took for granted that's the way men were. Then I got older and wiser and realized some men weren't like that. Many wanted to dominate."

Don and Eve would both be working at CCF headquarters on Seymour Street and would sometimes go out and talk and spend five cents on a cup of coffee—"a wild extravagance." The editorial offices were then moved to Hastings Street near Carroll where there was a volunteer staff. Don was paid $10 a week, the same rate as the man who physically distributed the paper. Occasionally Eve would help Don to correct the page-proofs before the paper went to press.

"For a while I took a live-in job—undergraduate nursing—caring for a woman in a hostel, but we kept in close contact and phoned each other regularly. One night when I was living at home with mother and father in a little two-room apartment, I was on my way to bed when Don phoned and asked me to a movie. I remember mother and dad thinking it was sort of nuts of me to get dressed again and go out with Don, but I did."

When they first met, Don had a room at the old Continental Hotel with just a bed and a gas plate, but it wasn't long before a room came empty where Eve lived on Hornby Street, near Davie, and "Don moved in and our life of sin began!"

Separate rooms were needed (at $8 a month each) because Don had severe asthma and had to sleep in a room with the windows closed. He would sit up late into the night breathing in his steaming asthma powder concoctions. Sixteen people in the house shared the one combined toilet, sink and bathroom and, since there was no water in the rented rooms, one can imagine the lineups for that particular household water source!

With no refrigeration available, they had to buy their food from day to day. Then they moved together to a two-room apartment on 16th Avenue for which they paid $16 a month. There is no record to indicate whether fresh-air fiend Eve accommodated to closed windows, or required Don to expose his asthmatic condition to Vancouver's outdoor elements.

It was mid-Depression and there was little money around. Eve noted that she had to figure in the cost of gas cooking to determine whether lamb, at 7 cents a pound, which took a long time to cook, was really any cheaper than T-bone steak, at 15 cents a pound, which one could fry in three or four minutes.

"We both thought it was just a good idea not to marry and I'm not quite sure why we decided to get married. Certainly our families didn't harass us in any way; they were all very friendly, pleasant and hospitable. I used to stay with Don's family at Langford outside Victoria and I then met his brother John and all his sisters: Molly, Idle, Connie and Sheena. Most of our friends were CCF. Occasionally my aunt would invite me to some 'do' or other with her better-off business friends at her place—Kensington Place on Beach Drive, one of the oldest swish apartment houses—but I didn't care too much for it and stopped that sort of thing.

"It was my suggestion, I think, that we get married. I don't think Don would have cared a hoot if we had never got married. It was totally out of character for us. If you had a civil wedding with a magistrate, that was $10, but a church wedding was $5. So we decided on the church—though neither of us had any use at all for religion—just to save five dollars.

"My mother was ill but my father and my aunt came to bear witness and sign the register. It took about three minutes and the minister said to Don, 'You may now salute your bride.' We didn't immediately understand what he meant. Then we thought it was so silly because we had been living together for two years and couldn't see kissing each other just to please the parson.

"My father and aunt went home and we went down to Robson Street, sat on a stool, had a hamburger and that was it. Now, I like celebrations. I like parties. But just because you're going to marry the person you love, why get dressed up and make a big ceremony of it? I can't bear weddings. I never could see any point in it. I think they are dreadful things.

"Actually, I think we got married on the strength of Don selling a story to a racing magazine. He was a fanatic about horse racing; he'd been going to racetracks since he was a child. We got on very well indeed for years but then I broke down again with TB and that was very hard on him.

"I went back to Tranquille for three months but then Don came; he didn't want me to stay there. It was just about the time of the blackouts because of the Japanese bombing of Pearl Harbour. We found an apartment first in an attic, two-and-a-half rooms with shared bathroom. I knew I wouldn't be able to climb those stairs. The back window looked out over the city and it was strange to watch the city grow dark during the blackouts.

"My doctor at Tranquille couldn't understand that I would rather stay with my husband in Vancouver and be bombed by the Japanese than go back up to Tranquille and be safe. Then Don found us a two-room flat on 12th Avenue on the ground floor looking out into a garden."

Don was bright. During the First World War when so many teachers went to war, Don became a so-called pupil-teacher. He passed his exams for Cambridge University with honours but he never attended. He also entered a competition for a true story about a personal experience, an adventure. He wrote a complete fabrication about carrying a phonograph into darkest Africa and playing Harry Lauder to the black people—and he won the prize! Of course he always told Eve never to believe what she read "because people will write anything to earn a living."

Don was writing fairly regularly for the *Vancouver Sun* and he wanted desperately to get to Santa Anita racetrack and write it up for the *Sun.* Eve had suggested the name *SunStar* since he didn't want to use his own name, and the paper agreed. It was illegal to take paying passengers in private cars but a person could advertise in the paper: *'Going to California; will share car.'* So Don and Eve got to California for $15 in gas money.

But Eve truly hated horse racing: "I think it's terrible they treat horses like that, but it's not as bad as polo. We both had passes, of course, for the club house. Then, by the third time we went down to Santa Anita, we had our own little MG-car, so I would leave Don at his beloved races and drive around and see the southern California countryside. I could go quite a long way in the four hours he was at the track. We could then escape Vancouver winters for about six weeks. It was better for his asthma and better for my TB."

Then Don somehow heard that the CBC needed a news editor. He applied to Ira Dilworth, the manager in charge of CBC in western Canada, packed along copies of his published stories to the interview—including items penned at the racetracks—and got the job. Eventually he became head of CBC Radio News in BC. The job certainly gave Don and Eve a little more security because, while Eve enjoyed nursing, she simply wasn't strong enough most of the time to pursue her profession.

For a while, Don had a strenuous schedule when the races were on at Hastings Park. He would get up at 5 a.m., work at CBC News till noon, write the horserace stories at the *Vancouver Sun* and then head to the races to make notes on the horses for the next day. On the way home he would buy fruit and vegetables and they would have salads and perhaps something from the deli. He was carefully looking after Eve as well as working a very long day.

Since Eve was again confined to bed with TB, she kept in touch with her world at that time through Don but mainly through the medium of her cherished bedside radio. It was probably then that she began her lifelong habit of jotting down her *aide memoire* "radio notes" in scribblers.

During that period, she had no visitors at all; she simply wasn't well enough. As she put it: "You just feel terribly, horribly ill and you're constantly very tired. It's an effort to get up to the bathroom, or even to turn in bed and you're very short of breath."

In time, she again recovered much of her strength and her life then took a decided turn for the better.

In the countryside, near Cranbrook. Eve helped look after ***Nancy Miles****, a child who had infantile paralysis. On her time off Eve would often borrow* ***Big Boy*** *from the local doctor who cared for Nancy. Riding horses was then Eve's first love and favourite recreation.*

Winifred** and **Ralph Grey** and daughters **Constance** and **Evelyn. *While Contie went on to 'Finishing School' in England, Eve opted for the socialist road favoured by her farmer-worker-writer father.*

Ralph Grey had lost his mother and three sisters to the scourge of TB in England and was deeply concerned about Eve entering nurse's training. He knew that very few precautions were taken in those days to protect nurses or trainees and a high percentage of them developed tuberculosis. "It became a major scandal," said Eve, "until public protests finally brought about improvements."

10 *"To Get the Future Going!"*

EVE MET DON'S BROTHER JOHN when the CCF was contesting a provincial election in BC. Don had taken Eve to meet his family at their home in Langford outside Victoria.

John Smith recalls first hearing Eve speak from the audience at a campaign meeting he had organized. "We needed speakers for the campaign so I didn't hesitate after that to call on her. She was an enthusiastic young member of the CCF with a good, strong speaking voice and I soon developed a high regard for her." And, no doubt, a great fondness.

John found her "quite effervescent" when she spoke, but soon learned that she didn't have strong reserves of energy. She would slip away from meetings when she tired and just quietly disappear and lie down somewhere. She seemed to look quite well to everyone but she needed these quiet times to rest and restore her strength for her next outing.

The CCF couldn't organize even a small meeting in the town of Esquimalt, but in the rural parts of the riding which surrounded Port Renfrew and Bamberton, Jordan River, Sooke and Langford, the CCF held many well-attended meetings and counted quite well in the vote in those areas.

Often called upon to provide an opening talk at such meetings, Eve soon became a popular speaker. She didn't mince her words. At party members' meetings, John recalled, she would sometimes startle her fellow CCFers by "warning against the liberals among us." This was just one aspect of her ongoing struggle to stiffen the political spines of party adherents and to hold them more closely to socialist ideals and principles.

"Private ownership will not resolve the problems of our society," she would say. Her answer, of course, was the social ownership of the means of production and distribution. "Eve was not going to waste her time promoting reform," said John. "She regarded reformism as fundamentally dishonest."

In one provincial election John was campaign organizer for

the CCF candidate, his brother Don. Significant differences between the two men, and between Eve and Don, came to the fore during that electoral contest. Unlike Eve, Don would not talk directly of capitalism or socialism. He preferred to stress specific CCF policies and programs, and emphasized those areas of social reform that he knew were of particular interest to his prospective supporters.

Eve was prepared for a quite different and longer-term political process, one including many tedious hours of research, writing, summer schools, seminars, endless meetings—to win people to socialism through appeals to the intellect. She considered socialist political education to be fundamental. But Don Smith had joined the camp of those who stressed the expediency of more immediate electoral success. Without political power so the party could change laws, they said, what was the exercise all about?

Don was also impatient, if not brusque, on the campaign trail. "He was not the sort of character," suggested John, "who could easily stand around and socialize and shake hands after meetings." Part of that, no doubt, was his problem with asthma, but he was also impatient with what he considered irrelevant chit-chat. He was always keen to get on to the next meeting, present himself as favourably as possible as a spokesman for the party and its policies, and then go home.

In one of his campaign speeches he made quite a point of the fact that Eve was the daughter of Ralph Grey who was related to Lord Earl Grey, the former Governor General of Canada, of Grey Cup fame. Eve was not happy that Don would emphasize this distant relationship simply to curry political support. Ralph Grey had been born to a branch of an aristocrat-aspiring English family but Eve would never mention it unless pressed. Even then she would always dismiss it as unimportant.

Early in their developing relationship, Eve felt that John Smith was a more sympatico colleague politically, and perhaps socially, than her husband. John took his politics quite seriously but he also knew how to enjoy the company of his friends and colleagues.

As well, he and Eve were among the dreamers who would allow their imaginations to picture the undoubted benefits to flow from the socialist society of the future. They were among the many exuberant young political leftists of their time who were markedly different from the more numerous, more self-oriented and election-absorbed partisans who gravitate to most political parties.

"In our finer moments," said John, "we would have high-flown visions, not of a workaday world, but one where we were all artists and craftsmen as well as workers. The human soul was going to flower. We were all high spirited when we got together. The work of the world was put behind us in our wilder flights of imagination and we soared to wherever our vision might take us."

The more visionary socialists assumed that resolving society's grievous economic problems would generate a great flowering of culture. Was this a gentle echo of the bleak industrial revolution's dreams of Medieval simplicity, devotion to honest hand-work, beauty in craftsmanship and closeness to nature?

Some writers have described such thinkers as "absurd escapists." But industry had certainly taken a hideous toll of the landscape and had created squalor and misery and urban decay in England's cities. A similar idealism motivated many in the early years of the Soviets when Bolsheviks believed that hammer-and-sickle designs could lead to social transformation by raising mass consciousness. It was feared that the removal of enjoyment from work along with the advance of science and technology would soon wither the soul and the esthetic senses.

But in the USSR, Stalin and his central planners had transformed the state into a monolithic, monopolist entity. He had produced an economy that had many of the drawbacks that Marx said were inherent in a capitalist monopoly.

Stalin managed to do much the opposite to what Marx had proposed. He had squeezed the workers to produce super-profits which were then channelled into a rapid, forced-march expansion of industry. This served the Soviet people well in wartime, producing in record time much of the armament required, in addition to the Allies' lend-lease matériel, to smash the German armies. But it had cut deeply into individual and family consumption. Very few resources were allocated to meeting the enormous pent up consumer demand for consumer goods.

All of which produced little to resemble the socialism that John and Eve and socialists the world over had dreamed about. The distorted Soviet economy was able, eventually, to rocket off dramatically into space exploration but could not produce sufficient pots, pans, stoves, kitchens and housing. Thus, while Canadian leftists thrilled to the rich, stirring, dramatic voices of the visiting *Red Army Chorus and Dance Ensemble*, they witnessed no great flowering of *popular* culture within the USSR.

Trotsky had even suggested that, under conditions of social equality, socialist men and women might all well reach the exalted levels of Beethoven and Goethe—a hopelessly romantic view.

Perhaps most miners and factory workers would have thought it sufficient that the use of technology would make their work less exhausting. Many got their annual holiday to enjoy the healing mineral waters of the Russian spas; few had sufficient leisure time to devote to an expansive cultural development.

While Stalin did his best to hide the horrors of his criminal state apparatus from the world, Eve, John and their comrades involved themselves, more accurately *immersed* themselves, in the urgent work at hand in Canada, the immediate, life-tending, soul-saving tasks required in the disastrous Depression.

They were trying desperately, as John put it, "to get the future going and put people to work. To take away this blockage—capitalism—which put people out of work and closed factories. The tools were there. Obviously the skills and capabilities were there; all you needed was a catalyst to bring them together and finally clear away this roadblock to progress.

"Social ownership of the means of production; that was what we were going to bring about. No doubt about it. We weren't afraid of expropriating industries. The sit-in technique that later developed might have been used to acquire production facilities if we had found, after winning electoral control, that the owners could block us through the courts."

These leftist activists in the CCF were not at all afraid of "going it alone" in one province, British Columbia.

"First of all, we didn't think we'd be alone for long. The bravest elements used to say, 'When we do take control here in BC we will take over all forestry and other major industry. We'll take the heights of the economy and make it all one big co-operative. We will trade as a block with the rest of the world.' It was to be legislated expropriation!"

There was much speculation that Lenin had latterly changed his view that socialism would follow rapidly on the heals of the monopoly stage of capitalism. He had also stressed the importance of co-operatives. Lenin had said: "We have the right to say that the simple development of cooperatives becomes identified for us with the development of socialism itself."

But Lenin was late, far too late, in sensing the dangers inherent in over-centralization of the command economy. He had warned, in his final days, of "a bureaucratic utopia." That was precisely what Stalin and his central planners had induced.

In Canada, one presumed, those capitalists would not be sitting idly while being relieved by the CCF, of their command of the "economic heights." Just what form was their opposition to expropriation expected to take?

For John Smith, the Spanish Civil War had driven home the limitations of what could be achieved if the CCF won legislative authority and actually used it against corporate Canada.

"Until that time we saw no cloud on the horizon which we couldn't overcome. We didn't think there could be any effective opposition to the great mass of the people we were going to educate and introduce to socialism. We felt there could be no real opposition to change from a handful of reactionaries."

Queried about the Left's reaction to what must have been sobering news of the Stalinist purges in the Soviet Union, and what effect this would have on their ability to gain public support for their planned undertakings, John Smith responded as follows:

"The crimes and terror of Stalin's regime only started to come to our attention with the purge trials during the years of the Spanish Civil War. But before that we saw Soviet workers battling ahead, closing the technological gap with the rest of the world, and moving from strength to strength.

"The main problem in Russia seemed to be the lack of individual, personal development. But we saw none of the problems that limited Russia as ones we would have to face: a phase of capitalist accumulation and struggles with a peasantry and the remnants of feudalism."

The leftist intellectuals of the CCF had an uneasy alliance with the labour movement. As John Smith saw it, "many in the CCF had a certain animosity toward unions as they had developed at that time. Many unions were more concerned with having a closed shop and preventing the unemployed from entering the labour market than anything else."

They then also often engaged, as did society in general, in

blatant racism against Canadian-born Japanese and Chinese in particular and Asian immigrants generally.

But John had little direct personal contact with unions. He worked mainly on his own around Langford painting houses, cutting firewood and filing saws. He was also involved in gardening and, not least, political education throughout the thirties.

In pre-war BC, politics was the usual sideshow, but in Europe many dark, lowering, ominous clouds—anti-unionism, anti-communism, anti-semitism, German nationalism and fascism—were gathering momentum.

July, 1960. "A friend, Edith, took this photo in John's cabin on the ***Louise.*** *I told her it was* 'highly immoral' *but she said,* 'Aw heck! Let people be nasty if they want!' *A good philosophy."*

11 *Rabble-rouser & Scribbler*

ONE OF EVE'S MOST RADICAL FRIENDS was the self-described political and labour agitator, Matt Glenday. In his early teen years, he learned his radical politics as he listened to speakers of the Independent Labour Party, preaching their socialist message on Scotland's famous Glasgow Green.

This is a summary of only the early, more colourful background and activities of Eve's long-time friend and socialist colleague, but what an event-filled life the young rabble-rouser led.

Matt Glenday arrived in San Francisco in 1905 and moved to BC shortly thereafter, transferring to the Carpenters' Union in Vancouver from Glasgow. He was the youngest delegate ever elected to the Building Trades Council.

Matt heard an organizer speak at Old City Hall on Main Street for the *Industrial Workers of the World*—the renowned *Wobblies*. The revolutionary syndicalism of the *IWW*—aiming to replace government with workers' syndicates—seemed like a great idea to the young radical, so he joined them.

The *IWW* joined with other workers, including western miners, in mistakenly seeking, in a major upsurge of union strength, an association with the revolutionary but all-too authoritarian Russian Bolsheviks.

But Glenday, unemployed for a short time in Vancouver, had much better luck in San Francisco. Within three days of his arrival a major earthquake struck and he found lots of work replacing destroyed buildings. Then he started on a tumultuous career as a rabble-rouser initiating minor quakes of his own.

As a labour activist, he helped spark the historic Free Speech fights in Oakland where in 1907 he joined the Socialist Party.

Free Speech struggles took place all the way up the west coast from San Diego to Victoria—and socialists were jailed in most cities along the way. During one such battle, Matt met Austin Lewis, the author-lecturer-attorney who defended some of the many socialists arrested in and around the Frisco Bay area.

The right to speak openly and carry the socialist message to workers on street corners (in the same manner, say, as the Salvation Army tried to "get all your coin on their drums") was the central issue then joined by the *Wobblies* and the Socialist Party. The struggle was critical to organizers like Glenday. If they had lost their right to address groups of workers, their rabble-rousing would have been severely restricted.

Always on the go, Matt Glenday moved on to New York in 1915 and became a business agent of local 2561 of the Carpenters Union. He participated in the big strike of 1917 when the union president, William Hutchison, suspended over seventeen thousand members of his union for balking at his directive to go back to work. They adamantly refused to do so because Hutchison had signed the deal with the contractors' association behind the backs of the union membership.

Matt charged into a meeting of about 5,000 union members in the Cooper Union building in downtown New York and initiated a wild melée when he vigorously opposed the order to return to work at a lower standard in an agreement made without the workers' prior knowledge and support. There was such an explosion of anger that the police had to be called to escort the union president from the meeting.

Matt and Sam Waskoff, another business agent, attended the National Convention of the Carpenters' Union in Fort Worth, Texas, to oppose the president. But they, along with many others, were prevented even from entering the convention hall.

Waskoff played a prominent role in the revolutionary activities in Russia at that time. Correspondents Rhys Williams and John Reid reported they were present when Waskoff led revolutionary forces to take over the telephone and telegraph system in Moscow. He was then responsible for sending out bogus telegrams to train dispatchers. The resulting confusion and chaos had counter-revolutionary forces moving in many wrong directions.

This great friend of Glenday's was also reliably reported by Williams to be one of the right-hand men of revolutionary leader Lenin. Waskoff died in 1922 on the Ukraine front fighting counter-revolutionary forces sponsored by the capitalist countries.

A Socialist Party of Canada organizer, Wilfred Gribble, who had taken a strong, anti-war stand in Canada, arrived in New York and helped get Matt a set of tools and a job. Gribble continued his anti-war efforts in New York.

There was considerable corruption in the unions in New York and the labour movement had no real socialist base there. Nevertheless, Glenday again led a floor fight against a czar of the building trades, Robert P. Brindell, attacking him for a campaign of graft. Although Brindell had close connections with people of high-flown status in the labour movement (such as Hutchison and Samuel Gompers) he was finally prosecuted by the famous liberal lawyer Samuel Untermeyer and sent to Sing Sing prison. For his part in this affair, Glenday was awarded a gold watch and $500.

In California again, in 1919, Matt helped raise funds for workers charged under the Criminal Syndicalist laws which declared many radical organizations illegal. When secret indictments were returned against those actively engaged in raising funds for the defence, Lewis, their labour lawyer, advised Matt and others to "leave the country without delay."

When Glenday arrived in Victoria, Canadian Immigration officials, aware of his radical background, tried to make him return to Seattle. But radicals could also be devious. He managed to get a temporary permit to enter Vancouver and got in touch with a helpful lawyer. A friend in the *One Big Union* loaned Glenday money for a deposit on a piece of land. His lawyer then notified Immigration that Matt had entered Canada as a British Subject, had taken up land, and therefore had a right to stay.

Glenday landed in Parksville in 1918 where he joined a working class political party, the Federated Labour Party. Like Matt, the FLP had no interest in reforming capitalism. It aimed at "the complete overthrow of the present system of property ownership and wealth production."

As a campaign manager, he plastered the town with election posters which agitated certain people. When a charge was laid against him he revelled in defending himself, demanding that his accusers prove their case. He told the court that all political parties put up posters and that the FLP would no doubt continue to do so. He further rubbed salt by saying "there will be a labour party long after the Chief of Police of Port Alberni is dead."

Glenday supported the work of FLP members Bob Skinner and Bill Hope who wrote both short- and long-term programs analyzing BC's social and economic conditions as they saw them. Matt learned from these radical planners. He credited Skinner and Hope with the substantive work which laid the foundation for the initial, strongly socialist principles and policies of the CCF.

Glenday went on to arrange a money transfer from the Munich Fund which was used to start a second CCF newspaper in BC, *The Federationist,* when *The Commonwealth* was folded by its private owner. He also drew attention to the "bore from within" approach of BC communists to the CCF, warning of complications that would arise if the CCF did not take a firm stand. The resulting fight led to the expulsion from the CCF of A.M. Stephens, president of a communist front, the *League for Peace and Democracy.*

Glenday was just one of many determined, committed, radical agitators who crossed paths—and exchanged affectionate personal and political barbs—with Eve, Don and John Smith in the chaotic years of political struggle after the founding of the CCF.

*

We quote here several excerpts from Glenday's lively, poignant, sometimes hilarious and, as Eve noted, "cheeky," correspondence with the Smiths.

To one of his earlier letters, Matt appended this slightly naughty portrait of Eve Grey:

ANALYST'S REPORT

Subject: Evelyn Grey

Your analyst has to report that this is one of the most difficult subjects he has dealt with over a long period of time. The conclusions enumerated below are, to the best of his belief, correct and reliable, but the girl is of such a nature as to defy a complete analysis.

Appearance:

Build: Slim, about 5'6" in height.

Complexion: Dark

Hair: Practically black. Smooth and lustrous. Short.

Eyes: Dark. Very big. (It should be particularly noted that the eyes of this subject are deceptive. They would give the impression of a sweet, gentle, ultra-feminine nature, which impression may be later confounded.)

Mouth: Intelligent. (Same remarks apply here as to the eyes.)

General Remarks on Appearance: The girl is exceedingly pretty, in a boyish way, and this fact makes her more dangerous than she would otherwise be.

Mentality:

It is here that the complexities of the subject's nature prove exceedingly difficult to analyze. It is probably a fact that had the girl lived a normal life she would be of the usual, attractive, party-going, bridge-playing, dancing type. It seems however that in some way or other, possibly because of continued ill health, she has taken up the study of socialism and, as might be expected of such a positive nature, she has turned to Marxism.

The contradiction of a boyish bob, dark vivid eyes, a sweet mouth, allied with the gross materialism and cynicism of Marxism, will be understood. The contradictions have produced in this case a girl of exceedingly dangerous character.

Your analyst has found her difficult to handle, since his brain is completely occupied in countering her impudent remarks whenever he meets her. Forced into a corner on the subject, the girl declared that beneath the hard exterior, all the usual feminine emotions ran riot. There is no doubt that if she possesses these emotions they *will* run riot, since the girl is intense in every way. But so far, your analyst has no reason to suppose that such emotions do exist as claimed.

The girl has a wider knowledge of her subject than possibly others and has the faculty of refraining from looking the part. This characteristic, we find, is her most dangerous weapon. There is no doubt that many unsuspecting girls have become friendly with her without realizing for one moment that she is a ruthless Marxist. It is practically impossible to warn others against her, as she can assume a touching "misunderstood" expression almost at will, even while taking steps in her mind to make another victim of Marxism.

The girl has considerable facility in the art of retort and argument, and if she can obtain the corner of a table on which to sit, and space in which to swing her attractive legs, it is practically impossible to deal with her. There is little doubt that her continued illness has so sharpened her mental faculties and developed her powers of thought that she can twist others of her sex around her fingers.

If she brings the eyes and the mouth into play it is extremely probable that she can do the same, to an even more pronounced degree, with the opposite sex. It is in this regard that your analyst would point out that such a girl must necessarily be a constant source of danger to a political movement. He would warn the Executive of the party to be on the qui vive for entanglements with Executive Board members. The girl is a Marxist of Marxians and may at any time go to work to ensure that the Executive turns the CCF into a 100 percent Marxian movement.

If it is true that beneath the Marxism she has, as she says, the usual feminine characteristics, the danger of such a girl around headquarters at this period in the history of the movement can well be imagined. There are all the potentialities of another Mata Hari here.

Summary:

A more complete report will be made later when your analyst has had further opportunity for observations. He will be compelled to raise his fees in this instance, as this is the toughest subject he has attempted to analyze and he has to accept insults of every description while engaging in even ordinary conversation with the girl.

The fact that she is very popular with other people makes the situation even more fraught with danger. She has lately joined an organization to which she refers as the "Unemployed Prostitutes." This fact should also be noted by the executive. It is, in this instance as in others, impossible to decide when she is telling the truth and when she is lying. It is extremely hard to believe that she would be unemployed in this particular line (see remarks on appearance). However, the girl remains, for the moment at least, very much an enigma.

*

One of his many letters from California urging Eve to struggle on, despite her recurring health problems, ended with this line:

See you don't overtax your health—and yet don't rest on your laurels. Matt.

As a prolific letter writer himself, Matt Glenday regularly prodded Eve to write more frequently. He also teased her endlessly about her passionate interest in ballet and in nature:

My Dearest Ballerina:

Quit chasing them butterflies for a night and send me some news. Otherwise I will have to take a header off the Golden Gate bridge. Your greatest FAN, Matt.

The editor of the BC CCF's newspaper did not always publish Glenday's scorching criticisms and critiques of the CCF's social democratic leadership. Matt regularly threatened to return to BC and again involve himself in its political and labour struggles:

Dear Darling Eve: "Matt" can make the Matterhorn's 14,780 ft. easier than Matt can get a few inches in the paper he helped launch for the eradication of capitalism. With love and curses. Matt.

Darling Eve-lyn: How is the educational committee getting along in bringing about the EVE-OLUTION?

So—they are not going to publish my review of Belden's book. Try and get a reading of Silken Curtain; then you will understand better how those labour fakirs work. Read it to those classes of yours.

I would like to visit one or two of those clubs when they have some of those right-wingers speaking. I might add my two cents worth.

Regards to Don & John. Matt

Eve thought Glenday idealized the working man and working class, but he would often comment on the apparent inability of "the workers" to make much of an impact on the political system and, regretfully, of his own current lack of involvement:

Dear Eve:

The most constructive thing I have done in ten years has been to keep my mouth shut, buy Willie Hearst's Sunday funnies, go to the beach and sit under a palm tree and watch the waves roll up on the beach and then recede. They look beautiful as they roll in. You think they're going someplace but they are like the workers. They have a chain on them that makes them topple over. They flash for a minute, and then peter out.

Your family tree is outstanding. The crown has blessed them with sword and arrows, the bent knee and bent back. I have no doubt but you will see that the picture is completed and get your neck stretched at the end of a rope. My sympathy to Don and John for the expense you will put them to.

Come down here when Don goes to Santa Anita.

Love &*Kisses,* this time only, Matt

Still another letter written from Carmel-By-The-Sea, California, commented on Eve's visit to Carmel and Matt's visit to Pender Island:

Lance Corporal Smith:

Sorry there were not enough heating pads, fur-lined coats, cough drops, aspirin and castor oil supplied to make your trip comfortable. You are on probation until next February when you will report to headquarters. You will either be demoted or promoted after a full investigation of your actions.

As you are always so busy, there is no reply to the "cheeky" letters you spoke of.

Thanks John, for telling the truth about our eats. I don't see why you don't sell that icebox; you never have anything in it except a little cat food.

If I ever go over the Hope-Princeton again, I will do the driving; my life is too precious to the revolutionary movement—even if it is not to you.

Your comments about the places that interested you sickened me. "Monuments to soldiers:" I know your party leader Winch kissed it; but please, even if you have, don't tell me. Let me have my illusions. At the rate John's going at the kitchen, I'm afraid Gabriel will sound his trumpet first.

P.S. Hope John will write and tell me how hard he works playing with his little paint brush. I have a promise from him that he will stay on the water wagon for two years; he has to keep that promise.

It's no use asking you to promise anything; you can always rationalize your actions. Anyway, with all your faults, I still admire you. I don't know why.

Love and Curses, Matt

With her friends Pauline and Beth, Eve took her turn with this delighted local pilot to see the Kamloops countryside from the air, a singular treat after years of confinement at nearby Tranquille San.

12 The Decidedly-Dissident Eve

ADHERING TO SOCIALIST CONVICTIONS when so many others had found it expedient to abandon them, meant Eve Smith had the courage to say and do those things that her instincts and her conscience told her were just and moral.

Eve's sense of morality defined and dovetailed with her definition of socialist ethics and if that made Eve a *bona fide* "dissident," so be it! But that role did not blend well with Don's.

The 1933 election marked the entry of the CCF into British Columbia provincial politics. The Tories won not even a single seat and their faltering performance helped the CCF to form the official opposition their first time out.

They won about one-third of the votes cast while the pugnacious Duff Pattullo's Liberals formed the government on the basis of a campaign of "socialized capitalism," an attempt to cut the ground from under the CCF.

In power, Pattullo waffled to the left to establish an industrial relations board, an agricultural marketing board, a reduced work week, better welfare services and a public works program to create employment.

Eve's husband Don Smith jumped into the fray to contest the Esquimalt riding on Vancouver Island during the CCF's second provincial contest in June 1937. Eve had mixed feelings about her husband's decision but dutifully supported him.

Eve was aware that Don intended to introduce her at a campaign rally that was broadcast on local radio, but she was not pleased that he called attention to the fact that relatives on her father's side had made political names for themselves. She did not consider them illustrious antecedents. Don Smith said:

"It is a long way from 1937, back to that day in 1832 when in the British House of Commons there was passed that first Reform Bill. Introduced by Lord John Russell and backed by the government with Earl Charles Grey as premier, the Reform Bill marked the first mile in a long, long trail.

"Tonight I introduce the last in that long line of Greys which came down through Grey, Governor-General of Canada and the wartime Foreign Secretary of Great Britain, Lord Grey of Fallodon. It is with great pleasure that I introduce the great granddaughter of the man who, with Lord John Russell, started the British people on the path of parliamentary reform and, incidentally, the last of a family which has carved its name deeply in the history of Great Britain and the Dominions, Miss Evelyn Grey."

Eve noted, in response, that "the most peculiar aspect of speaking tonight is not that I should be speaking on behalf of the CCF but that there should be exactly the same cry of 'Utopian Radicalism' raised in connection with this movement as there was when the Reform Bill was introduced into the British House of Commons over a century ago.

"The Reform Bill extended the franchise so that the privilege of voting on representatives to Parliament and other important issues was no longer confined exclusively to the wealthy, landed aristocracy.

"The necessity for this legislation arose from the fact that the newly developing merchant class was seeking to gain power in government in order to bring about changes necessary in the methods of production and exchange. This could be done only by electing people who could represent their interests."

While Eve agreed to make that comment, as a socialist, she preferred no mention be made of "the G.G. connection." She also wanted Don to stake out a more militant socialist position.

Eve's experience of dissent was highly individual. The concentrated effort in reading, researching, debating at meetings, writing articles, making speeches and the responsibility of taking public positions on issues, was to shape her entire life.

The very act of research assumed the nature of investigative journalism for Eve. She had a passion to learn in detail how the social and economic systems worked, and in whose interests. She would write anywhere for answers to her queries.

She learned through experience the thrill of discovering new information. The joy in learning often surprised and enthralled her, and was essential to her becoming more thoughtful about issues and more likely to reshape her earlier tendency toward acceptance of too simplistic theories and solutions. But while she appreciated the complexity of the issues that fascinated her, she never wavered from her faith in socialist solutions.

Eve did not cast aside her long held political convictions. She had studied the classic Marxian analysis and held it closely as central to her belief system.

Also, she found it quite extraordinary that so many people, including some of her close friends, could hold and cherish religious beliefs that she considered fundamentally at odds with common sense, even "downright silly" as she told one interviewer.

Eve Smith was as Eve Smith wrote. There was no split between an authorial persona and her true self. She was an outstanding example of the dictum: to thine own self be true. She had the capacity to be honest with herself and quite direct with others. She would even allow, on a rare occasion, that she was capable of being persuaded of the merits of a different policy, but not if it seemed to her to deviate from socialist principle.

But for Eve to write something simply to be personally popular or to entertain was of no interest to her. Nor had she the slightest concern that any view she presented would provoke indignation or be found troublesome by a conformist society.

Eve harboured no illusions about the effects of her writing on society. She measured as victories the receipt of letters stating the writers had been inspired to change their attitudes and practices with respect to politics or conservation. She was thrilled that her efforts, as she approached old age, were still taken seriously; she felt vindicated in her work and validated as a useful human being.

Her ability to reach out to people, to win converts to her points of view, to her causes, and to revel in such victories, helped sustain her determination to struggle on, to use her restricted energies to the full. She took courage in the belief that the cumulative effect of small, individual changes on our society, on the world, could be enormous.

Eve, as dissident, not only disagreed with the essential characteristics of the capitalist system, she had the courage to express herself in opposition to it consistently and unequivocally. In this respect she differed greatly from many self-described "convinced socialists" of the early CCF period who found it convenient constantly to adapt and reshape their views to such a degree that their policies were hardly distinguishable from those of the old parties—and, in the end, were equally ineffectual.

As the CCF fought its internal wars between the soft-pedalling social democratic leadership and its more working class radicals, time had slipped by and Premier Pattullo had positioned himself to take advantage of the CCF's disarray.

Unusual for a Liberal of his time, Pattullo offered what he called "socialized credit" to keep private BC industries from going under in the depths of Canada's Despression, despite a substantial provincial debt of over $160,000,000.

The CCF had finally pushed aside the Rev. Robert Connell at the insistence of the Left, including Eve, Don and John Smith, and had replaced him with the more colourful, much more dynamic leader, the fiery, socialist-talking Harold Winch.

Winch had an extraordinary political vigour and a passionate style of speech-making matched by his all-too-apparent need for alcohol to ease the seeming pain of his restless leadership and his highly dramatic public performances.

Despite the years of Depression, the sit-ins and the "On-to-Ottawa" march of the unemployed, the CCF, whether held back by infighting over policy or still very much involved in a slow building process, could only hold its own at seven seats when Pattullo pulled the plug and once again captured public support.

The heroics of the flamboyant Winch notwithstanding, Pattullo won thirty-one of forty-eight seats, a personal triumph of political style over substance. It set a pattern to be followed later during the long Social Credit reign of W.A.C. Bennett, the hardware merchant from Kelowna, who would dramatically seize the moment and project himself into the premiership.

The politically astute Pattullo had brought in his reformist "Mini-New-Deal" but did little to change the status quo in terms of the relative position of working class British Columbians vis-a-vis the growing power of the entrepreneurial merchant class.

The CCF leftists continued through the 1939-1945 war until the early 1950's to exert what influence they could on the CCF party in BC and its elected social democrat members at Victoria.

But as a person who later chose to absent herself from the party which would abandon its principles and "take the capitalist road," so to speak, Eve felt no pangs of guilt whatsoever in vigorously attacking at party meetings any weak, watered-down, ineffectual policies advocated by her erstwhile political associates.

Eve's dissidence took the form of moral resistance—a force of conscience—that did not permit her to backtrack. It simply never would have occurred to her to repent her views or actions for any conceivable personal gain. It was not in her character to do so.

She concluded, sadly, it was simpler for most people to follow a leader, just as religious people might cling to an organization offering authority figures. It would be easier still, she reckoned, if political leaders would perform an occasional mythical miracle, as well—but they hadn't yet managed it.

Eve deplored that so many people would surrender their freedom of thought and action rather than value and treasure it and use it creatively. Too many people sought spiritual and political leaders and accepted their leadership without question in a community of worship that too often rendered their critical faculties almost mute. For the leader it was too often a matter of opportunism. But for the follower, Eve felt, there is the much greater danger of unthinking conformism.

In the environment of "the party," many found it convenient, too, to "go along and get along" with the leaders. Close and amicable relations were certainly easier to sustain. The dissident had to be prepared to be viewed as "a disagreeable person." A veritable pain in the butt.

If CCFers were heretics repudiating the capitalist system (in truth, a majority were not), then there should have been *many* heresies tolerated. Eve wanted to expose and openly debate the full range of views brought forward by members of the party. She was disappointed that there were so many "woolly-minded, applauding sheep, unused or too lazy to think for themselves."

The CCF presumed to act as an intellectually superior movement, but it was the dissidents in the party who comprised the moral opposition to electoral politics for its own sake.

These were the forceful opponents to the Canadian politics epitomized by the Conservative Prime Minister R.B. Bennett who dared to offer unemployed workers an insulting five cents a day to keep their aggrieved minds and assaulted bodies together.

So long as the CCF tolerated a healthy degree of diversity of views and enjoined its members to hammer out their differences on the floor of party conventions, Eve felt, it could maintain a substantial degree of party unity and essential cohesiveness. Members given the opportunity at least to state their varied opinions were much more likely to continue to contribute their time, energy, money and loyalty.

But the social democratic leaders grew increasingly intolerant of diversity. With fewer opportunities to express their views, more members began, as Eve suggests, to leave the reading, studying and planning of policy to "the leaders and their hired hands." Co-inciding with M.J. Coldwell's period as national leader, a follow-the-leader syndrome soon took hold.

The authoritarian tendencies of hired secretaries such as David Lewis began to assert themselves with a vengeance. In Lewis' case, his entrenched European anti-communism was of a particularly virulent variety. He was prone to equate almost any criticism of the CCF's social democratic leadership and policies with communism. In any event, it became habitual and convenient to so label the party dissidents who, ironically, worked dilligently (if not with Lewis' degree of misplaced fervour) to keep the CCF free of communist party influence.

Eve found she could not trust the leaders of the party to continue to hold genuinely democratic conventions or to sustain party processes which allowed the power of ideas to speak freely for themselves. Simply stating that the party was democratic did not make it so. She reasoned that diversity of thought is an essential tenet of any democratic institution, and fundamental to a political movement intent on bringing about greater fairness and equality in society.

She could not in the end continue to support a party that abandoned political education, paid mere lip service to internal democracy, allowed its leaders to ignore party policies, and increasingly tended to be controlled by self-perpetuating cliques.

For Eve and hundreds more, this was tantamount to a new version of old party élitism—albeit with a deceptive new face.

Eve Smith and many fellow leftists fought for almost twenty years to democratize the party process and to hold it to socialist "principles." She felt these were the basic and essential elements and that they were adequately outlined in the CCF's enduringly controversial original *Regina Manifesto.*

But that was not a unanimous view among leftists and the conflict over the *Manifesto* requires further exploration.

13 *Never Resting, Rarely Content*

THE ABUSE OF POWER, whether by corporate entrepreneurs, government officials or those in leadership positions in her own party, aroused Eve Smith's moral indignation and energized the rebel in her—never buried far below her cheery exterior.

Eve was a committed political animal in this sense: she had made a sustained effort to inform herself of the basic underpinnings of socialist thought.

She championed the CCF's much-maligned *Regina Manifesto.* For many, even on the Left, it was a highly suspect political benchmark, purporting as it did to represent the diverse views of Marxists, trade unionists, farmer-populists, academics, social gospel preachers and social democrats. How many actually read it?

Reportedly written in the main by Frank Underhill who later denounced it and became a Liberal, the document served for a time—approximately 1933 to 1951—to represent and channel Eve's abhorrence of economic inequity and inhumanity.

While Eve's political views seemed based as much on moral outrage as economic analysis, her party's leaders were often unable to demonstrate either genuine outrage or qualitative economic analysis.

While the leaders' electoral ambitions were their overriding concerns, they were well down the list of Eve's priorities. She rated political education first and she was pleased to be asked to serve, initially, as Ernie Winch's "assistant" on the BC CCF's political education committee. Later, when it was recognized she was doing most of the work involved, she chaired that committee.

Still, Eve had no thought of running for any party or public office and maintained a cautiously suspect view of those who sought election, including her husband, Don. Whatever their motives, Eve did not fully share them. Nor was she uncritical of rank-and-file party members.

"The people in the CCF were from all walks of life and seemed to mix fairly well. But there was a certain amount of worship of the MPs and MLAs, the 'look-to-the-leader' sort of thing, instead of studying and understanding for oneself, and drawing one's own conclusions.

"The other thing you sometimes found on the Left was an idealization of the working class. We had a very good friend, Matt Glenday, a Scot, and I think you could say that Matt idealized the working class.

"We had another friend engaged in working class activity all his life who said that the working class is *always* in the right, even when it's wrong. If you analyze that, it makes sense. As the exploited class, they *are* in the right, insofar as they are being exploited.

"And if you are driven by hunger to steal, you might feel, 'We do the work, why shouldn't we be entitled to more?' The Marquis de Sade is quoted by Simone de Beauvoir as saying, 'My child, the harshness of the rich justifies the knavery of the poor.' "

Eve aggravated her relationships with officials of the party every time she set the truth, as she saw it, ahead of any party political expediency. She was one of thousands of CCF members who saw the *Regina Manifesto* as something to cling to. They happily identified with "not resting content until capitalism has been eliminated."

This aggressive stance, they felt, clearly separated the "socialist" intent of the CCF from the older, corporate-supporting Liberal and Conservative parties. And Eve and John Smith were surely among the more restless, discontented and committed of the leftists seeking to abolish capitalism.

As electoral successes brought the party closer to power provincially in the 1940's, most of those who ran for party office (and the party's appointed officials) regarded the CCF's 1933 guiding *Manifesto* as something of an anomoly and a handicap—a temporary embarrassment. For them, the manifesto had served its purpose for a time: it had attracted socialists and intellectuals who had given the party increased visibility and credibility, and had involved them in building the political machinery essential to winning legislative seats and electing MPs to Parliament.

After listening to one national CCF convention's interminable wrangle on whether to enshrine or abandon its infamous *Regina Manifesto*, this journalist wrote: "The party has been infested with *Manifestosis Canadiensis*, our own version of the Australian rabbit infestation, myxomatosis. The disease induces rabid emotionalism, bug-eyes and frothing at the mouth. It is potentially fatal, and only rarely do infected party members develop a degree of immunity to it. Any number of humorous injections will not necessarily reduce the severity of the symptoms."

Of course at every election Grits and Tories and their cheerleaders in the media and corporate worlds castigated the CCF's supposed intent to nationalize every farm and every corner grocery store. Thus, it was not difficult to wildly exaggerate the party's program and to frighten voters: to grasp the essentials of socialism, even the adumbrated version of it promoted by the CCF, required a little thought and study. After the 1940's, few took on that onerous task. "Socialism" subsequently became a less understood concept—and a much harder political sell.

The *Manifesto*—in the view of office-seeking, ambitious party activists—was too specific, too socialistic, indeed an albatross around their necks. But it became a rallying symbol for thousands of party members of everything that was distinctive about the CCF: the party's determination to put the corporate-based economy under the firm control of a socialist state whose objective would be "production to meet people's needs rather than profit."

The party's socialists certainly had a vision of a better society, one that excited and inspired them. The vision was democratic and egalitarian. So it was a shock to them when party officials tried to substitute social democracy for socialism.

One part of this effort was the attempt to proscribe certain publications that dared to criticize the Labour party—"our sister party"—in Britain.

Of course it was both insulting and farcical to suggest to intelligent, independent-minded radicals with deeply enquiring minds that certain leaflets espousing "wrong-headed" ideas might lead them astray. It was an ill-considered attempt by party rightists to exercise mind control over their often brighter and better-read fellow members. Worse still, the next step was to threaten expulsion—political excommunication—from participation in this supposedly democratically-functioning party.

Party members, previously, had been encouraged to engage in research and study and to propose policy options. Indeed, it had been the coming together of groups of political thinkers, social theorists and activists in local study clubs across the nation that had encouraged and precipitated the birth of this socialist-social democratic, co-operative commonwealth movement.

However they viewed it, the "party brass" were terrified that any *bona fide* socialist content in the CCF's election materials would leave the party open to ridicule and the derision of the conservative press.

As reformers, they wanted political power. But they desperately sought acceptance by those they perceived as their social superiors, and that provided another reason to elect non-working-class leaders.

Meeting before, during and after conventions as a "left caucus," or still later as a "socialist fellowship," the CCF leftists in BC were viewed as a serious threat to the party's social democratic leadership. The Left's advocates were told unequivocally that "there must be no party within the party." The "brass" were quite humourless about it. The ultimatum became: either pledge your allegiance to the social democratic leadership or get out! Over time, many socialist thinkers and party activists did just that.

The CCF's mild, social democratic reformism, as advocated by party secretary David Lewis and as enunciated by party leader M.J. Coldwell, prevailed. This reformism moved the party into electoral machine liberalism and adoption of policies with little to distinguish them. Eve knew they would do little or nothing to change the relative economic status of the working class.

Eve collected press clippings. She wanted documentation of the CCF's failures—and its weaknesses. Among these was one quoting M.J. Coldwell, who deigned to say to a post-convention press conference: "I am pleased that *my* policies are supported by *my* followers." Eve was scandalized and once again directly challenged the party leader.

Repeatedly called to account in letters from Eve for his disregard for the party's policies, as determined by federal conventions, Coldwell eventually wrote: "Mrs. Smith: Madam, *kindly do not write to me, ever again!*"

Much earlier than most party members, Eve Smith saw in the 1940's where this lack of integrity, this non-adherence to democratic process was leading the CCF.

Eve feared any governmental form that handed too much decision-making power to either politicians (with their 'handlers') or bureaucrats. She regarded rebellion against the abuse of power by politicians and corporations as her right and her moral duty.

Eve understood Marx's philosophy as one of faith in people to liberate themselves and realize their potential. She believed fervently in this Marxist Humanist brand of socialism. When it came to "interpreting" Marx, Eve wisely recommended that each individual read Marx directly for herself, as opposed to ploughing through the endless variety of available *opinions about* Marx.

From her reading Eve concluded that Erich Fromm had viewed Marx and Marxism correctly. Fromm had also urged his readers to "go to the source." It was Fromm, after all, who as late as 1961 first brought to North American readers the translation of Marx's *Economic and Philosophical Manuscripts* (translated by B.T. Bottomore) in Fromm's book *Marx's Concept of Man.*

In her writings, Eve took pains to be as transparent and as free from difficult-to-fathom concepts as possible. Her intention, always, was to define and clarify the issues, never to obfuscate.

Not all her socialist colleagues were as clear in their thinking. Political debate among the leftists centred too often on individuality. To each his own truth. To each his own dollar-a-bottle political prescription, albeit an elixir most often "based" on Marx.

One could argue, and Eve did, that the very purpose of the Left was to generate controversy and debate and to provide intelligent, forward-looking socialist options. Alas, the former was more easily realized than the latter.

Canada's Left, collectively, held and proselytized many visions of a better society. These would have to be reconciled or somehow accommodated before socialists could participate with any great enthusiasm, or to any great effect, in party politics. It was an accommodation that the CCF was singularly unsuccessful in making. (The NDP had no intention of trying.)

On the contrary, a strenuous effort was made, if publicly denied, to exclude socialists and socialist thinking from the Co-operative Commonwealth Federation. In 1958, the CCF's troublesome *Manifesto* would be superseded, finally, by a more clearly "social democratic" document, the Winnipeg *Declaration*.

Despite the frequent and erroneous media declarations to the contrary, "socialism" disappeared from the CCF long before its attempted unity embrace with organized labour in 1961.

Eve Smith, *here at 58, kept herself strong and fit through gardening, swimming and household chores. But repeated bouts with TB confined her to bed for nine or ten years, left her with shortness of breath and required that she take a long rest every afternoon of her adult life.*

14 *Eve Speaks on Eugene Debs*

THE AMERICAN SOCIALIST LEADER Eugene Victor Debs had been a major political figure in the US of the early 1900's and a particular source of inspiration for Eve Smith. As one of his biographers said, "his name lives on long after those of his detractors and those instrumental in persecuting him were forgotten."

Most Canadians in the 1940's were unaware of the history of socialist politics in the US, and Eve Smith, fascinated by Debs who had received over 900,000 votes in his socialist candidacy to be president of the United States, wanted British Columbians to learn about him. She was a popular guest speaker and her talks on the historic figure of Eugene V. Debs, his life and times, and the lessons that might be learned from his life were well received.

Eve deplored the increasing remoteness and affectation she witnessed in the CCF's leaders. She wanted another leader, like J.S. Woodsworth, a "common man" who rubbed shoulders with the working class, knew their problems from personal experience, and got his hands into the dishwater—a man, indeed, like Eugene Debs.

This is an abbreviated version of her lecture:

*

As socialists, we do not believe in the 'Great Man' theory. That is, that great men make history. Nor do we believe that events are ordained by any god/father figure. We believe that conditions and circumstances develop people's thinking and actions. And that people, in turn, try to change and modify those conditions. Thus, ideas and conditions act and interact, one on another.

If ever a man reacted to his environment, it was Eugene Debs. The way he developed and changed his ideas and actions to meet changing conditions is one of the things that makes a study of his life and times of great interest to us.

Unlike some people who have become 'great' in the eyes of their fellow men, Debs deserved recognition, for he was great in his very simplicity, in the fact that though honours and adulation were showered on him, he never left the rank and file. His fellow workers were always his personal friends and his love for them, his understanding and sympathy for their troubles, were sincere, not something just put on like a cloak for the platform. He felt a great loyalty to his class and even before the days when he embraced socialism, he deeply felt that class loyalty.

But perhaps his ability to learn from experience and change his tactics to meet changing conditions, is the most important thing that we can learn and remember about him.

Debs did not start life as a socialist. Socialism came to him relatively late. He went through a period of believing that the wrongs and injustices and inequalities of the society that he lived in could be set right under capitalism. He was enthused, first, by craft unionism, then industrial unionism, then political action—supporting Grover Cleaveland, then a separate People's Party, and finally he embraced scientific socialism as the only solution to abolish wage slavery and the profit system.

The era in which Debs grew up was that of the Robber Barons, an era when every ounce of profit was being gouged out of the workers and every means, no matter how brutal or illegal, was used by these Robber Barons to prevent workers from forming their own organizations —workers' unions.

These were tumultuous times—before the end of the century. If Debs had lived in relatively quiet times he probably would not have made such a mark. But, as it was, he rose to great heights as an ardent fighter for his fellow workers, an agitator and crusader, always struggling against an array of power that was lined up against the working class: the capitalists, the government, the judiciary, the paid officers of the state, the pulpit, the militia . . . and Debs never lost an opportunity to expose those elements.

Debs has been portrayed as a sort of folksy Hoosier character rather than the militant trade unionist and socialist that he was. He recognized the odds against implementing the principles of socialism and he rejected the success he could have enjoyed as a labour leader, making a lot of money and securing his future. He well understood the corrupting influence of respectability and chose the hard way.

Early in his life he was a railroader, firing engines, a very dangerous job in those days. Men were often killed, safety devices were not always employed. There were faulty tracks; railcars often rammed together. Debs organized the brakemen, switchmen and carmen into one union. The necessity of having one strong body of rail workers became obvious to him.

Long before he was a socialist, Debs was strongly pro-worker. He saw that they produced the wealth but did not benefit from that production. It was only a few years previously that he had been opposed to strikes, saying that they led to anarchy and were against the laws of the land. Strange words from the man who was later to be so prominent in one of the most important of all strikes, the Pullman Strike of 1894.

Debs played a major part in the Pullman Strike, that great contest between workers and owners. Debs and others who were active in the strike were jailed on a charge of 'conspiracy to obstruct the mails.' Considered more dangerous, Debs got six months in jail, the other leaders only three. But this experience brought home to him how all the institutions of capitalism are ranged against the working class: the corporations, the courts, the press, the armed forces, the pulpit.

That famous attorney, Clarence Darrow, had been retained by the Chicago and Northwestern Railway Managers Association but he was so disgusted with the manner in which the railway workers were treated and the way the strike was handled that he left that lucrative position and became counsel for the rail workers and other unionists in many important and historic labour incidents.

While serving his six months in Woodstock jail, Debs was sent books and pamphlets on socialism. An ardent young man came to see him and brought him Marx's *Capital*. As one author said: 'A tough and pragmatic trade unionist entered the jail; a radical, well on the way to socialism, departed six months later.'

When Debs returned to Chicago, something like 100,000 people lined the streets to greet and cheer him. In a speech at a labour rally, Debs had something to say about the aftermath of the Haymarket riots. He described the sentences meted out to the active participants as 'judicial murders.' The Haymarket incidents arose from the struggles of working men to reduce their work day to eight hours and to use what they had previously thought to be their right to free speech to agitate and propagandize for it. Agit-prop.

By 1900 Debs was the candidate for the combined Socialist

Labour and Social Democratic parties. The 100,000 votes he received encouraged the two parties to officially combine, a major stride forward in the organization of socialist activities. The ruthlessness of the capitalists and the eager co-operation of government officials in their anti-labour activities was teaching the workers that socialism was the only hope for them. Debs consistently proclaimed the issue was between capitalism and socialism, despotism and democracy.

In 1905 Debs helped to organize the famous *IWW* union, the *Industrial Workers of the World*, who became known as *The Wobblies*. He maintained that the American Federation of Labour that was initially formed to help its workers was now the tool of capitalists in the exploitation of workers. He said the AFL's go-slow philosophy of gradually improving conditions under capitalism (and often stepping in to stop labour actions) helped the owning class. Debs' objective was to have all of labour organized into one big and powerful labour body.

Debs also continued the struggle for the political education of working people, political awareness and democratic action. He did not favour the tactics of direct, militant action, often used by the IWW, though he certainly understood the reasons for it. Violence of every description was used against the IWW by the owners of industry.

The vote for women was advocated by Debs long before he became a socialist. As a young man he had belonged to a literary society in his home town of Terre Haute. Visiting speakers included Wendell Phillips, the slave abolitionist, and Robert Ingersoll, the atheist. But when Debs suggested Susan B. Anthony be invited to speak, others in the group refused to go along. A woman who went around advocating the vote for women was just too much! Always persistent, Debs went ahead on his own, invited Anthony to speak, hired the hall and made all the arrangements. He then escorted her from the rail station himself.

The First World War caused a major split in the socialist ranks. A majority actually opposed military action. But a strong minority who were nationalists first and, at best, only lukewarm to socialism, walked out of the party, supported the war, and aided one capitalist government against another.

Although not a pacifist, Debs opposed the 1914-1918 war because he saw no point in workers participating in an essentially capitalist crisis and spoke out strongly against worker involvement in it. When socialists were arrested under the Espionage Act he spoke in their support and was then himself arrested.

Debs was charged with 'uttering words intended to cause insubordination and disloyalty' within the military forces of the United States and with 'inciting resistance to war!'

In his speech to the jury, Debs said: 'I admit being opposed to the present form of government. I admit being opposed to the present social system. I am doing what little I can, to bring about a change that shall do away with the rule of the great body of the people by relatively small groups, and establish in this country an industrial and social democracy. What you may choose to do with me is of little consequence. It is American institutions which are on trial here before a court of American citizens.'

That court of Americans convicted Debs and he was given a ten-year sentence. So this man, who had spent his lifetime fighting for his fellow workers, was jailed because he refused to fight against his fellow men.

President Woodrow Wilson steadfastly refused to pardon Debs after the war. But, in the year 1920, convict number 9653 at Atlanta Jail was nominated presidential candidate for the Socialist Party. Debs, in jail, polled over 900,000 votes. President Harding eventually pardoned Eugene Debs, by then an old man, in 1921.

Debs had taken up the cause of the victimized, the underpaid, those discriminated against—in short, the casualties of capitalism. Debs took up prison reform, insisting that most criminals were products of the capitalist system, and that only with the abolition of capitalism and the advent of socialism could people live decently and properly develop.

With capitalism 'progressing' in its inevitable manner: great fortunes amassed by the few and great poverty and exploitation ever increasing, the Depression just over the horizon, the old socialist fighter quietly died and passed out of the struggle.

But Debs' ideas live on. The example of his integrity and his life's work is there for us to learn from—if we so choose.

Eve Smith loved her ponies, "dear Cheyenne and Pico." *She bought Cheyenne in 1952 when he was three and looked after him for over thirty years at her small, South Pender Island acreage.*

15 *Choosing Not To Make War*

1939 BROUGHT WAR AGAIN to Eve and Don Smith, to their friends, their politics, their lives. It brought the enormous anxiety and disruption which only a war could visit upon them.

Eve clearly remembered the fundamental controversy at that time, the debate among her socialist colleagues, about whether they could possibly support Canada's participation in another world war—just twenty-one years after the armistice of 1918.

Some of Eve's comrades thought there would be no war. Don felt certain there *would* be. He and most of his family were dead set against participating. John was vehemently opposed. Their sister Connie joined the CWACs ('Quacks!'), the Canadian Women's Army Corps, as a way to finance her postwar training as a nurse.

It was a genuine shock to Eve Smith that the majority of CCF members would so readily abandon party policy and leave their leader, J.S. Woodsworth, virtually alone in the House of Commons in opposing Canada's participation in a "capitalist war." She was astonished that so many CCF members would put "patriotism" before the "socialist principle" of opposition to such a war.

"They believed that Hitler was terrible, as I did," Eve said. "Through the later years of the Depression we had been exposing Hitler and his anti-Semitism and his concentration camps. We knew what was going on and we tried to do something about it.

"But we were opposed to working class people going off and killing each other just for the sake of profiting General Motors and Gulf Oil. We argued that going to war was doing precisely what your enemy was doing: being mindlessly destructive."

For Eve the issue of democratic choice was paramount. In her strongly held view, one could support the war and enlist, or not. But, she reasoned, when you are supposedly fighting for democracy, how could you then possibly support conscription which deprived many thousands of Canadians of their democratic right to oppose the war and not participate in it?

BC's Premier Pattullo once again astutely put forward a public works program and offered co-operation with Ottawa as part of his 1941 wartime election platform.

The CCF doubled their number of MLAs to fourteen, the Tories won twelve seats and the Liberals found themselves four short of a majority, dropping to twenty-one seats.

But the CCF had won almost precisely one voter in three with 33.36 percent of the popular vote and seemed on their way to electoral power. They were even ahead of the Pattullo-led Liberals at 32.94 percent and the resurgent Tories with 30.91percent.

The Liberals avoided defeat by voting in convention for a new leader, John Hart, to take them into an anti-CCF wartime coalition government with the Tories: Coalition 33—CCF 14.

The "socialist principle," as Eve called it, of "opposition to a capitalist war" became absolutely central in their lives when Don's brother John, who spoke out strongly against the war, was conscripted. "We would have hidden John if he had been agreeable. We would have paid for him to live somewhere else and not join the army, but he said it was not in his character to hide out."

Anti-war sentiment, however, was waning. The anti-militarist syndicalist elements in the union movement had substantially diminished. But John Smith, younger than Don by four years, refused to "go active." Don had asthma which disqualified him from service. Their brother, Lloyd, was in England. He became a conscientious objector and never got into uniform.

Thousands of "no-go's," French-Canadian oppositionists, conscientious and political objectors, including John Smith, were gathered at such army camps as Vernon and Terrace, BC, supposedly preparing to guard Canada's west coast (which authorities considered vulnerable) against any possible Japanese incursion.

As absurd as that possibility seemed, there were incidents that alarmed government officials and precipitated the movement of these unwilling troopers. On June 20, 1942, a Japanese ship actually shelled the lighthouse on Estevan Point on Vancouver Island. Japanese troops captured two remote islands, Attu and Kiska, at the extreme end of the US-owned Aleutian Islands.

In 1942-43 the Alaska Highway was quickly planned and rapidly pushed forward—2300 kilometres of it in eight months—by US Army engineers. A Japanese invasion apparently seemed a real threat to Canadian and US politicians and their military.

In a federally-endorsed criminal action, 23,000 people of Japanese extraction, two-thirds of them Canadian born, were unceremoniously uprooted by local authorities from their businesses and farms and carted off to interior ghost towns or set to work on Alberta beet farms. Their land, their boats and other property were brutally confiscated in a blatantly racist expropriation, and sold—without a thought being given to compensation. Only the CCF opposed these actions.

Even after the war when there was no possible excuse for it, they were callously and disgracefully mistreated. They were given the option of accepting transport to Japan or "dispersal in Canada, somewhere east of the Rockies."

At the tender age of twenty-five, John Smith found himself in a leadership position among the conscripts, many of whom were in their teen years or early twenties. When word got out to them that the military had decided to renege on its agreement with these men and to ship them to Halifax for embarkation to the war in Europe, they responded by locking up their officers and demanding meetings with the army's top brass.

By any measure, it was mutiny in the ranks, pure and simple. To break the strike, and to prevent all-out riots on several western military bases, the government had to negotiate with their representatives, John among them. Finally, the men were given a small amount of spending money, sent home for a holiday, and given the unspecified option of hiding out or going overseas on an inactive, non-violent basis. John Smith opted for the latter and shipped to London via Halifax to observe the warring capitalists from somewhat closer up—tending a quartermaster's stores.

John wrote to Eve at length, and often, from England. She, in turn, kept him informed of events, political and otherwise, at home. He shipped two small paintings to Eve which adorn, still, a wall of the Smith home on South Pender Island.

Although stricken again with TB, Eve monitored the situation by listening mostly to CBC Radio in her bedroom. At first the CCF held out briefly against conscription. Their initial theme was "conscript wealth and matériel, not men!"

The national leader, M.J. Coldwell, demanded Canada sell war goods, munitions, tanks and so on to Britain "for cash on the barrelhead." Eve thought this pronouncement "too immoral for words!" Then the party brass changed their tune and started talking in favour of conscription and forcing men to go and fight. Eve was incensed.

"I was lying on my bed and I heard Grace McInnes and Harold Winch on radio urging people to go to war and they said these very words: 'It is not fair to the ones who are going overseas to have others staying at home; therefore to be fair, you have to have conscription.' Now, can you imagine such Orwellian double-talk as that? If I hadn't heard them myself on radio, I would hardly have believed that anyone could talk such gibberish!

"For those who wanted to go, well, they had volunteered. It was their right. But there was nothing fair, for those who didn't wish to go, to be forced to kill others and be killed—just to help H.R. MacMillan and Crown Zellerbach boost their profits."

As a matter of principle, many on the Left simply could not support the war. If it was a principle, you couldn't compromise; otherwise it wasn't a principle. To change their minds would have been political expediency.

*

There are at least two 'truths' about wars, one would think. First, few would agree to fight them if they understood the full, irrational verity of them or could foresee their horrific and terrifying human costs. Secondly, the politicians and militarists who can suddenly puff themselves up as "passionate patriots and upholders of truth, faith and country," certainly believe that in defending their personal property and/or "the nation's security," any amount of truth suppression and lying can be justified.

*

Prime Minister Mackenzie King held out against conscription until he judged the political balance of forces to have changed. French Canadians, by and large (despite the Nazi occupation of France) were fiercely determined not to be drawn into another war fought by imperial Britain. Quebec, in the view of some of King's ministers, was close to revolution on the issue so he felt obliged politically to equivocate. He did so in this classically King, if laughable, manner: "There will be conscription if necessary, but not necessarily conscription."

The Smiths' anti-war position during World War II was very much a minority one within the CCF. There was much genuine pacifism but the issue was a complex one. Patriotism, for one thing, was not generally as fashionable among the Left. They were among those least likely to accept the "my country, right or wrong" brand of eager, unquestioning patriotism of those who just couldn't wait to get into battle.

But many on the Left took what they considered a "realistic" view and considered themselves morally bound to oppose the horrific evil of Nazism which sent millions to their deaths. Some also felt the nightmarish possibility of German stormtroopers overrunning Canada not a total impossibility. Many others, of course, had strong personal ties to the United Kingdom—the "old country" whence their parents had come or where their parents or grandparents lived with the dangers and deprivation.

The nationalism of Canada's superpatriots was aggressive in nature, attributing virtues beyond criticism to one's country and to fighting for one's flag. But, the majority of Canadians, somewhat reticently patriotic, were astonished by their US neighbours. Wrapped in jingoism and their star-spangled banner from birth, they seemed collectively to snap to attention, hands on hearts, prepared to die for America, apple pie, General Motors and the Supreme Allied commander—their very own General "Ike" Eisenhower. US propagandists did their best to glorify war, and if stocks just happened to skyrocket in value? Well, that only proved that war was a good thing for corporate USA.

As still more news arrived of Nazi atrocities, the consensus became overwhelming in Canada: the German juggernaut had to be stopped, rolled back and put out of commission along with the splenetic, hate-preaching Nazi party that had spawned it.

But were the Smiths and the anti-war activists who shared their perspective, the pacifists and conscientious objectors, any less moral and courageous than those who offered genuine, enthusiastic, or perhaps even mindless, support for the war? Perhaps too often in history it has been the ill-considered decisions of the democratic majority that have prevailed.

During the war years, the political mood of many in Canada's armed forces changed. If they were going to risk their lives abroad they would be much more insistent on a decent, more humane, more sharing society to return to. This led many to take another look at the CCF which had been struggling for twelve long years to elect tiny groups of MPs to Ottawa and small numbers of MLAs to provincial legislatures.

The Soviet peoples and their heroic Red Army were another

factor. They had become our wartime allies, "true comrades-in-arms." The people pushing War Savings Bonds said so! Canadians were proud of the association, filled with admiration for those who eventually lost twenty million people in smashing the formidable German war machine. If these people were "socialists," could the Canadian version be all that bad?

But Canadian workers in wartime were not, in the main, hellbent on putting an end to capitalism. Quite a few of our more politicized returning soldiers were keen to "bring to birth a new world from the ashes of the old." Many more were determined to promote economic and social change and the CCF seemed, at least potentially, a promising political option.

But after the war was finally concluded in both Europe and the Pacific, Premier Hart won thirty-seven seats in an October, 1945 campaign. The CCF dropped to ten.

The Coalition won 55.8 percent. The CCF, while losing seats, climbed to 37.6 percent. The LPP (communist), in their best effort, won 3.5 percent—but no seats.

Social Credit, soon to be revitalized in a daring move by a long-time Tory, W.A.C. Bennett, won less than 0.5 percent.

Across Canada, CCF membership increased from 20,000 in 1942 to over 100,000 in 1944, the same year the Saskatchewan CCF won overwhelmingly. Ontario had elected thirty-four CCFers in 1943. It seemed a cheering time for the CCF's social democratic brand of "socialism."

There was little enthusiasm, however, on the socialist Left.

Social democrats might very well attempt to design programs as "equalizers" to help elevate the "socially disadvantaged." But serious leftists knew there would be immediate, entrenched opposition by those who held effective corporate power.

Any well-designed programs that effectively challenged the economic status quo would bring the advocates of capitalism unhindered by "fuzzy-minded" socialist planners immediately into the fray to slap down any such serious initiatives.

The socialist Left knew in their hearts and heads that only by building mass popular organizations prepared to struggle for their rights and interests could they make any real difference. A majority of the Left for years urged the CCF political pussycats to somehow change into triumphal socialist tigers challenging the power élite. But the CCF kits developed no claws—and few clues.

16 *Not a Shrinking Violet*

EVE INSISTED ON PARTY DEMOCRACY and fought for rank-and-file control of the CCF's political agenda. She did so, vigorously, even as her party became increasingly less committed to open and democratic processes. The CCF was also backing away from its democratizing tradition of encouraging intensive political education.

Neither the CCF Left nor Right were cohesive or homologous in their socialist and social democratic views, respectively. But it was much easier for the Right to unite around its primary goal: its obsession to win elections, to "take power," than it was for the Left to consistently agree on its goals and strategies.

Too many leftists enjoyed the roles that seemed to be their lot: the persecuted underdog, the uncompromising policy purist, or that of the bright, thrusting debater, caught up in a self-realized version of a supposed "scientific" and "dialectical" process.

Too few of the leftists would admit among themselves to the possibility of theoretical or policy error, much less to the strategic need to change a long-held view of a rapidly-changing world. At times, it seemed, it mattered not at all that "the workers," their target audience, simply couldn't understand what on earth some of the self-absorbed, self-appointed leaders-to-the-left were talking about.

The sometimes obscurantist language employed by some 1930's to 50's Marxian socialists when in full, flamboyant flight, could often leave their theoretically-challenged audiences perhaps impressed, but linguistically and politically overdosed—and more likely to take their chances with those old-party pols, the ones speaking for those sleazy capitalists who, despite everything, were occasionally creating jobs and paying wages.

But generally, the socialists in the CCF, when they managed to consider such issues with a degree of realism, knew perfectly well that the social-democratic Right of the party (the more politically ambitious, the hellbent-for-election, the focused-on-power, the hangers-on and camp followers—there were always more of them!) would elect a majority among party executives and councils, and therefore control the appointed positions—all of the conventional machinery of electoral power politics.

They would also control the nominating conventions in most constituencies and, in most cases, freeze out any leftist aspirants who tried to buck the rightists' social democratic views and their predominance in the party.

Another problem area never tackled by the Left was, and remains, the extraordinary practice, now an entrenched tradition, of allowing its party leader, while in opposition, to control completely the appointment of *his* chief grousers-in-opposition—the ministry critics.

More crucially, the party leader, when called upon to form a government, would select only politically sympatico and controllable buddies for cabinet. He could ignore any vigorous or highly competent leftists whom he feared might occasionally embarrass the new government by publicly advocating implementation of the party's policies as determined by democratic conventions.

To the Left, such policies were considered sacrosanct "instructions" from the party's ranks to the cabinet. To the Rightist leader, these represented mere expressions of the party hoi polloi—the rabble—that could be ignored with impunity. Party conventions, treated more as social gatherings, became much less important in the determination of party principles and directions.

Any token leftist elevated to head a ministry would remain in position only "at the pleasure" of the premier. Such appointments offered opportunities for the leader to "educate" the odd man out, to witness his fellow appointees' obsequious approval of every pronouncement, however tentative, pathetic or unwise, by the all-powerful, the leader, seated in the chair most tall with the upholstery most plush.

It is somewhat more in the UK tradition of cabinet building to include representatives of different "power centres" and to tolerate in cabinet the strong expression of various trends of opinion within the party. But Canadian social democrats have allowed their leaders to be their "be-all and end-all" in terms of the exercise of control and political power. Eve Smith correctly anticipated the results of that corrupting practice.

Some serious thought might produce a more democratic

practice—and much-improved cabinets—wherein a degree of healthy, dynamic tension and intelligent, honest debate on policy could replace what has posed as leadership.

As it happened, there was, among many on the Left, a certain ambivalence in their love-hate relationship with their party. One could see an obvious measure of resignation, even half-heartedness, in their fight for party democracy. It seemed that they didn't expect, or even wish, to win the tactical skirmishes to control the party apparatus. Many on the Left were content to leave the mundane, dismal stuff of machine politics to those who cared more for it.

They would be damned, however, if their rightist colleagues would be allowed to control party policy without first enduring a debate or, on occasion (depending on the heat of the issue and the Left's ability to sustain the fight) a scorching, chew-'em-up and spit-'em-out confrontation.

Unity of purpose, party wide, was rare. Let the confounded party hacks retain most of the elected positions. It was socialist principles and policies that mattered. The rest of it was window dressing, the mechanics of politics—essential perhaps, but of secondary importance.

Internal political education was a matter usually left to the provincial sections of the CCF but there were occasional clashes when the Ontario-strong federal party would try to bring their far-west partner, the socialist-inclined, sometimes erratic and unpredictable BC CCFers, into line with the mild, social democratic thrust of the Ottawa office.

One such occasion involved Eve Smith directly and very personally. It was a pivotal event among the cumulative, internal changes in party practices, attitudes and policies that prompted many leftists to leave the party. This was the infamous, so-called "Literature Incident" at the 1950 national party convention held in Vancouver.

Eve Smith, in the thick of it, did not incite this confrontation, but neither did she seek accommodation with the forces she felt were wrecking the CCF and destroying the Left's opportunity to construct a democratic and socialist party in Canada. Compromising with the devil was not her style.

Eve chaired the BC CCF's political education committee and, it is fair to say, worked, unpaid, like an inspired Trojan at the task, ordering and making available a wide variety of socialist literature. The books and pamphlets secured by democratic decision by her committee, were advertised and often reviewed in the BC CCF newspaper and were ordered and distributed, with the blessing of the party's executive, from the party's provincial office.

CCF clubs throughout the province made liberal use of this material in their study of a variety of socialist models and economic and social issues. There was no dispute in BC over this practice until the federal party's national secretary, David Lewis, was apprised that the known leftist, Eve Smith, was stationed at her well-stocked literature table just outside the convention hall, in a corridor of the Vancouver Hotel.

The secretary's eye was drawn to the source of several pamphlets as the Socialist Party of Great Britain. The Oxford scholar, Lewis, on friendly terms with the British Labour Party's right-wing leader, Hugh Gaitskell, was shown that one of the pamphlets was critical of Gaitskell's rightward drift, a policy also favoured by Lewis. He saw red, or perhaps thought he had spotted a Red, and demanded that Eve remove the offensive pamphlet immediately.

Having the authority of education chair, and fully expecting the BC executive, which approved the sale of socialist pamphlets, to back her, Eve refused. She emphatically defended her right to keep the suspect leaflet available on her table. The hubbub attracted the notice of party members nearby, including the CCF Premier of Saskatchewan, Tommy Douglas, also capable of irrational, anti-communist bluster, and prone to parrot Lewis's views. Douglas, a one time amateur pugilist as well as preacher, had a strongly pugnacious side to him, although better known as a witty speaker and charming compromiser. He, too, presumed to see a dangerous Red in the conscientious person of the literature chair, Eve Smith. He joined, stridently, in this provocative and politically divisive exercise, supposedly to safeguard the sensitive and tender minds of Ontario social democrats from the dangerous reading material indulged in by the more intellectually curious BC socialists by censoring their reading material.

Lewis and Douglas may not have realized that Eve was simply doing the approved work she had been appointed to do. But they were certainly aware of the strongly socialist set of views held by many rank-and-file BC members. Douglas was clever enough, in Saskatchewan, to try to keep his party solidly behind him. He liked to smile and soothe: "We need both wings to fly."

Lewis, however, lost no opportunity to ridicule leftist CCFers about their "out-of-step" views and, arrogantly, to see and portray himself as the sole, effective defender of the party against the always "imminent danger" of a Commie takeover.

In truth, the leaflet merely provided a pretext for Lewis to once again foam and fulminate against the threatening Reds. He would first create the scarecrow-strawman and then demolish it with heated, if phoney, intensity.

Like father, like son: a few years later in Regina, an all-party campaign meeting had heard from the CCF provincial treasurer, Clarence Fines, and the other candidates and were listening courteously while the gentle LPP (Communist) candidate, Nelson Clarke, was gently chiding the CCF government for not doing more. Suddenly, there was a violent interruption as the young Steve Lewis, in Regina for a summer job with a crown corporation, astonished the audience by leaping to his feet to stridently denounce the baffled Clarke, accuse him of sharing responsibility for the Hungarian bloodbath and other dastardly Soviet deeds.

Reginans were somewhat shocked by the vehemence of the intervention. It served them well enough to adhere to democracy, allow the LPP candidate his ten minutes, greet him cheerfully on the street and make side bets that his party would receive more or less than their usual hundred-and-twenty votes.

Some Reginans certainly did get hopping angry over politics. At that time, 1956, my little puddle-jumper V-Dub was chased down a Regina main street by a rather large black limo, its horn blaring. Its driver, a wealthy physician, was incensed by my "Re-elect Fines" CCF window sign. He screeched to a stop beside me at the stoplight and roared at me: "Five-hundred dollars Fines gets his ass kicked out of there! Get your money into Richardson's!" The tires screeched again and away he went.

The stockbroker staff were not at all nonplussed when I trudged in with a paper bag full of bills to risk my life's savings. Fines won handsomely, and so did I. My winnings paid off the balance of my car loan.

But the gross intolerance toward Canada's home-grown leftists—or anyone taking a socialist position anywhere to the left of the Coldwell-era cold warriors—earned the undying enmity of the CCF Left, many of whom described the Lewises as "social fascists."

There had been previous instances at CCF gatherings where non-party members, including those considered "pesky Trotskyites" and "pamphlet pushers" from sundry other political groups, had been asked, usually with courtesy and good humour, to cease and desist from setting up literature tables and "harassing" CCF members. Trotskyists from the League for Socialist Action were particularly vigorous, in their efforts to recruit members, in bearding CCF members in the corridors and inviting them to LSA forums. But Eve was no "pesky Trot;" she chaired the BC party's education committee. And, as Lewis soon discovered, Eve Smith was no shrinking violet!

But this particular "literature incident," because of the arrogant, accusatory manner in which Lewis provoked it and addressed it from the convention podium, and because leftists were incensed by the steady dilution and diminution of CCF policies, became a turning point in the somewhat tumultuous history of the BC section of the CCF.

Eve resolutely stood her ground against Lewis and others at the convention. Later, she carefully wrote up her notes of this "happening" and the discussions, debates and repercussions which inevitably followed such a highly-charged dispute:

The Literature Incident

The incident started with a man named Eggeston from Trail, not a delegate, who came to the table and violently threw a pamphlet onto the floor. It was titled: *Is the British Labour Policy the Way to Socialism?* I asked if he had read it, and he had not. He demanded that I remove the pamphlet and called it, "god-damned Trotskyist stuff." I explained that the publisher of the pamphlet, the Socialist Party of Great Britain, was not in fact a Trotskyist organization. He was very offensive and threatened to call David Lewis who was standing nearby. I asked him to do so.

Lewis arrived and the Saskatchewan Premier, Tommy Douglas, also came up. I asked if they had read the pamphlet. They had not but demanded I remove it. I then asked how they knew what it was about. Lewis termed it Trotskyist and I informed him that it was not. I think, incidentally, it is a pity that the National Secretary is ignorant of what the SPGB stands for.

One of them made the remark that it criticized the British Labour Party! I remarked that M.J. Coldwell, the CCF national leader, had been making speeches about respecting minorities, and how democratic the CCF was. Had I taken Coldwell's remarks too literally? My brother-in-law, John Smith, came up and suggested that, because of Mr. Lewis's rudeness, he should take the pamphlet to the convention platform. Belligerent and unpleasant, Lewis went off to attack Mrs Smith.

Lewis grabbed the microphone and made wild appeals against "this woman" and her literature "criticizing our sister party in Great Britain." In spite of the speeches of BC delegates, including MPs, MLAs and the BC leader, Harold Winch, that the socialist literature should be available to those who cared to read it and in support of the BC CCF education committee, the federal delegates (with large numbers from Ontario) did what was expected of them. They sustained the position of the national secretary against BC's literature chairman.

I then took the microphone from Madame Thérese Casgrain, who had been chairing the convention, briefly attempting to explain my position. There were howls of protest with both sides shouting at each other. Having helped to precipitate the needless controversy, Douglas appealed for unity.

After the platform scene, I returned to the table where Donald MacDonald, another national party official, was removing practically all of the socialist pamphlets. I asked him to let me go by to get my purse and he made no reply. I suggested to him that the Mayor of Chicago burnt books; he might do likewise. Finally, pushed aside and not allowed past him, I asked if he would like me to call the police. He then allowed me to get my purse.

Of course the idea of banning literature is distasteful to democratically-minded people. That literature from a party, many of whose members helped in the formation of the CCF, should be banned on the basis that it "criticized our sister party," is a matter of grave concern to people who advocate, and believe in, freedom of speech.

As a result of the very biased and distorted version of this affair put out by the national office, and then by the BC CCF administration committee under the signatures of Arthur Turner and Jessie Mendels, the provincial executive "condemned Eve Smith for her actions at the convention, regretted deeply the sending of a letter to the capitalist press explaining (her side of) the issue, and dismissed Eve Smith as Education Chairman."

How close is the CCF to becoming a Fascist organization when it comes to an appointee taking the platform, shouting to the delegates that the pamphlet he was wildly waving was critical of a sister party, and that "this woman was pushing its sale," and the mob howls down a suggestion that the said woman, the accused person, be allowed to speak? It seemed not many steps from the Mayfair Ballroom at the Vancouver Hotel to Hitler's Sportsplatz in Berlin!

The question arises: is this movement going to accept such censorship? If the chairman of the committee had been informed in advance that only certain types of literature could be displayed, she would have had the opportunity to resign in protest.

This is but a natural corollary of the greatly modified form of "socialism" that is being handed down to us by our leaders. When it is found necessary to suppress certain schools of thought within the movement, it then becomes necessary to use ruthless methods for that suppression, because suppression and ruthlessness go hand in hand.

This incident is just one more in a long line of differences that has developed dissatisfaction among socialists in the BC CCF, and has led to the formation of the Socialist Fellowship. (End of Eve's notes.)

*

After the convention, a great many of the BC delegates and visitor-members were annoyed. They had seen, over time, how the CCF had been moving to the Right and forsaking its original *Regina Manifesto* principles which stated that the CCF would end capitalism and use the nation's resources in the interests of its citizens, not of profits for the few.

Those most worked up by this new insult—being told, in effect, what they could or could not read—gathered across the street in the Georgia Hotel ballroom. There were about eighty people and talk centred on the literature incident. Many considered it much more than a mere "incident." They had now to think seriously about the whole drift of the party to the Right, about the federal delegates' "shocking" support of the censorship appeal by David Lewis, and the question of censorship within the party.

One woman objected to Eve taking the microphone from the hands of the chairman to defend herself but the great majority supported Eve's actions, finding them entirely consistent with her role as education chair, and her obvious right to speak in her own defence when subjected to such an attack.

It was their view that the movement's continual swing away from socialist education and toward "falling into line" with the leader had to be addressed. They decided they must meet regularly, in socialist fellowship, to develop their approach and strategy for future participation in the party.

*

Postscript: In her **Report on Literature** to the provincial executive in August, 1950, Eve pointed out that "the now banned pamphlet" which had so incensed Lewis and Douglas, "had been on sale for nearly a year" by the BC CCF at various locations, including the provincial office, its associated Boag House, its summer schools and at many other meetings.

Eve had regularly sent updated lists of "all literature on sale at the CCF office to all CCF clubs, Council members, MLAs and MPs, the Women's Council and 30 other individuals" with never a whimper or protest from anyone.

But now they had supinely joined the federal office in proscribing the socialist literature and dumping their own education chair in order to conform to the newly-defined censorship policy of the federal party office.

It was, for many, just one more step towards abandoning internal political education, discouraging study of socialism and, in fact, dismissing any further pretense of socialist content in the party itself.

As Eve summarized in her report:

"If the CCF 'leadership' has decided to ban all literature that criticizes the British Labour Party, then *it will have to ban all socialist classics, as they all analyze and expose the fallacies of the reform movements that have arisen from time to time.*"

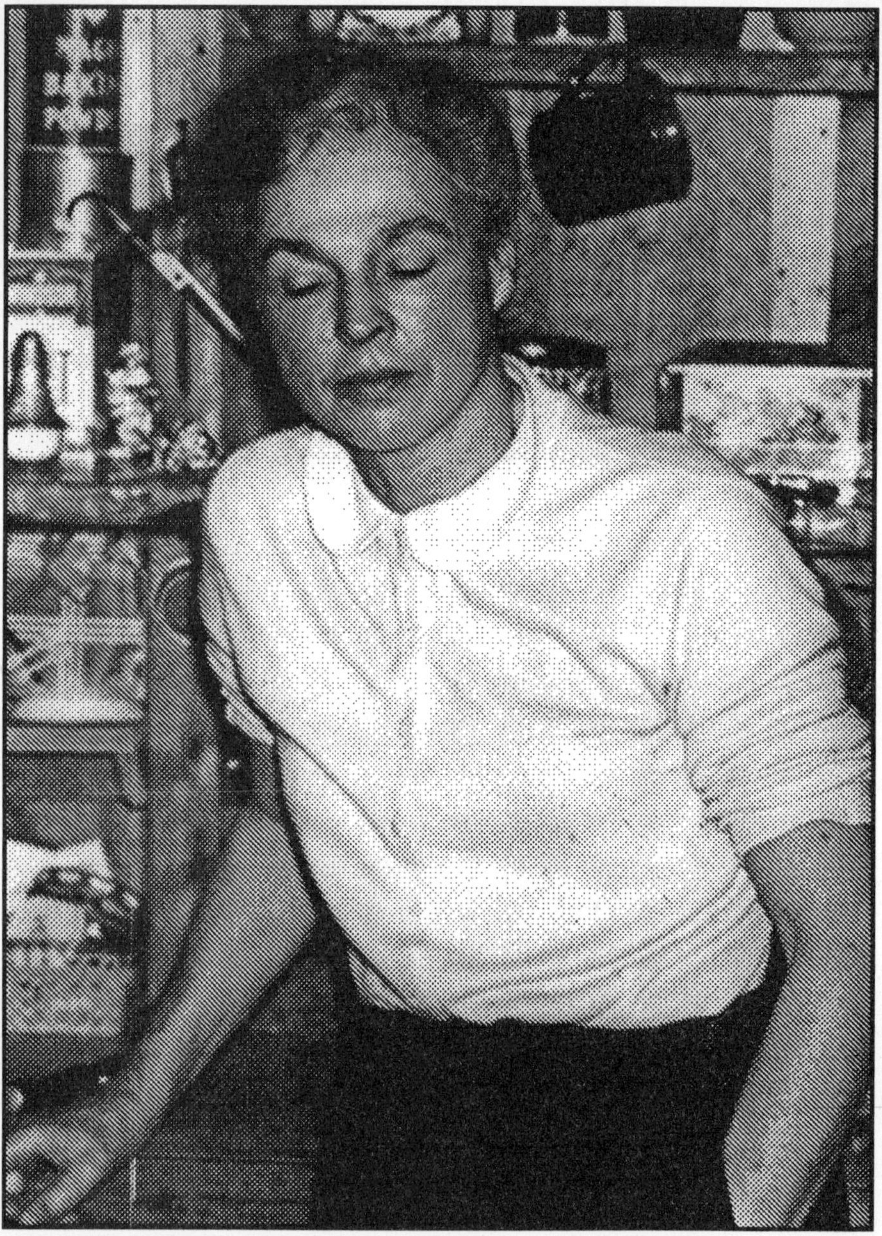

The feisty Eve was among the first of many CCF leftists who understood that the CCF leadership feared full discussion of policies and would take extreme measures to stifle it. Eve championed open debate of differences as an essential process within any party that purported to be democratic.

17 *A Fellowship of the Left*

THAT GEORGIA HOTEL MEETING precipitated the formation of the loosely-knit Socialist Fellowship. It comprised CCF members in BC who demanded the right, *within* the party, to study, discuss and promote socialist philosophy, principles, policies and programs.

Members of the Fellowship rejected out of hand the CCF National Office diktat that they should limit their interests to the reformist views and publications approved by the party leader and party officials.

Without such openness in the party, Eve Smith and many fellow socialists felt, CCF members would be better advised to participate in *other* educational groups where discussion and promotion of socialism was not proscribed.

It was difficult enough, they said, to have to fight off the continuing efforts of the social democrats at Ottawa to downgrade socialist policy. But it was an alarming state of affairs to have the BC CCF provincial executive adopt a position of non-support for their own, executive-appointed, committee chair.

As one angry critic put it, "They endorsed the actions of two hired national officials by allowing Eve Smith to take the rap."

In forming the Socialist Fellowship, the socialist Left of the CCF in BC had opened up a new forum with an enthusiastic membership of the alienated CCF Left—a solid socialist core that seemed to have strong potential for growth.

For many months Eve played a prominent role as the person in charge of planning the agendas, sending out meeting notices, summarizing discussions and decisions, and forwarding minutes to a growing list of interested CCF clubs and individual members.

There was the most intense feeling, among those who attended the Fellowship meetings and debated the issues, that it was their responsibility, their goal, if anyone could, to somehow grab the CCF by the scruff of the neck and drag it back to its original socialist principles and policies. But there were, as always on the CCF's socialist Left, many and varied views on how this could best be done.

Colin Cameron, one-time CCF MLA, later an MP and one of the Left's most vocal proponents, was among those who first supported the idea of a Socialist Fellowship as a sort of study group with an educational function. But Colin and other S.F. participants firmly resisted the idea of the Fellowship formally proposing resolutions to CCF clubs and having them sent on to party councils and conventions.

That act, firmly endorsed and principally organized by Eve Smith in her attempts to reinvigorate socialist concepts within the CCF, became the central issue which divided adherents of the Fellowship.

Colin Cameron and others knew that sending out resolutions to clubs and constituency associations was crossing the line between mere group study/discussion of socialist issues, and organizing effective socialist activity as Eve was doing. Forming "a party within the party," as defined by the provincial executive, was clearly understood to be "unnacceptable" activity.

Two letters to Eve from Colin Cameron written early in 1951 underline that Cameron, among others, would not be tied to the Socialist Fellowship if it meant losing his ability to function actively as a spokesman for the Left *within* the party:

Cassidy P.O. January 23, '51

. . . Now, for your questions: No, we have not organised ourselves here and to be quite frank, we do not intend to, as we do not consider the formal organisation of a group within the CCF will be to the advantage of the socialist movement. Many of us (I had a long talk with Alistair the other day) are greatly perturbed over the trend of events within the Fellowship, and from correspondence I have had, I gather this disquiet is shared by many in Vancouver.

My conception of the function of a left-wing group is that of education within the mass of the movement, not the organisation of a separatist movement within it which appears to be happening now. The sort of thing you did at Point Grey with your talk on Eugene Debs, the sort of thing Burrard is doing with study groups, and the continual presentation of the socialist point of view at club meetings. I know that some at that time (initial, post-convention meeting) wanted to organise a separate group within the CCF, but I also remember that the idea was decisively rejected.

All this business of organising and caucusing and creating little select groups creates a furtive and conspiratorial atmosphere about what should be a perfectly open and legitimate sponsorship and encouragement to socialist education.

Nor do I agree with this business of planting resolutions which are always as obvious as the proverbial backhouse on a rock! If a resolution has any value—a somewhat doubtful point to my mind—it is derived from having arisen within the group sponsoring it as a result of their own thinking. A resolution arriving any other way is completely phoney and consequently worse than useless as it deceives the promoters as to the actual support for the idea contained in it.

In my opinion, the Socialist Fellowship should confine itself to discussing ways and means of spreading knowledge of socialism throughout the membership and to carrying out ideas for this purpose. We must always remember that the dough is more important than the yeast which can only effervesce on its own to no purpose unless thoroughly mixed into the dough.

In regard to the resolution on the UN, I think it is silly, to be blunt. I am as well aware as anyone of the shortcomings of the UN, which are inevitable. But I am also well aware, as should be anyone who has read today's or yesterday's papers, of its value in spite of its shortcomings. We may amuse ourselves by calling it a den of capitalist iniquity, but the fact remains that without it, we would today be plunged in war.

I shall be over at the Council meeting . . . and if this resolution appears I shall oppose it, as I refuse to associate myself with what seems to me to be a silly and childish position. Let me put it to you this way. There is not and cannot be a socialist national government anywhere, for it is a contradition in terms. But until the world has been reorganised on a non-national, socialist basis, there will be and must be governments. Any organisation which brings those governments together for discussion is an immense advance on the state of affairs where each nation state sat in a hermetically sealed box. To pretend that it is of no value because it is not a socialist world organisation is so silly as to pretend there is no value in minimum wage laws, or hours of work acts, because we hope to see the day when the wage system will go.

At the Council meeting, we should concentrate on . . . (urging that) it is time now to retrace our steps and, as we set our course anew, it is necessary for the CCF to remember whose were the voices which set us on our now obviously tragically wrong course.

If we manage ourselves well, the left wing can come out of this council meeting in control of the BC section's policies. But if we present silly resolutions and make fools of ourselves, then the reactionaries will come out stronger than ever.

I expect this will not please you but it is as well there should be no illusion as to my attitude and that of those contacted over here.

Sincerely yours, Colin Cameron.

*

Again, in February, Cameron held to his doubtful proposition that the Left "could have" overwhelmed the Right, and emphasized that he was *not* a dues-paying member of the S.F.:

Dear Eve:

I had hoped to be able to see you last weekend but was unable to do so, and there seemed little point in phoning merely to wrangle over the wire.

Since the Council meeting I am more than ever convinced of the correctness of my position. Due to the march of events, the Right was in the position where it could have been completely routed by the Left. But the S.F. had succeeded in putting the Left in a false position and consequently on the defensive when it should have been on the offensive.

The whole elaborate mechanism (on paper) suggested by the minutes laid us wide open to the charge of being a disruptive inner caucus. This impression was borne out by some of the resolutions, in particular the one which idiotically proclaims the work of the Fellowship as of greater importance than work for the CCF. Even if one takes (the) view that the Fellowship constitutes the brain of the CCF (and I am doubtful of that since reading the silly resolutions and observing the silly behaviour of some), this would still be as stupid as to declare that one should care for his brain and let the rest of his body go to hell.

There is still plenty of work for socialists to do in the CCF. To do it they need the stimulation of meeting and discussion. The publication of the mimeographed sheet is useful and, of course, must be financed as must your correspondence with individuals throughout the province.

But let us have no more of these resolutions planted hither and yon—resolutions which obviously will not receive support from the majority of CCF members.

I enclose $5.00 which I ought to have sent long since as a contribution *(not dues)* to the work of the Fellowship.

Adios, Colin

*

Asked to address a CCF nominating meeting at that time, Eve

continued to emphasize the importance to the CCF of political education:

It was said at a recent nominating convention that 95 percent of the audience at public meetings were CCF supporters—and that it was a waste of time talking policy to them, that it would merely be a wasted effort to convert the converted!

Well, I say: On the contrary! Let our public meetings be educational, not necessarily 'dry!' Educational meetings can be much more interesting than mere 'rallies.'

We took a group of girls to the Hotel Vancouver to hear a constructive, practical explanation of public ownership. They weren't talked down to. They understood it, and they enjoyed it.

This movement must decide whether or not it is going to be a socialist movement, or merely a social democratic party. Those terms now represent two schools of thought that I know we all understand quite well. I am not going to waste our time giving definitions of Marxian Socialism and democratic socialism, except to say that Marxian Socialism is essentially democratic.

*

Eve's speeches were enthusiastically applauded for the clarity of her message and her unambiguous adherence to democratic and socialist principles. This was a welcome antidote to the usual cheerleading, rah-rah, vote-for-us exhortations of less well versed CCFers who became politically ambitious candidates.

To weaken the party's goals, she would stress, was to give up the game entirely. Many CCFers were proud of her unequivocal stand and those numbers were growing. Her ongoing organizational efforts had seen to that.

Still, this was a time of considerable anxiety, ferment and agonizing self-appraisal among the party's leftists. When Eve mailed the minutes of the S.F. meetings to the "loose alliance" of socialist-leaning CCF clubs and individuals, letters came pouring into her home office. The writers wanted to learn more, to inform others clubs of their own activities, and to be kept informed.

Few of her correspondents managed, in their excitement and turmoil, so rapid a reversal as the gentleman from New Westminster who wrote:

May 9, 1951

Dear Mrs Smith:

There is not the slightest doubt in my mind that the CCF is today the best medium for democratic socialist action.

My answer is: Stay in the CCF and work in the clubs. I support left-wing socialism, but whatever action I take is my own. I agree with you that control must remain in the hands of the membership.

Comradely yours, Georges J.B. LaFrance

P.S. Your correspondence is very much welcomed.

*

May 12/51

Dear Mrs Smith:

I have thrown away as useless my membership in the CCF; as the sudden, complete realization that my beliefs in revolutionary political action have become completely incompatible with the reform political action of the CCF.

This is now leading me in search of a party that will fill this need and if you believe that the Socialist Party of Canada is the answer, contact me at once. Otherwise, I shall be forced to join the L.P.P. (Labour Progressive [Communist] Party).

Comradely yours, Georges

*

There occurs at times in politics an intense nastiness that deeply disturbs fair-minded people. There was the accusation repeated by some of the leading CCF social democrats that the Fellowship was "Trotskyist" in its political orientation. This was a deliberate misnomer conveniently thrown at political enemies or "undesirables." It was designed to cause maximum distress and deliberately used "to put certain people under a cloud."

Doug Cameron records that he had heard that assertion, "but the simple fact is, it was never true. It was the Fellowship members, in fact, who kept the CCF more or less clear of Trotskyists and Trotskyism and Stalinists and Stalinism.

"Some of both groups tried to influence the policies of the S.F. but I don't think there's ever been such a group of puritans anywhere (as the S.F. membership). We wouldn't allow our commitment to pure, unadulterated socialism to be corrupted by killers of that kind—like Trotsky, Stalin and Lenin.

"They were driven out. Anybody who tried to raise a sectarian, non-CCF, set of principles was ruthlessly driven out.

"But the right-wing tactic of the Grace MacInnises and David Lewises had always been smear and innuendo. They tried to discredit people by whatever label they felt would be most damning in public opinion. It still goes on. But it was the Left of the CCF that got rid of the communists."

Doug Cameron and others contended that Gordon Dowding, who later became a CCF MLA and a Speaker of the Legislature, helped organize a substantial group who sought membership in the Fellowship with less than pure motives. The implication was that they swamped the S.F. with members who would vote for its dissolution when the pressure was on.

At one point a number of Fellowship members accepted the invitation of Dave Stupich, the resident fixture, some said "fixer," of the Nanaimo CCF club, to hold a mini-convention of the Fellowship. There was an inexpensive weekend ferry available and quite a number from the lower mainland set off for Nanaimo. The sessions went well until, as Eve reports, some of the delegates decided, at a break, "to make game of M.J. Coldwell."

"Some of us put on an impromptu skit. Coldwell had been getting stout so his 'impersonator' had to have a pillow stuffed behind his shirt. There were five or six of us sitting in the 'audience' making comments to and about M.J. It was 'M.J. this' and 'M.J. that' sort of thing. He was such a pompous person with his little satellites hanging around him. I jumped up and made some silly sort of motion, and the 'chairman,' of course, as was usually the case with the Left at federal conventions, disallowed it.

"It was all innocent enough, we thought, but our skit, which was put on in the spirit of good fun, did have the effect of shocking some of the more staid Vancouver Islanders. Stupich felt we shouldn't have made game of Coldwell, since he was, after all, the elected leader.

"Anyway, that meeting was our swan song, in a way. We really didn't have much say from then on, although the Socialist Fellowship was active for a while."

*

The Socialist Fellowship was one of many attempts by leftists in the CCF—and later in the NDP's aptly-named *Waffle*—to co-ordinate their efforts to examine the economy, develop socialist-based policies, and present a somewhat more united leftist front to the party's councils and conventions.

It also provided a social framework for private bitching sessions about the people "down east" who had "sold us out!" For many, the man they held most responsible for "the sellout," their favourite party *bete noire,* was Toronto lawyer, dedicated anti-communist and friend of right-wing union leaders, David Lewis.

At one S.F. meeting Eve spoke out sharply and lucidly to counter the right-wing influence emanating from Ottawa as members discussed the Fellowship's future:

Diversity of Opinion Within the Party

"On this matter of CCF speakers and writers expressing different points of view in public, I would like to say that I am very much in agreement with that principle. There are many controversial issues in the world today and we do not have pat answers for everything that arises. But the public should be aware that we exist and that we discuss things. Surely one way of interesting people in the CCF is to have full discussions. Then they can decide for themselves what they support.

"I do not propose that we allow our speakers to oppose some policy that has been democratically decided upon in a convention. But we have the machinery for dealing with such persons. We have expelled people for opposing CCF policy, A.M. Stephen, for example, and rightly so."

*

To the Co-operative Commonwealth's "Coldwell Clique" at Ottawa, the Socialist Fellowship seemed to be "nothing less than an underground front trying to interfere with CCF policy."

To the person who reported this "national office view" to a meeting of the Fellowship, Eve had her reply. As John Smith and many others maintained, Eve wanted to cut through the nonsense of reformism, the gradual diminishing of principle and weakening of policy until there was nothing left worth supporting. On this occasion she once again clarified the issue:

"But that is *precisely* what we want to do," she admonished. "We want to interfere with the attempt to eliminate or dilute CCF policy. If we are to be of any use, we must have some ability to affect policy in the CCF.

"Let us consider why we came into being. The daily newspapers have given us publicity and we may well pick up support for our views all over the place. If we simply fade away or dissolve, we are letting all these people down. They are saying, for example, that 'At last a group is going to lead an anti-war stand!' "

*

The combative, defiant Eve Smith had not the slightest trepidation about being expelled from the CCF. She knew how she would deal with it. Unlike Colin Cameron and Dorothy Steeves whose views and public statements were influenced and moderated by their ambition to be among the leadership group themselves and to become elected MLAs, Eve was inhibited by no such concerns and was free to focus on principle, policy and process.

After all the years of internal struggles that she had engaged in for party democracy and socialist content in policy, she was not about to hide her light under a bushel basket. Certainly not one full of obfuscation:

"If we are suspended, it will create a tremendous furore in the CCF and fair-minded people will insist that we be heard. We have been struggling for this free expression for years. Let's use it!

"Compromise has been the downfall of many socialist groups. Let's fight for the Socialist Fellowship within the CCF and not be thrown out.

"We must carry on because socialist activity has been nullified by the CCF. If we fight and win, our position will be stronger than ever, and so will the CCF.

"If a large enough group stands together, we can win; but we must all make ourselves known and heard.

"Let's stay (in the party) and fight. The national and provincial leaders will be exposed if they try disallowing freedom of speech and freedom of association.

"Let's have faith in rank-and-file members to support us."

*

The Socialist Fellowship continued to hold its meetings, usually at the Hillside CCF Club. Members insisted they didn't wish to disrupt the CCF; they simply wanted to bring it back to its original principles as enunciated in the venerable *Regina Manifesto*.

Some of the members of the CCF who attended meetings of the S.F. periodically were Colin Cameron, Dorothy Steeves, future party leader Bob Strachan, Ed Olson, Jack O'Brien, Lefty Morgan and perhaps several dozen of the more active leftists in party clubs from the lower mainland and Vancouver Island.

By the summer of 1951 the relatively short-lived Socialist Fellowship had been disrupted by differences between the members as to its purpose and especially its process—and by the provincial executive's directive to disband or face expulsion.

Many members like Eve and John were unable to accept the strained logic of the party executive that by directly relating party policies to socialist principles, and by using every available strategy and option to promote such policies among socialists active in CCF clubs throughout the province, they had somehow violated some unwritten, supposedly democratic, party principle.

As perhaps too few others did, Eve saw through the demand for the dissolution of the S.F. as a fearful attempt by the party's right wing to maintain its stranglehold on the reins of party power and ensure its control of any future elected caucus and provincial and/or federal government.

But a small group of quite admirable leftists such as Colin Cameron felt they could somehow finesse control of the party executive and council by the sheer logic of their leftist positions. And if passion in delivery was what was required to win the day, Colin Cameron, better than most, would be able to provide the essential fervour, ardour and Scottish eloquence in full measure.

*

Years later, Doug Cameron happened upon such a group, including Colin: "I was at Colin's granddaughter's first birthday party. I had not seen Colin and Gretchen since I had left the party in 1951. This was probably in 1963 and Anne and I and Kirsten, our daughter, arrived. There they all were in the backyard discussing politics. Talking about the same people. Carrying on in the same manner. 'Now if we can just get this resolution passed . . . .' 'Yes, Colin, that's right, we've got to get that bastard so-and-so . .'

"It was a sort of time warp; you go out one door and come in through another twelve years later and they're saying the same things about the same people and carrying on the same Machiavellian little cabals . . ."

*

Many of the same people who had worked in the S.F. became involved in a new Social Science Forum which met on Davie Street to examine social policy issues relevant to British Columbia lives of the 1950's. The S.F. continued to hold occasional meetings but Eve became ill once again and was unable to continue her conscientious efforts to focus the political debates.

But the old proscription against having a "party within the party" had succeeded in disrupting the Fellowship's continuity,

Eve was an enthusiastic organic gardener who practised what she learned from books. Guests enjoyed simple, wholesome meals and ate from plates on their laps. There were no 'non-essential' tables or settings.

splitting off some members who feared expulsion, or simply discouraging people from involvement.

Some Fellowship members, including some of the brightest, hardest-working intellectuals among the party's key working class participants, had wearied of the weight and freight of too much internal party struggle, some of it nasty, bitter and emotionally draining. Many of them chose this period to resign from the CCF to put their energies to work elsewhere.

Losing so many enthusiasts, activists and key party workers undoubtedly greatly weakened the CCF and in large part accounted for its continuing inability to broaden its electoral support. This widespread alienation was a direct result of abandoning the socio-economic policies distinguishing it from others parties.

True democrats tend by nature, thought the idealistic Eve Smith, toward tolerance of diversity and pluralism of views. But, when the CCF began to fail that test, she and hundreds like her had to look elsewhere. Now without a party to directly influence, the dissenters became enemies in principle of the party establishment. Their considerable collective capability, creative drive, energy and enthusiasm was lost to the CCF.

Some founded a number of single-issue organizations which channeled their energies. Others worked in government, making important contributions to Canada's socio-political development. Many were persuaded, reluctantly, that there were worthwhile pursuits in life other than politics. They quietly packed up their manifestos and retired from the minefield of political combat.

Whatever their reasons, many simply left. They sensed correctly that Canadians confronted by a choice of two centre-right, corporate-supporting parties, the Liberals and CCF/social democrats, would opt for "the real thing," Liberals rather than pseudo-Liberals—the Soc-Dems that Liberal Prime Minister Louis St. Laurent would later suggest were merely "Liberals-in-a-hurry."

Most social democrats, having abandoned their initial *raison d'etre:* clear, vibrant "socialist" policies, lost their sense of mission, their integrity and self respect. They wandered aimlessly over the political map, publicly agonized over their self-banished, now-vanished, constantly-moving political goal-posts, and prayerfully tested public opinion polls. They became mired in a quagmire of self doubt and a misguided search for a popular new "formula."

Sadly, they lack conviction, passion, believability . . . and purpose.

18 A Perspective on "Socialism"

THE "SOCIALIST" STATES OF OUR WORLD, always in crisis, were undergoing an acute, navel-gazing confidence check in the 1970's. One form or another of "socialism" had taken hold in many countries, in many modalities—certainly enough "experiments" to excite the hopes of socialists everywhere.

Many felt that the "forthcoming" economic gains in these newly-socialist states would lead to the "inevitable triumph" of socialism in many more states. Few expected them to self destruct.

To bring here a measure of perspective to the yearnings of Eve Smith and other Canadian leftists of the 1930's to 1950's, we offer this cursory look into "socialism." (Some readers may prefer to move on to lighter subject matter in the next chapter.)

One should observe, first, that many of these new, self-described "socialist" régimes popping up around the world were still young and largely unproven. Confidence in them was tempered.

Just thirty years earlier in the 1940's, "socialism" was to be found only in one country, the Soviet Union. Socialists pridefully proclaimed that only through the might of the Soviet "socialist" state were Hitler's hordes finally crushed in 1945.

But they had been astounded and appalled to learn of the murdered and exiled millions, the gulag, and the incarceration of dissidents in grim psychiatric jails. By any yardstick, these were hardly measures to be applauded as either democratic or socialist initiatives—certainly not by socialists such as Eve Smith.

Still, *some* Canadian leftists inexplicably remained apologists for Stalin's sordid, megalomaniacal and inhuman depravity.

In 1949, the People's Liberation Army triumphed and "set China on the path to building socialism." Then, one after another, so many nations revolted that, by the 1970's, close to half the world's peoples lived under nominally socialist regimes.

The world's leading capitalists, too, were deeply revolted. "Experts" and right-wing "think tanks on socialism" proliferated. Socialism became *the* major concern of Western capitalism.

Many new African and Asian "socialist" states added to US corporate angst and fears of an eclipsed future with crumbling market economies. Then, more immediately disturbing, revolutionary Cubans triumphed a mere ten-minute jet ride from Miami and panic set in. The CIA drafted many bizarre plots to kill Castro and John Kennedy eventually backed its ill-conceived and abortive invasion plan. Additional disturbing news was on the way.

The US monied élite looked on in disbelief as still another socialist bombshell exploded. The Chilean people had actually *elected* a Marxist president! Salvador Allende had dared to give socialism its *second* base in the Latin hemisphere. Enough! *Basta!*

It was no longer just the US-Soviet standoff at the Big Nukes Corral. CIA agents, with Secretary of State Henry Kissinger pulling strings for President Nixon, soon orchestrated General Pinochet's military murder of Allende at the Presidential palacio.

But few expected the extent of the madness to come. The world had yet to see the napalmed bodies and chemically-defoliated landscape of Vietnam. The United States would commit half a million military to "defend US interests" in an attempt to stop the socialist advance in southeast Asia.

The astonishing Kennedy-Johnson-Nixon war on Vietnam failed totally. The socialist cadres-in-black-pyjamas had emerged from their underground tunnels to smash the US war machine and force its governing élite into traumatized submission. Nixon, the compleat liar, called it "an honourable peace."

An overriding question remained for Democratic Socialists. Just how well were these new "socialist" economies serving their people? Eve Smith's adopted prescription: "public ownership of the means of production and distribution," had been supposed not only to *deliver* but to *guarantee* to deliver better, more equitable, freer, participatory societies, had it not?

Was the medicine working? Were the resulting régimes worth the bad taste left from the violent revolutions? From Poland to Mozambique, from China to Cuba, the answer was: "Not so well as expected." And from many, a resounding *"No!"*

What went wrong? These experiments with dictatorial *state,* as opposed to *social* ownership (did *anyone* consider them classic examples of socialism?) resulted in horrendously authoritarian, bureaucratized economies, far removed from Eve's concept of "democratic and socialist" societies.

Where were the expected benefits to working people? Full employment? But what was the nature of the jobs? Pride in the technological achievements of a socialist economy? Surely, but rockets, missiles and Sputnik space probes were not adequate substitutes for democratic forms. May Day military parades and goose-stepping around Lenin's tomb proved inadequate inspiration for sagging Soviet spirits. And the magnificent East German "socialist" athletes who astonished the world? How many of these muscular fraus were pumped up frauds bloated by steroids?

Socialists had been justificably cynical of the West's version of democracy: the buying of elections through saturation advertising, for example. Surely the one-party "socialist" states presented opportunities for a superior democratic process to flower?

If only some of these male-ego-dominated central committees had had the wit to add a few Eve Smiths or Emma Goldmans to their number—strong women unwilling to defer to the leadership! Would they then have failed so miserably to reflect genuine socialist and humanist values?

In the near-total absence of democratic upward pressures, the bureaucrats became comfortably befuddled, greedily self-aggrandized, lazy and otherwise unfit to serve socialist idealism.

Instead of incorporating the human ideals of freedom, equality and participatory democracy, the centralized economies had generally created a stultifying, even stupifying, degree of bureaucratization and of blind adherence to the dictates of ruling élites.

No matter how lengthy the verbal exhortations, the bureaucracies lacked creativity and responsiveness. Instead of liberating the creative forces of working people and instilling greater individual and collective responsibility, the central committees fostered a cowed, frightened work force. The leaders failed to create a basis for dynamic interaction between the leaders and the led.

In Cuba, many outsiders had witnessed new, democratic forms of local elections and participation at block and municipal levels. Local initiatives were encouraged and supported in such matters as community gardens, greenbelts and voluntary work in production. But the party's hierarchy stifled local proposals relating to the fundamental essentials of socialism: the right of full participation by workers in setting national goals for the economy; the advance of human freedoms and civil rights; and structured, undeniable, democratic opportunities to evaluate and change the people at key decision-making levels: the maximum leaders, politburos, central committees and military commands.

Barring such options, the leaders were free to institutionalize the anti-socialist pattern of *non-participation* of citizens. They established no framework allowing workers to influence vital discussions on plans to achieve their stated needs and desires.

Establishing state ownership of the means of production and enforcing centralized state planning did not promote a spirit-liberating enthusiasm for change. The Stalinist drive to industrialize the Soviet economy ended workers' dreams of industrial democracy and turned the concept of a socialist democracy on its head.

Also—disastrously—the Soviet bloc countries, in achieving great technological capacity, also created environmental nightmares for working people, their children and their communities. The natural physical environment suffered horrific degradation, helping sap the health and spirit of Soviet society.

Rather than freeing people to decide on the equitable distribution of improvements resulting from socio-economic planning, the bureaucrats and the power-grasping party cliques they fearfully obeyed, promoted their own self-interest. In truth, a monstrous fraud was perpetrated on the Soviet peoples.

Similarly in other new "socialist" régimes, the hopes of millions of idealistic socialist adherents, worldwide, including Eve and John Smith, gradually evaporated in profound disillusionment. This shattering of lifelong dreams was no small thing.

Socialists understood this as a quite extraordinary betrayal. And socialism betrayed became equated with socialism as failure—a failed system. But no amount of tinkering with a system that denied open, creative involvement could save it. The very word "socialism" became defiled political terminology. These discredited régimes could no longer merit the loyalty and support of socialist proponents and intellectuals throughout the world.

The distorted practice had failed the theory. What theory? In plain language, a socialist society had an essential main purpose: that the requirements necessary to life of every member of society would be satisfied. That would develop from the expansion of material wealth and enrichment of intellectual culture.

People would obviously have differing abilities and personal goals. But automatons they would not be. As material economic conditions improved, a socialist model of society would have the capacity to satisfy differing needs.

Just as in a family, the community would consider the needs of *all*. That's what socialism, for most of the Left, was all about. But socialist thinkers had failed to anticipate and properly plan the requirements of their states.

Even the Lenins and the Trotskys, while brilliant analysts and writers, had no plan to democratize the leadership process. Without guaranteed leadership renewal, the way was open for an egomaniac like Stalin to abort democratic forms. The people were thus deprived of personal participation and real political power.

The creation of the "new man, socialist man," so well idealized by the writing and example of Ernesto Che Guevara in Cuba, became the goal. He was to be a selfless, idealistic, caring, responsible worker-citizen, spurred by a broadly-shared civic duty and moral incentive. But this heroic concept was largely lost sight of as a socialist goal. For the most part, workers were offered only personal acquisition, an opportunity merely to aspire to join the privileged of the party or the bureaucracy, or both, as incentive.

The first mate of the Russian cargo transport I hitched a ride on from Havana to St. John, candidly told me, in proficient and brutally frank English: "If I can manage to cover my ass for another two years I'll be eligible for membership in the party and my wife and I will be guaranteed the good life from then on." As to equal opportunities under the Soviet system? He laughed.

Under Stalin's ruthless direction, the technical bureaucrats stressed purely economic goals—ever higher production numbers— based on greater exploitation of workers and resources.

But had the socialist thinkers promoted objectives based on meeting real human needs? designing and building more livable human communities? acknowledging and respecting the natural world rather than exploiting it as a mere "resource" for people? promoting a better, safer and more stimulating quality to their lives, both at work and at home?

Eve Smith and other BC socialists deplored the continuing distortion of such socialist objectives. Similarly, she soon recognized that the CCF's leadership, fearing genuine discussion and dissent, had systematically stifled debate rather than welcoming it as an essential facet of any democratic movement or association.

Without dissent and debate, the free flow of ideas was suppressed. The results were: distrust; a process focused on *con-*

trol of the political instrument, the party; the permanent loss of so many of the ablest, most enthusiastic members; the counter-productive elimination of political education; the revision of party policy to reflect the opportunistic policies of uncertain leaders; and policy based too often on pointless polling of an ill-informed public. Who, indeed, would inform and educate that public?

While "socialism" abroad achieved state power by convincing people it was preferable to czarist-enforced feudal structures or Chinese Kuomintang militarism or neo-colonial exploitation, it nevertheless failed to develop or sustain the participatory, democratic forms essential to socialism.

What might have become exciting socialist experiments became authoritarian, competitive régimes. Rather than by-passing the worst forms of capitalist exploitation (as the early Bolsheviks had hoped) the Soviet leaders succeeded only in postponing that painful instability for seventy years. Capitalism with its perverse ideology and inhuman premises would weaken any remaining bonds of solidarity and feelings of mutual concern.

Capitalism, in all its inequitable, exploitative, criminally-enhanced glory, has engulfed post-Soviet citizenry with economic and social chaos. Russian citizens could be forgiven when they said: "If *this* is western democracy, let's go back and reform the socialist system we had. Anything would be better than this!"

Soviet-style socialism, by the 1980's, had ceased to be regarded as an "inevitable" improvement on capitalist democracy. The only wonder, in the Soviet bloc, was the speed with which it was dismantled under the extraordinary leadership of Gorbachev. And, as we now know, he won his position as USSR General Secretary in a politburo election by only one vote—his own!

*

How might "socialism" better have been defined to make it both relevant and responsive to this century? Eve Smith, as a thoughtful critic of the CCF from day one, and of the socialist experiments abroad, had many ideas in common with socialists the world over who demanded and promoted a more democratic and responsive politics. What had they been fighting for?

Surely the goals of socialism must include, as Eve Smith stressed, the freest expression of individuality in political, social and cultural relations. Would such openness not have established a society with healthy norms of political participation, sanctification of the environment, plus mandatory responsibility for improving socio-economic standards for all peoples?

Those who attempted to define societal goals under real-life or would-be socialist economies failed to address *any* of these questions with sufficient foresight and clarity of thought.

Was the socialist's faith in the human capacity for self-determination and co-operative governance misplaced? If not, does the replacement of private by *public* control over resources and production and sharing merely represent a correct *beginning* made towards a "new socialism" which would clearly define the process and conditions for the ongoing enlargement and continuous redefinition of peoples' self-determination?

Socialist idealists, of course, maintain that socialism hasn't failed—but *had never been tried!* They persist in their argument that capitalism *has*, largely, failed. Certainly it will be indefensible, in the 2000's, that two to three percent of the earth's population will continue to own and control between 80 and 90 percent of real productive assets. This hardly represents a notable improvement over feudal times. Capitalism continues to work well—but for only a relative few.

Under socialism, in the versions available for study to date, the parties of self-perpetuating élites have proved only minimally more capable, or less, of meeting human needs than the capitalist élites. If these egregious distortions of economic power are somehow to be rectified (and if the privileges of enormous personal fortunes amassed under capitalism are to be forfeited, in time) what should replace them?

In free-wheeling capitalist societies, the great majority remain unable to purchase a share in the system sufficient to sustain their well-being. Reforming such systems has confounded the best efforts of democrats, social democrats, liberals and reformers over the generations. In Canada one child in three still lives in poverty.

Is there available an alternative socio-economic-governmental system which places a much higher value on the qualities of human existence, and on all facets of our ecological systems? It may well be time for political thinkers to start again with clean slates. No person with appropriate answers should be reticent to divulge them to this weary, waiting world.

In the meantime, surely the term "socialism" has outlived its usefulness. As Eve pointed out, "it means very different things to different people." Its continued use serves only to confuse, rather then enlighten. The word has become one more part of the outdated, much-polluted political culture that must be discarded. Similarly, for Canadian journalists to continue referring to social democrats as "socialists" is incorrect, misleading and foolish.

Do we want, however, to throw out the much-abused socialist baby with the bloodied bathwater? Surely while planners labour to devise a better-structured, much more participatory governmental form, they could do much worse than seriously analyze, evaluate and retain the best of the socio-political idealism exemplified in the extraordinary global struggles for socialism.

Countless heroic efforts toward human emancipation and betterment have ensued this past century under the rubric of "socialism." Enormous effort has been expended to destroy the old and unworthy régimes, but astonishingly little has been done to ensure successor states would be better equipped to govern.

Whatever new structures might emerge from such studies, they should not be regarded—as Marxian socialism once was by far too many—as beyond criticism, somehow perfectly perfect, despite its many insufficiencies. In roundly and correctly condemning capitalism, socialists too easily accepted the whole Marxian skein of wool without ever sufficiently unwinding its complex, labyrinthine layers and investigating whether the various strands when knit, produced an inhabitable whole.

In planning ahead we cannot ignore the fact that the basic truths of socialism have been enormously popular. The fact that authoritarian personalities gravitated to "socialist" leadership should not shock us, especially when we have seen such emphasis on *economic* development at the expense of *human* development. That process surely needs to be more fully understood.

Many socialists, as Eve Smith said, "accepted" the socio-economic critiques of Marx and Engels without ever having studied them. Was it much wonder then that, given the opportunity and power to implement socialism, too many socialist "believers" remained as essentially confused about methodology as they were indeterminate about appropriate societal goals?

One must expect that the devotees of any *New Social System* to be given birth will be passionate advocates. But we enter a plea here that they not be so arrogant (and oblivious of history) as to suggest their new Wo-manifesto (or whatever) will be blessed, a la

Mary, with an immaculate conception or a trouble-free gestation.

Any new socio-political system will not be trouble-free. It will require constant care and nurturing, just as a child, so it can grow in strength, wisdom and maturity. Also, in my view, it must continually be tested in the light of such simple virtues of honesty, concern and responsibility which were exemplified by Eve Smith. Such tests necessarily constantly challenge the status quo.

Any decent new society will certainly have to overcome today's existing inequalities of the human condition. Otherwise, the exercise of equal rights in the future will not be sustainable. Economies based, as they are now in the industrialized nations, on illegitimate concentrations of power and privilege simply cannot and will not produce decent societies.

People in future decades may well choose, as Eve Smith did (in a spasm of youthful enthusiasm to resolve the grim social problems she witnesssed in the Depression) to examine these weighty matters seriously and in depth, and adopt what may seem a reasonable set of political and human values with extraordinary zeal and commitment—and continue in that direction with unrelenting impetus.

That would be entirely admirable, no doubt.

An alternative is to examine the political players and processes as a somewhat more detached political sociologist, social anthropologist or investigative journalist might approach them —approximating my own folly in this regard.

Certainly, in this writer's view, a person who deliberately thrusts only one foot into the political soup to give it a provocative and perhaps invigorating stir—and then carefully retrieves that foot to observe and analyse the ensuing ripples—also has a useful and positive role to play.

One might observe too that no matter the choice of political elixir one samples, there is a danger that what might begin as a tentative enquiry into socio-political theory (or political hucksterism as the case may be) may well prove an obsessive fascination.

There is, even in Canada, a pharmacopia of political nostrums which are more apt to intrigue and infect the unwary individual (journalist, social theorist, or planner) than to cure social ills. Instead of submitting to any such lure and risk possible contamination, one might better conclude, as my perceptive and wise Irish mother instinctively did: *"Politics? It's a mug's game."*

Doug Cameron with Eve in her South Pender Island workplace. She enjoyed cheerful banter or debate with many friends, including Cameron, an early political associate and long-time buddy.

19 *That Great Gettin'-up Mornin'*

AMONG THE NOMINAL LEFTISTS EMBROILED with the CCF and its youth movement, the CCYM, was political maverick Doug Cameron. His youthful critique of the CCF brought him to Eve Smith's attention and he became a close friend to Eve and John from the 1940's onward. He considered Eve Smith "the most thoroughly consistent human being I've ever known."

The young Cameron's political baptism included, as we will see in this interview, certain elements of farce. But his youthful exuberance gave way in time, with the guidance of Eve and John Smith and others, to a perceptive appraisal of the 1940's-1950's CCF that many leftists might consider valid.

Cameron's Norwegian, cigar-maker, trade union activist grandfather presented him with useful tools on his 14th birthday which set his mind to work casually probing the CCF's policy postures during his teen years. Young Doug found two books wrapped in brown paper, direct from the Chicago publisher, the *Communist Manifesto* and *Value, Price and Profit*, by Karl Marx.

His grandfather and his mother voted CCF so, as Cameron said, "it had always been part and parcel of the family, like corn flakes." When a young friend, Larry Cole, proselytized him into attending Co-operative Commonwealth Youth Movement (CCYM) meetings, Doug did so "more out of boredom and curiosity than any political conviction.

"I showed up at a youth club in Burnaby on a cold, bitter January night in 1947 to witness the improbable spectacle of the club splitting up over alleged immorality. Another club was formed that night by the very straight-laced, right-wing members." Cameron sat with the remaining rump, call it the Left group. Overall, he thought the evening incredible, entertaining enough to relieve his boredom for a while, but not politically illuminating.

Shortly after joining the club, Doug found himself the subject of controversy. As one of two club delegates nominated to attend a provincial CCYM convention in Victoria, he was startled that much of the first morning was spent trying to unseat him as a delegate! But the youthful politicos finally exhausted that subject and allowed him to remain.

Once again, however, vague questions were posed about possible sexual hanky-panky, heaven forbid, among the pubescent youth, and mismanagement of CCYM funds, which amounted to petty cash at most. "None of this," laughed Cameron, "had anything to do with the future of the CCF or the welfare of BC. It was so parochial and unbelievable. Even worse, on the homeward-bound ferry, a chap named Ray tried to recruit me as an ally in this little war he was waging against the CCYM executive."

The political provocateur in Cameron couldn't resist the opportunity this presented: "I suggested he send a letter to all CCYM clubs and he dutifully wrote it all down as I dictated."

Cameron started with his critique that the policies of the CCF and CCYM "would only lead to the establishment of a pseudo-socialist society in Canada—and I added some more gibberish" which Ray then enthusiastically typed, copied and sent out.

To young Doug's great delight, "all Hell broke loose." But Cameron claims there was more than youthful hellery motivating him. "I felt that if the working class of Canada had to depend on this collection of comedians, where were we? I could see they had no deeply-held political convictions. They seemed a small group of people who wanted to be elected for the direct benefit of the sessional indemnities, or to receive the largesse their party might one day dispense if they made it to government.

"Suffering some disillusionment, I started arguing with my grandfather and, I have to admit, made his last few years a misery. In his old age all he could do was hope that some of the things he talked about and worked for were finally going to happen.

"In the last year of his life he was hoping Joe Stalin and his Red Army would gallop across the Atlantic, then across Canada, and establish the workers' paradise in BC— by force if necessary.

"This only exacerbated our arguments. I often wondered whether I had precipitated his final stroke." Cameron's hyperbole notwithstanding, the grandfather offered his grandson some good and practical advice. He said, "If you disagree with the CCF so much, why the hell don't you quit?" Said Cameron, "I should have, there and then."

But Cameron hung in, no doubt revelling in the rumpus caused by the letter critical of CCF policies that he had helped Ray to concoct. When it came to the attention of the provincial executive, "they decided they'd have to shoot down us loonies out in Burnaby before things got totally out of hand."

Doug was learning, first hand, about the left-right schisms endemic within the CCF. "Grace MacInnis came and told us to be good children and work hard to elect a CCF government. Colin Cameron came as well, but exhibited his carefully-couched concerns about the same policies that the CCYMers had questioned."

Then the remarkable, politically articulate George Weaver surfaced. "He certainly knew his Marxism and in that sense towered over everyone else in the CCF at that time. But he depended upon the goodwill, almost the charity, of the Winches, Ernie and Harold. He was used by them to gun down the intellectual Left of the party. But in his later days, he must have suffered pangs of conscience. His theosophy seemed to take hold of him.

"Weaver was interested in acquiring twelve disciples. He wanted to be able to transmogrify himself into the Godhead, Nirvana, and he fancied that here, perhaps, were his twelve disciples. Whether he was truly recruiting for himself, in terms of his own religious motivation, or whether he had decided the party had strayed too far, I don't know, but he came to our defence.

"Frankly, we didn't know what we were talking about. I certainly didn't and he immediately told me so. I cheerfully admitted he was absolutely right, but it didn't take long, with his help, to understand the issues in a much more profound way."

Thus encouraged and enlightened, Cameron made the following claims: "I bamboozled a friend, Norman Wood, to join the New Westminster CCF club with me. We then wrote a juvenile plagiarism of the *Regina Manifesto* and distributed it throughout the CCYM and that really did start a riot. The Burnaby CCF decided to smother us with a big philosophic and political pillow, so they convened a meeting. It was jammed to the rafters."

Conveniently, Cameron developed a flubug and left his friend Norman Wood to bear the wrath of his local party, that is until George Weaver again stepped in. "He put the right wing to rout, just as he had previously put the left wing to rout. The policy battle had been crystallizing in the party. This meeting just triggered it and it boiled over to the executive level as well.

"They had to decide once again whether to allow this sort of democratic discussion within the party. Colin Cameron and Gretchen Steeves and others (always pleased to recruit supporters of their own positions) decided to support us. There was nothing wrong, they decided, with giving young people their head. There were others, however, who wanted 'to exterminate this cancer' right off the bat.

"References started to appear in the *CCF News.* Weaver's column moved magically from right wing to left wing, much to the consternation of the Winches, Grace MacInnis and Tom Alsbury, who then carried on a vicious vendetta against George Weaver.

"Then one day I received a note which said:

'Dear Comrade, I have read what you said in your letter to the paper and I agree with you. Can you come to supper (date and time) at 3525 West 27th Avenue? Comradely yours, Eve Smith.'

Eve, too, was busy recruiting!

"Much to my mother's consternation (she couldn't understand why anyone would go to somebody's place for supper when you didn't know who they were), I went off to meet Eve Smith. Mother thought this must be some *femme fatale* who was going to lead me astray. I was half hoping it might be true.

"Then I met Eve Smith and John Smith and found, yes indeed, here finally were people who understood things the way I did. But they understood politics in a much more profound, intellectual and articulate way, certainly, than I did. John and Eve, you see, could deal with the CCF from its formation and give its history within a chronological and intellectual context, and that to me was remarkable.

"I was just twenty and we became friends and allies! There were a number of others involved, including a number of young women in the Point Grey club who did not see the world in the conventional sense that their mothers did. They would tell you straight if you were out of line. They felt they had every right to lead lives as creative and rewarding as any men."

What Eve Smith always considered a 'healthy debate' on policies within the party also served to promote and widen the left-right policy divisions within the CCF and CCYM. There was particular concern that the UK Labour party was using troops to defeat a Longshoremen's strike. Said Cameron, "It was a traumatic development to see this ruthless Labour government trying to put capitalism back on its feet. They were prepared to do almost anything to the working class in the process."

There had also been the prospect in BC of the CCF forming a government and the Left was seriously concerned that those who might get elected, the Winches, MacInnises and others, had neither substantive policies nor socialist convictions. As Doug Cameron described them, "Their objective, their principle, their policy, the consummation of all their desires was to form a cabinet and perhaps to implement some mild reforms."

There was no longer any pretense on the Left (with the exception of the Canadian Communist Party—which conveniently changed its name for a period to the Labour Progressive Party) about the failure of Stalin's régime in the Soviet Union to develop a socialist state.

"It had a monstrous government which resulted in the discrediting or disappearance of many Stalinist parties throughout the world as well as Trotskyist groups. It wasn't 'a workers' state' or even 'a degenerated workers' state' as Trotsky claimed. We were all involved in the ying and the yang, if you like, of socialism, social democracy and the recurring schisms and ruptures of party politics."

Doug Cameron then underlined one of the central issues, a critical difference of opinion among leftists. In his view, "the *Regina Manifesto* never did reflect or codify the views of the large majority of the members of the CCF. Not any more than the revolutionary preambles to US trade union constitutions ever reflected the views of Sam Gompers and all the other porkchoppers. Those *Wobbly*-like preambles said they all believed in 'that great-gettin'-up-mornin' and emancipation. Only after the Second World War did they rewrite those constitutions and take out those socialistic-sounding preambles.

"If you wanted to abolish the private means of wealth production in the sense of ownership of the mines and railways and auto companies and have that ownership in common (instead of leaving it all to the Fords and Rockefellers) . . . well, that was *the* dividing line for many of us.

"To illustrate the point, I saw recently on television that in the event of an accident in (coal baron) Dunsmuir's coal mines, he had ordered that the mules and horses would be sent up to the surface first, *before* the miners, because the animals were considered more valuable. As Marx said, miners in Germany, France, Glace Bay and Wales had more in common than they ever had with the owning class, the bureaucracy or the church.

"But the 1914 Socialist International was the end of socialism as a realistic political objective. The parties divided along nationalist, rather than internationalist, lines. The German socialists supported the Kaiser and the rest went their separate ways as appendages of their nation states.

"There are still small groups, the Socialist Party of Great Britain is one, who reassure each other that Marx's prophesies eventually will be fulfilled, that 'history and the stars in heaven are moving toward socialism.' Despite the fact that history seems to be moving in a quite horrible, malignant, self-destructive direction. One member said, 'I can't envision wages under socialism, or money, or private ownership.' Those were the criteria. So, if you accepted any of those despite their cruel and pernicious aspects, you were simply a reformist.

"On the other hand, reform the capitalist and you've reformed capitalism. That has always been the majority view. I'm sure I might get substantial disagreement from the Smiths on that point. They believe there was a betrayal of socialism in the CCF. I don't believe there ever has been a betrayal.

"David Lewis was used as the ramrod of the establishment in the CCF to just run the left-wing rebels into the ground, which he did ruthlessly but effectively on most occasions. Unfortunately, for the Right, there will always be, I think, a small group of idealists who will keep throwing sand into the political machinery, and the leftists include the most effective party workers, the best organized and the most committed."

Doug Cameron felt that when the Left was either run out of the CCF provincial parties (or too discouraged to continue providing ideas, intellectual stimulus or campaign work for ineffectual politicians) the leaders such as Barrett and Blakeney simply put their own intellectually-barren stamp on *their* parties. In effect, each of them became his own party of one!

"Barrett and Blakeney stayed on long after they were finished politically. Barrett not only got rid of his opposition, he effectively got rid of the party.

"However, in the early fifties, Eve still felt it was possible to turn the party back to its roots in the *Regina Manifesto*. I contend that it was only the drafters who (temporarily?) had that ideological commitment, not the party members. But I don't think Eve ever made that distinction. She felt the *Manifesto* was an expression of the party members and if they followed that intellectual guidepost, inevitably they would be successful politically.

"But the CCF should have ended shortly after the war when Mackenzie King tried to bring M.J. Coldwell into his cabinet as labour minister. If King had succeeded, the great majority of CCFers would have been swept into the Liberal party. However, the Liberal backbenchers just erupted in opposition. But King was way ahead of his party in weighing the potential political benefits of merging with the CCF.

"Over time, Eve lost any expectation that party politics would make much difference. It's not likely she believed the world is a lost cause as I did. Anything I've ever joined, I've managed to work my way out of.

"Party politics is just a snare, a delusion. But you can change things by fighting specific issues and you do it by organizing people around a particular issue, whether it's in the factory, in the streets, or wherever. But if you start with a large 'P' political party, and try to generate political issues within that, you're just due for endless frustration and disappointment.

"In the context of this lunatic world, which is totally out of control and which can't be brought under control, having *the* answer, knowing *the* secret, isn't going to help you. It's just going to make your mental stress greater than those who don't care, don't know, and furthermore don't want to know."

To illustrate his contempt for CCF party politics, Doug Cameron then described how Eve had once volunteered him as a CCF speaker in White Rock. He was not then a party member, but was still "hanging around" the CCF.

"It was a black, rainy night and Eve turned off the highway onto someone's lawn and drove right up to the house. And there was this startled chap looking out his window into our headlights. Eve said, 'No, this isn't it,' put the car into reverse, and I often wondered what we had done to his lovely lawn!

"Eventually we found this group of twenty-five elderly people. I doubt they had ever thought about one serious issue in their lives, but suddenly there was an election and life would begin, paradise would be achieved with the election of the CCF. So I gave what I thought was a thorough and exhaustive analysis of how bloody awful the world was. Then the chair asked for questions.

"This elderly fellow in the front row said, 'We all know what's wrong with the world; we want to know what it's going to be like under socialism. That's why we came tonight.' They wanted divine revelation. They wanted to know what it would be like on 'That Great Gettin'-up Mornin' when they entered the Kingdom of Heaven. So I looked down at them and thought, 'Why not send them home happy?'

"I stole those lovely phrases: 'I can't envision money under socialism, I can't envision wages, I can't envision private enterprise, etcetera. I gave them all the old razamataz and they all went home happy with smiles on their faces, and not wanting to deal with the world as it was. It is a secular religion for most of them.

"But . . . the *one* thing they couldn't stand about Eve and John was their *consistency*. They had heard them make the same critiques from 1933 until 1951 and they *hated* them for it. They couldn't stand that commitment to principle, that consistency."

***John Smith** enjoyed visitors, the family pets, reading from the constantly-expanding home library, and his beloved organic gardening—perhaps in reverse order. He won prizes at the local fair almost every year for his delicious, organically-grown vegetables.*

20 A Fixation on Fluoridation

ALUMINUM COMPANIES HAD A WASTE PRODUCT for sale, sodium fluoride, a highly toxic poison. The best they could manage, initially, was to sell it at 15 cents a pound as rat poison, hardly worth the cost of transporting it to market.

Then a bright corporate marketing official decided in the mid-fifties that a refined version of the product could be promoted and sold to local governments to be dumped into municipal water supplies. Our teeth suddenly needed saving. Sodium fluoride, not calcium fluoride, it was decided, would do the trick.

Suddenly there was enormous publicity and propaganda in favour of fluoridation. Eve Smith kept an advertisement she cut from one of the chemical company journals saying aluminum fluoride "would be a bonanza for the aluminum companies" who would now make millions from the stuff left over from their aluminum smelting operations.

This immediately gave birth to the anti-fluoridationist movement, hundreds of people who were soon being beat up by the aluminum companies as "rat poison cranks and crackpots." Among the "crackpots" campaigning vociferously against fluoridation was the best-known radio broadcaster in Ontario, Gordon Sinclair, later a participant in the popular TV program *Front Page Challenge*. He was heard regularly, on his top-rated CFRB news and opinion program, castigating the aluminum companies and city councils for "introducing rat poison into our water supply."

Among the many lesser known but most active opponents of fluoridation in BC were Eve and Don Smith, John Smith and Doug Cameron.

To promote their new "bonanza," the aluminum companies hired doctors and lawyers to promote fluoridation to parent-teacher associations and city councils across North America. Soon the fluorides were introduced to municipal water supplies, often without the public being made aware of it, and the battle was on. What followed, as Eve described it, was "an enormous uproar.

"When they found this had been put over on them many people were furious and they started demanding that the fluoride be removed or not added without a municipal vote."

An issue of *Fluoridation News* published a long list of cities and towns in the United States whose local councils had voted against fluoride, or whose citizens had voted against it or had voted to have it removed.

"In Canada, the aluminum companies got their propaganda mills really rolling. Soon you would go to your dentist and he would want to paint your teeth with fluoride. So we set up a huge and very active anti-fluoride citizens' committee.

"Our main argument was the question of freedom of choice. No one had the right to put a chemical or drug into our water. People would say, 'Well, you accept chlorination; why not fluoridation?' The argument was made that chlorine cleans the water and oxidizes as it comes out of the tap. If you want to be very fussy you can take your water off a few hours before you drink it, and whatever is left of the chlorine will sink to the bottom. The basic difference is that sodium fluoride acts on you, your bones and your teeth.

"The pro-fluoride people said it will stop cavities. You should have it from infancy. In fact, your mother should take it before you're born! Well, there are plenty of minerals that are essential to our bodies, but no one has been able to prove that sodium fluoride is. It was just a huge money-making promotion driven by advertising and propaganda. If ever money prompted people to tell lies, that was one glaring example.

"At a Socialist Party of Canada (BC branch) meeting in Vancouver I said I wanted to speak about our anti-fluoridation campaign. Two or three people said, 'What does this have to do with socialism?' So I asked whether they wanted their city council to put a drug into the water they had to drink when they had no other source of water. If you become convinced that fluoride is good for you, you can buy tablets and dissolve them in your own glass of water and it's very inexpensive.

"They allowed me to speak when I pointed out it was a basic issue concerning freedom. I felt it had been proven beyond a shadow of a doubt that fluoridation was harmful, caused brittle bones and mottled teeth, even at one part per million. We also went into the issue of nutrition's role in the prevention of tooth decay—eating natural foods such as raw fruit and vegetables, avoiding sugar and not eating candy.

"There was a referendum on fluoridation in Vancouver in 1958 and it was defeated by two-thirds of the voters. We went to city council in delegations and presented our case. We had documentation of the dangers of fluoride from some of the top scientists of the world. We had books and pamphlets written by chemists, doctors, dentists and chemical engineers.

"But the power of the aluminum companies was brought to bear in many places. There was a dentist who was editor of the dental journal in Seattle, a Dr McQuinney. He wrote an editorial against fluoridation and was fired. A public health doctor in Trail took a public stand against fluoridation and they sent him way up north as punishment. There was case after case like that.

"Vancouver radio stations had fluoridation proponents on and we would insist they air the other side of the debate. John went on CJOR and we called in our support. People felt strongly about it and we had a terrific organization, even though we were all attacked as cranks and crackpots and faddists."

As the CBC News Director in Vancouver, Don Smith had occasion to be directly involved in the fluoridation controversy while at work. Some of the local dentists in Vancouver had asked one of the aluminum companies' hired guns, a doctor from Washington, D.C., to speak on the CBC.

Northern Times newsmagazine (quoting a highly-respected biologist) later referred to such "professionals" who accepted huge sums of money in exchange for leaving their professional integrity as scientists trampled under foot, as "prostitutes of the biological sciences" or, if one preferred, "bio-whores." So the doctor and his entourage arrived at the newsroom where Don, forewarned of their pending arrival, had prepared for them.

"They talked for a while until Don said, 'We have a set of questions we will ask you on air.' The doctor then said very decisively that *he* would arrange what questions were to be asked, nobody else! Then Don said, 'This is publicly-owned radio and we feel that we, living in Vancouver, have the right to ask you the questions that Vancouver people wish to have asked, and the first question is, what is the difference between calcium fluoride and sodium fluoride. We have heard people say there is no difference and we think that there is and the people of Vancouver would like to ask you that.'

"But the doctor said 'No, I won't answer that question.' So Don told him he couldn't put him on the air on CBC unless he agreed to answer all the questions he wanted to pose. The doctor and his entourage then went out and had a little conference. When they returned they still insisted the doctor would not answer Don's questions. And Don told them, 'In that case there will be no program.' "

Don Smith then asked the doctor whether he gave his own children sodium fluoride tablets with their water. The doctor admitted he did not, and the interview was over. But Eve and Don had to persuade even the CBC to give equal time to both sides of the debate.

"Finally they agreed to provide time for Dr Boucher, a naturopathic physician who had been quite a leading person against fluoridation, and someone we thought would be very good on air. But when we phoned him, he said he really didn't have time to prepare." However, the good doctor was not to be let off the hook so easily as all that.

"Don and I sat up most of the night pulling a speech together for him. He came over, read it two or three times, then went to the CBC and gave the talk.The fight went on for years and, I suppose, in some places, it's still going on."

Doug Cameron explained his part in the campaign: "I helped John and Eve with the anti-fluoridation battle without a great commitment other than the fact that I don't like mass medication any more than I like mass hysteria, mass murder or mass movements. I'm suspicious of them all. But certainly I did not believe that people should be subjected to fluoridation in view of their age differences, their particular health needs and all the rest of it."

It's unreasonable, no doubt, to suggest that the proponents of fluoridation were all in the pay of the aluminum companies. Reputable scientists examining the evidence arrived at different conclusions from their assessments of much conflicting information. But it might be entirely reasonable to suggest that some hired scientists' conclusions were influenced by the fat consulting fees they received directly from the aluminum companies.

21 *Eve's Road to Pender Island*

EVE'S ROOTS IN THE GULF ISLANDS were so strong and deep that it seemed inevitable she would return. Once she had given due thought and consideration to the move, she found the physical and mental adjustment from the hustle of Vancouver to the peace of South Pender Island relatively easy to make.

For one thing, in 1952 she was forty-eight, and it seemed time to commit herself to the Gulf Islands if she was ever to do so. Then, too, her mother had left her $4,000 and Eve could think of no finer or wiser investment than "a piece of the Islands."

Another complication that had a bearing on her decision to move to Pender was her growing affection for her husband's younger brother John, and her probable disaffection for Don.

When pressed about this Eve said, "John? Oh well, I just fell in love with him!" She hastened to add, "there had been no falling out" with her husband. It was simply an honest, respectful growing apart as they developed differing interests, and they were wise enough to continue the amicable relations they had always had.

Still, her decision to move to South Pender Island was not taken lightly. "I was leaving my home and leaving Don. It seemed sort of mean. I didn't exactly admire myself for it."

But Eve retained her dedication to the cause of socialism while Don had changed some of his views, including some they had both once considered socialist. Eve recalled chiding Don for "his regrettable backtracking."

Don was considered the intellectual of the Smith family. So much so that "nothing much was expected of the rest of us," said John. Don showed not the slightest interest in growing vegetables. John, who had some background in gardening, helped Eve to start a garden in Don and Eve's back yard in Vancouver.

John had a room in Kitsilano and saw a lot of Eve. As one friend noted, "John was around quite a bit. In fact, at times he was certainly the star boarder."

On one occasion Eve and John went off to Gabriola Island

together and, as one friend attests, "Eve very much enjoyed her unusual situation," i.e. having the two brothers attending her, and enjoying good times with both of them. And why not?

"Eve was special, a unique personality," said her friend. "She was keenly interested in people. She loved gossip. She *adored* gossip. Her life was constricted in some ways, partly because of limited energy, shortness of breath, and the need to rest most mid-afternoons, all problems related to her several bouts with TB. But still, there was focus in her activities; she had this unusual curiosity and a great range of interests! The world is just catching up with her now!"

When Eve left Vancouver, it seemed to some that it was more like Don was leaving Eve because his passionate interest in life was horses—racing horses. Indeed Don, as a racing aficionado, would head to the racetrack at every opportunity, even to far away Santa Anita. Friends felt he was a fanatic about it. While Eve loved horses too, riding at every chance, even participating in local dressage trials in her teen years, she strongly disapproved of the cruelty she felt was very much a part of horse racing.

Eve finally took the plunge and paid $3,000 for three acres of shrubbery and glorious, restfully-treed waterfront, on South Pender Island. She felt she was home, and it *was*, literally, a plunge: Eve thoroughly enjoyed swimming in the ocean waters bordering her property. Its comparative isolation allowed her the extra pleasure of swimming in the buff, but not without a neighbour or two making a bit of a fuss about it.

Eve's cousin Herbert Spalding who lived on the other side of South Pender owned a small, portable sawmill producing lumber from his own trees. All the cedar siding and flooring for Eve's house came through his mill from trees on the island, but much of the lumber for framing the house was scavenged from the beach. A carpenter name Bob Loosmore and John worked for ten days on the one-room home, starting on the May 24th weekend.

"John's sister, Connie, and I came over and camped. We used to get wood off the beach and make campfires and make the breakfasts and other meals while the men worked. They worked literally from dawn to dusk. Later John built on two additional rooms, our bedrooms.

"I was pretty much alone for six months and it was lovely. John used to come over for a day or two or a week when he wasn't working. But in the many years after we built the place and before we came to live on Pender, we lent the place to anyone who could come. There were seven Smiths and they all came in turn and brought their children, all except Don. We had friends over to our Vancouver house but he never wanted to go visiting. He was a very isolated person. He had bad asthma and he never got accustomed to visiting. John is the most gregarious one in that family."

Eve and Don had bought their home in Vancouver for $8,000. It was sold, eventually, for more than fifty times that amount, according to John. Eve was not surprised, years later, when Don would sometimes send money to his sisters and occasionally to her, although she claimed not to need it.

Don was a confident and talented writer, able to turn his hand from newspaper reporting to colour stories on the horses, political speeches, editing the CCF paper, and then to editing news at the CBC. "But," said John, "he had a certain contempt for literary discussions." As BC's CBC Radio News Director, Don was a busy newsman with few if any literary pretensions, while John prided himself on his literary acumen and ability to quote chapter and—under the influence of vodka—sometimes endless verse.

Eve finally moved permanently to South Pender in 1962 when she was fifty-eight. John arrived to stay a few months later. He had worked regularly as a painter in Vancouver. Eve had met a number of artistic people there, including Ira Schwartz, a classical pianist, who was a friend of Lauren Harris. John was "given a free hand for five years" by the Group of Seven artist to do the painting at his Belmont Drive home just off 10th Avenue.

As his house painting skills became better known on Pender, John got enough work after a year or so to support himself on the island. He also bought three acres nearby and built a house on it which he rented out for additional income. But, said Eve, "Once John got settled in he didn't want to leave."

After Eve had been on Pender for about a year, Eve received a message from Connie informing her that Don was very ill. He had seemed almost cured of his asthma problems when she had left, but he had suffered a severe attack of asthma. She took a taxi all the way to the ferry at Nanaimo at no small expense to get to Don's side as quickly as possible.

She stayed on for six weeks to care for him. "This was good because it opened up our friendship again. He said he hoped I would consider the house mine and stay there whenever I came to Vancouver, so I did." Over the years, when she was still reasonably well, Eve would head to Vancouver or Victoria on occasion to see her beloved ballets and to attend concerts. Said one close friend, "She was bonkers about ballet."

Another contemporary insists that Eve was quite naively convinced, for a period of time, that Don in Vancouver was unaware that John had periodically joined her on South Pender. In fact, all her friends were quite open-minded about her remaining married and friendly with one brother while living with the other. "None of my friends, to do them justice, ever seemed to disapprove of me; they just went right on being friends."

But somehow John was given the impression that some of his new neighbours considered that "living together while not married was quite sinful. It took some of them a few years to realize that Eve was a straight-forward person."

Eve was among the first to join the *Voice of Women* and she felt close to many of the members. "At that time we were all good friends. They were a really sincere, strong group of women. There were a few men as well, including Martin Rossander. Oh, I've heard there were certain jealousies and that women would sort of pick at each other sometimes. But I've only heard about it; I've never seen it."

Living on the island did not cut her off from her investigations and research. Indeed, she became much more focused. "The libraries were always very good about finding and sending books. And I subscribed to many periodicals from the States and from England as well as Canada. I read all sorts of books and magazines on conservation, wildlife, ecology and organic gardening."

Once a year, at least, Eve and John would take a trip "out" from Pender to visit friends or relations or just to experience a different seascape or landscape. "People were quite amused," said John, "to learn we had taken a holiday to nearby Quadra Island." But it was quite useful in forcing them to leave their regular pursuits behind for a few days. "Eve couldn't write her letters and I couldn't garden." (It was during a holiday at Rebecca Spit that they heard on their portable radio that President Allende of Chile had been assassinated.)

"We bought these lots," said Eve, "partly to keep them as wild land. More than half of our three acres was left as wild land—it's still untouched. The front garden area was already cleared when we came because there had been a house here years ago built by settlers named Drummond. They were friends of my parents but their house burned down."

Eve started a garden soon after her arrival, the one she and John later called "the home garden," and John turned the sod for her. When he was away she would spend a couple of hours each morning and afternoon on her hands and knees picking out the bracken roots. These went into her first compost pile while the stones and smaller rocks went onto the trail down from the road.

"Then I would go down to Gowlland Point and fill two buckets with well-dried sheep manure, and then plant the sort of things we could leave—root crops like carrots and beets—so when we returned we'd have food to harvest. I kept a list, just for fun, of the seeds I planted and how long they took to come up.

"When John would come for a few days he would work on the garden fence or the garden hut or the woodshed. I had the garden for the first three years until I developed TB again.

"Ever since I first had TB it was a rule of law that I had a two-hour rest after lunch. I would get so tired, that was the only way I could keep going.

"All we had was a tub and a washboard and John helped with the laundry. But I've always done the housework. A typical day would start with lighting the little camp cookstove and heater. I'd make breakfast—I did all the cooking—and I always made all our bread. We might go down to the beach and collect any lumber that had drifted ashore. In the summer I slept outside under the trees."

Eve and John made or enhanced friendships with people who sometimes badly needed a getaway for a few days from the stresses of life in the city. Just knowing the place was open for their use when they needed it was a comfort to many.

"We would have visitors all summer long. We didn't do much in the way of entertaining, although we sometimes had people for supper. We would go to the Gills' place once a week and play chess, or the two of us would play chess after supper, or read. I would often go to bed early and John would read.

"Sometimes I would be walking in the woods and I'd find a new-born calf that couldn't suck. I'd go to Hope's and she would fetch it home and teach it how to suck. I'd been brought up with boats so for a time we had a little rowboat. But when I got sick John got rid of it because it was too much trouble hauling it up.

"We did our shopping at Bedwell in an old-fashioned country store where you could get food, kitchenware and even hardware. John Freeman would often give us a lift in his Jeep. He was the mailman and he married my cousin, Bea Spalding. He would collect our mail three days a week and take it to the wharf at Bedwell, then row his little boat through the canal to Browning Harbour. The taximan would then take it to Port Washington. From there it went around to Hope Bay to be sorted at the post office in Corbett's Store and then redistributed.

"We used to have Community Club meetings in our homes. Most people came and we would discuss the problems of the island, like highways and spraying, or our opposition to hunting and whether we would allow Bedwell Harbour to be built.

"We saw quite a bit of the Jennens, the sheep herders. Their sheep farm was just over the hill a half mile away in a very fertile valley. The sheep would be rounded up and spend the night on Gowlland Point, especially in lambing season. We used to watch them playing and gambolling about. They would actually play 'I'm the king of the castle,' each trying to stay atop the hill. Then they'd race around the edge of the beach to the end, stop a while, then have another race. As it got darker they'd be sorted out by their mothers who each knew the bleet of their own babies.

"We just loved having the sheep around and I always had a pet sheep or two who would come up to the house. One day we were sitting in the living room and one of the old ewes looked at me through the door and came right up to me. People were so amused with the sheep coming into the house.

"Another time a lamb was born just beside our back step and it became a sort of pet. I would have a pet lamb like this every year, but every spring they would be rounded up and the younger ones taken off to be butchered and you had to get used to that.

"Then there was this big old ewe who would stand on her hind legs, put her forefeet against the wall and push her head in through the window to get an apple. Once when we had a group of kids here we had six sheep coming around the edge of the hut, all of them quite tame and looking for apples. We had such fun with them.

"Some people wanted enclosures for the sheep. One man

said, 'You could actually see manure on the road!' And I laughed, 'Isn't that awful in a rural community! I hope you picked it up and took it home to your garden.' But one good thing sheep do is keep the long grass down and the trails open; that reduces the fire hazard. Of course, I don't believe in killing them to eat them.

"But the majority of residents, some of them non-resident owners, voted to have the sheep kept behind bars, as it were. Yet, it wasn't a reasonable thing."

So, you were either for sheep or against them. Some people never spoke to their neighbours again after the bylaw was enacted requiring the police to impound stray sheep. But there were humorous moments. One farmer was a bit of a wit. A couple of policemen confronted him when they had received a complaint about five stray sheep. "Are these your sheep?" they demanded. He said, "No, I don't know them at all. I don't recognize the expression on their faces." Then another farmer, a bystander, said, "I guess there's nothing we can do; I don't know them either!"

"Uninformed democracy isn't always so wonderful," said Eve. "It may sound great that a majority favours a log boom, or clearcut logging or to have sheep placed in pens, but that doesn't mean these are good things. We need better-informed people to make democracy work well." A point Eve would make repeatedly.

Another issue was spraying. "We stopped the spraying here. But then the whole issue would start up again. They sprayed 2-4-D on the foliage along the roadside which makes it stand there dry and bare and dead."

Eve was an inveterate note taker. She would record what had happened at meetings when she returned home. She would scribble away while the radio was on, making certain to reference the program, the date, the subject matter and the various opinions expressed. She kept dozens of spiral notebooks labelled "Radio Notes." John marvelled at this industry while he was quite content to just listen—and then, perhaps, to forget most of it.

"We'd get up in the dark," said John, "to take advantage of every bit of daylight. And we kept busy. Eve was marvellous at polishing oil lamps. She had contempt for people who didn't keep their lamps clean. For brief periods she had a high energy level. Eve always preferred to eat at home; she didn't like going to cafés. If we planned even a short trip she would make sandwiches. Even as a girl she had done that. She was always packing food away."

John would give some visitors the impression of deep brooding or of engaging his mind in private philosophical thought. It was Eve who would animately engage their guests. She always seemed to know precisely how she felt and where she stood. "Eve certainly didn't suffer from too much introspection," said John. "She didn't go around wondering what attitude to take."

John had earlier delighted in getting to know Eve's father, a retiring sort of person, a self-educated man who could quote many great writers such as Dostoevsky and Tolstoy. "Ralph Grey," he said, "was one of the quietest, most human characters you'd care to meet." John would also quote authors and poets and Eve no doubt saw and admired some of her father's qualities in John.

Speaking about the Gulf Islands years later, Eve said this: "There are advantages and disadvantages. I think it's far better to live here even though they are becoming so urbanized and citified. You can't prevent the horrors of 'civilization;' but you can get some benefits. We have home care now and resident doctors and that enables some of us old folks to remain in our homes."

But not everyone was enthused about Eve's intended "retreat" to the islands. She had mentioned it to her radical correspondent, Matt Glenday, in Carmel, California. Matt replied in his usual "cheeky" tone:

Dear Eve: Carmel, June 9, 1952

I suppose you are building your shack on South Pender Island.

The defeat of the anti-revolutionary forces in BC can now await your pleasure and enjoyment, as you dilly-dally away your time, becoming a beachcomber picking up discarded things drifted up on the beach.

The fires you light from it won't light the road to the Revolution that I thought was in your heart.

I have reconciled myself to hear that you never went to a meeting to heckle those betrayers of the working class movement, and that you never used that ability you had a few years ago to organize group action against them.

Talent you have, but it is now going to hybronate (sic) on the Island of South Pender, ten miles from contact with the rest of the world. Sleep peacefully on your dream island.

With love, kisses and curses—and may your tongue hang out for the lack of water on the island when the revolutionary forces land on that place. Matt

22 *Nukes and Other Hazards*

THE FIRST ANTI-NUCLEAR GROUP Eve was involved with was *Radiation Hazards* in Vancouver. It was formed in 1958 when Eve was again confined to bed but John Smith and Doug Cameron, among many others, became actively involved.

The group made a serious attempt to study many of the problems associated with nuclear tests, power plants and other sources of radiation. They studied the rapidly-proliferating literature including the latest books, anti-nuclear group publications and professional monographs. They formed study groups and brought in renowned experts such as Dr Linus Pauling to speak at many well-attended public meetings.

Eve remembered her mother's reaction to the announcement that the atom was first split: "I don't like this at all." Millions, worldwide, felt a similar, instinctive reaction against the looming potential for nuclear disasters.

"For years we worked on educating people about radiation hazards. We were very active. Dr Pauling came twice to lecture on the subject. We had huge meetings and filled the Orpheum theatre to overflowing. Bob Strachan, the CCF leader, was there and the Liberal party leader, but Premier WACky Bennett didn't show up. Vic Cathers was there representing the BC Federation of Labour which supported the rallies. Pauling was wonderful. He stayed and answered questions far into the night."

By 1962, several anti-nuclear groups had formed in BC. These included *Citizens for Survival*, the *Focus Society*, and the *Gibsons Committee for Nuclear Disarmament.* These groups federated into an umbrella organization, the *League for Total Disarmament.* Based on the principle of non-violence, the League stated its "unalterable opposition to any government manufacturing, possessing or testing nuclear weapons" and supported all practical moves toward world peace.

The aims of the *Citizens For Survival* group were typical of similar groups across Canada, including the organization active at

Canadian universities, the *Combined Universities Campaign for Nuclear Disarmament* (CUCND).

Citizens for Survival said it would actively oppose the production, testing and use of nuclear, bacteriological and chemical weapons; oppose war as an instrument of national policy; urge the Canadian government to disarm unilaterally, withdraw from all military alliances and pursue a policy of neutrality.

Further, the groups demanded "a continuing accounting from government of actions taken to protect the population from radioactive contamination of food, water and air by industry, scientific research, and fallout from nuclear tests."

It was recognized that nuclear hazards originated from sources other than nuclear bomb testing, although that concern, along with the ever-present, horrific threat of a nuclear holocaust, was paramount.

"All of us," said Eve, "refused x-rays unless they were absolutely necessary. We would argue when doctors and dentists wanted x-rays for no apparent valid professional reason." Many of them just took x-rays because they were available. Perhaps others thought if there was one chance in thousands of finding something on an x-ray, it was worth the health risks involved in radiation. But members of *Radiation Hazards* often found that the professionals knew little or nothing of the effects of radiation within their own workplaces.

"I remember going to my gynecologist and I gave him a bit of a lecture on the hazards of x-ray radiation to the genetic pool. Then I said, 'Well, I guess I have a nerve telling *you* all this.' But then he said, 'No, I didn't know anything about that!' Imagine a gynecologist who didn't know that a woman who was pregnant shouldn't have an x-ray!"

At the time there was a major propaganda effort to make it appear that low-level radiation didn't matter. But many authorities on the subject, Dr Pauling, Dr Bartell, Tamplin, Goffman and Dr Caldicott, all stressed the dangers of low-level radiation. Several claimed that all radiation does *some* damage.

The *Radiation Hazards* group joined the *League for Total Disarmament* and other groups to sponsor several marches. One was to the Japanese Gardens at UBC on the anniversary of the date a nuclear bomb was dropped on Hiroshima. Eve went along to demonstrate her solidarity with the marchers, riding in a car most of the way since she couldn't walk very far.

The popular *Vancouver Sun* columnist, Jack Scott, reported on and encouraged participation in the marches in his widely-read column.

The question of keeping US nuclear weapons out of Canada became a major issue in the 1963 federal election. John Diefenbaker, the Tory P.M. who was not on good terms with, nor held in high esteem by, President Kennedy, waffled on the question but finally agreed to allow the US to bring nuclear warheads to Canada to arm the Bomarc missiles.

The Liberal Official Opposition leader, Mike Pearson, had developed a cosy relationship with (and received election planning advice from) the Kennedy clique which was then engaged in escalating its military involvement in Vietnam. After dithering, the Liberals submitted to heavy diplomatic pressure, surrendered Canadian sovereignty, declared their firm support for US nuclear policy and welcomed US nuclear warheads to our territory.

As an NDP candidate running a vigorous anti-nuclear campaign that year (as well as debating and exposing the "gutless, weak, so-called 'nationalist' economic policy" of the Liberal candidate, Walter Gordon) I spoke over a portable loud speaker system, repeatedly attacking the "lapdog" Liberal nuclear policy. I was reassured to see scores of Toronto-Davenport housewives standing on their front verandas warmly applauding my anti-nuclear message. I wasn't surprised when the NDP vote shot up from 6 percent to almost 25 percent in that riding. I *was* surprised when Gordon congratulated me on our anti-nuclear position.

Twice in 1963, BC groups travelled to Comox on Vancouver Island and sat down outside the gates of the US Air Force base. As Eve reported, "Prime Minister Lester Pearson who had, ironically, won the Nobel Prize for Peace, wasn't in office two seconds before he allowed the US Air Force to bring those warheads to Comox."

The Comox-Courtenay area in BC was one of two Canadian Forces bases acknowledged to have received US nuclear weapons. The *League* emphasized that the weapons stationed at the Comox RCAF/USAF base and elsewhere did not defend anyone and did not act as a deterrent. What alarmed thinking Canadians is these bombs had the capacity to incinerate millions of human beings.

Approximately 400 demonstrators attended the first protest. They had allied themselves "with all those who, legally or illegally, openly or clandestinely, had resisted participation in the arms race of their respective governments."

A cavalcade of 48 cars with 250 people arrived by ferry from Vancouver. They were joined by 150 more marchers ranging in age from 8 to 82. The marches started at Courtenay with people joining in where they could along the way, or at the Comox base.

Many of them, including Eve, stayed at the base for a week. She did not camp out overnight but, rather than put her health at risk, stayed with a friend in town and joined in the daily demonstrations. The marchers moved from gate to gate which would be locked before, or just as, the demonstrators arrived.

The resolute demonstrators camped in a farmer's field which had been loaned to the cause. They held meetings there and in the local sports arena. Eve reported, "We leafleted the town but the base was the main provider of jobs for the town which really lived off the air base. Money talks. It was 'economic determinism'—as somebody once said." Keeping as active as possible, Eve wrote a number of articles about the marches at that time.

In April the following year, another group demonstrated against the government's "bunker" at Nanaimo. This was a fairly large "fallout shelter" called a Regional Emergency Government Headquarters. Controlled by the military, it was a rather muddle-headed plan designed to preserve government officials and military leaders during and after a nuclear war.

This was BC's version of the fully-equipped "Diefenbunker" in the Ottawa area named, of course, after the Tory PM. In an hilarious speech about it, MP Harold Winch said "the bureaucrats had thought of everything; in case someone had a heart attack inall the excitement, they had even provided refrigeration for *one* corpse!" The government knew perfectly well that the privileged officials selected to inhabit these bunkers had no better prospect of surviving a nuclear attack than those left outside.

Again the *League for Total Disarmament* was in the forefront of the demonstration, offering transportation to the bunker site and handing out leaflets. Members worked hard to explode the myth that people could survive a nuclear war merely by closing their eyes to reality and hiding in a hole in the ground.

The League also poured cold water on the "balance of fear" argument which held that by having United States nuclear bombs on Canada's soil, the Canadian government was joining in the so-called nuclear deterrent. But, as the *League* again and again emphasized, the only safe shelter from the insanity of nuclear war was peace with binding accords.

"No amount of earth and concrete will shelter us from the consequences of war," said their statement.

The Smiths' friend, Doug Cameron, described how he was among the first to be involved in the *Radiation Hazards* group: "I saw a little ad indicating that some people were concerned about nuclear testing and were holding a meeting at the Unitarian Church on West 10th Ave. I was one of about three men sitting among fifteen or more women.

"The women were outstanding. Bright, articulate, determined, absolutely incredible. I couldn't imagine any group of twenty or so men being in the same class. But the women had little or no experience in organizations and weren't sure how to get their project started. This was in April or May of 1960.

"For my part, I had a daughter who was about to be born and nuclear testing was a personal concern. The motivation was the same for these women. They were worried about the effects on their children of Strontium 90 and Iodine 141 and all the other by-products of nuclear radiation.

"They were about to adjourn and were discussing when to hold another meeting so I spoke up and suggested they consider holding a large public meeting in August on the 15th anniversary of the dropping of the atomic bomb on Hiroshima. They put me on that committee and we all got to work. Shortly after that these *Radiation Hazards Committees* spread all over BC.

"John and Eve got involved. We rented the Kerrisdale Arena and the women brought in Dr Hugh Keenleyside and other speakers. The BC Federation of Labour helped organize it."

This writer represented "the Fed" at an odd meeting at that time at Keenleyside's home. T.C. Douglas, Alex MacDonald and others were to attempt to persuade the prestigious fellow to run as a federal NDP candidate. But the man nervously kept disappearing to an upstairs level as though to physically avoid the question. His "strategy" worked. The question was never seriously posed. But he spoke out strongly against nuclear weapons in Canada.

"The arena was jammed; it was unbelievable," Cameron reported. "These women had developed a slogan: *'No More Hiroshimas!'* and that slogan was picked up and went around the world.

"There were several large meetings of that kind. But slowly, the inevitable happened as the membership grew. Some people started to say, 'Now we don't want to be perceived as against the established social order with the government as the enemy.' So, are you going to operate within the capitalist system, or are you going to operate outside it so you can change the system?

"We defeated a move to have our group join the *Canadian Committee for Nuclear Responsibility*, but a committee was formed to determine how we could best work with that group and they recommended a merger with them. So, just as was the case with the CCF, they organized, sold memberships and we were swallowed up by a majority whose policy was not to rock the boat."

Cameron also said he was not prepared to work with the *BC Peace Council* because of its Communist Party influence. He said they were "the worst of the worst, whether deliberate dupes or unintentional dupes."

Starting with these early, anti-nuclear, anti-war demonstrations, the people of BC were in the forefront in Canada of efforts to educate Canadians about the many questions related to human survival this century.

The peace groups, initially derided as emotionally unstable or mentally unbalanced "peaceniks," (or even as "Commie dupes") have helped to educate British Columbians to the point where Vancouver has periodically held some of the largest pro-peace, anti-war demonstrations in North America.

The *League for Total Disarmament* underlined that the subject of arms control had been on the agenda of every United Nations General Assembly since its founding in 1946, and that world spending on armaments had reached a staggering 120 billions of dollars by 1964 and "continues to rise at a fantastic rate." It showed that the arms race began and continued on the basis of unilateral initiatives by first one side and then the other; and that it could be reversed only by unilateral initiatives for peace. The military budgets, here and elsewhere, they reasoned, could better be spent on life-nurturing rather than life-destroying activities.

The League sought also to "create a bond between those people on both sides of the Iron Curtain who in their daily lives resist their rulers' war machines."

The official declaration that the city of Vancouver was a "Nuclear-Free Zone" was another positive step in that direction.

But years later, US nuclear-armed warships still sought entry to Vancouver waters.

Despite the disintegration of the Soviet Union and its satellites in Europe, the nuclear threat persists in other forms as many other nations, Israel, South Africa, Indian, Pakistan and Iraq among them, continued to develop their capacity to make "The Bomb."

Clearly, the need continues for education about the stupidity and the enormous cost of war, and preparations for war. Canadians owe a vote of thanks to all those who struggled in those postwar years to publicize the nuclear threat and to popularize what seemed to many initially as a rather "kooky" concept: demonstrating and marching for peace.

Eve Smith is remembered as one of the stalwart, courageous, disciplined few who helped establish such groups, and for her participation in all the pro-peace, anti-war demonstrations that her precarious health status permitted.

As the number of nuclear power plants increased in Canada, there were again many individuals who were prepared to ridicule those who fought against them. Eve continued her personal efforts to warn the public and to answer the nuclear proponents. This is but one of scores of letters she wrote on that subject:

April 26, 1975

Editor, *Vancouver Sun,* Sir:

Replying to Mr Tim Padmore on nuclear plants and how those who oppose any increase of radioactive materials in our environment are 'hysterical:' I would like to remind him that anyone who opposes the orthodox is 'hysterical' or 'emotional' or 'crackpot.'

Not many years ago those of us who exposed DDT and others of the chlorinated hydrocarbons and herbicides were 'emotional' and 'crackpots.'

The government and the producers of these chemical poisons were advocating their use long after proof of their hazards had been published and exposed.

Many top-ranking scientists tell us that nuclear plants are not 'clean' or 'safe,' so why should we believe the proponents of nuclear power?

Tim Padmore says that 'solar power is expensive.' So is the James Bay development, the Mackenzie Valley Pipeline, Athabaska Tar Sands, in money, and more important, in destruction of the land and living things.

One platform for offshore oil exploration costs $100 million.

Solar cells store energy. Wind mills can store energy. Methane gas from city and farm can be used for heating and operating stationary machinery. All these things are off the drawing board and in use.

We are backward in Canada.

Mr Padmore stresses the minute likelihood of death due to nuclear accidents, but what about sickness that doesn't kill? And cancer, leukemia and genetic complications?

Indeed, the lack of care exhibited by the promoters of nuclear plants is enough to cause hysteria.

Eve Smith

The Smiths' South Pender Island home, one-time refuge for hippies, draft dodgers, deserters, visiting social planners, and centre for Eve Smith's environmental rabble-rousing and ecological networking.

23 *Happy Home, Hippy Haven*

THE GULF ISLANDS IN THE FIFTIES were relatively uninhabited, unspoiled, and still largely a farming community. They provided a perfect place for anyone seeking a temporary refuge, a place to rest an anxious mind. Indeed, the Smiths' cabin was designed, in part, to restore care-worn spirits. So they built their haven and they thought they knew who would come. But those who later came seeking peaceful sanctum were hardly the revolutionaries Matt Glenday might have wished for.

There was a group of Canadians and expatriot US citizens in Vancouver who assisted draft dodgers and deserters from the US armed forces. So Eve and John registered there, offering to take one person "for a week or two in the summer until he could get used to being in Canada and away from home."

A young man named Ian Sommerville arrived and stayed in the Smiths' hut, just by their back door, for three months. "He was always very pleasant, never the slightest bit of trouble. Before he left, Ian said, 'If I am ever in jail and going to be hanged and they ask me what I want for my last supper, I'll say I want an Eve Smith meal.' Oh dear, it seems so ironic doesn't it? You could have your special beefsteak and strawberries dinner—and then a rope around your neck!"

As more hippies gradually straggled onto the island, they would find their way with packs on their backs to the Smiths' never-locked door and ask whether there was a place they could camp. They were always welcomed.

"There were quite a few people like Jeannie Anderson, Bill Plasket, Rick Gordon among those younger, temporary residents on the island. Some lived in houses of non-resident owners, perhaps doing some work instead of paying rent, or paying very low rent. Others were renting and sharing a house with four or five people. Still others camped in the woods on Alan Brooks' land or on Wyn Spalding's place, or wherever they could find a haven."

John Smith delighted in having the hippies camp on his land.

"It was quite a pleasant scene," he said. "Some of them had put up quite a nice teepee." In return they cut wood or helped John with his garden. He was several times "accused of harbouring hippies. *Harbouring* them!" Nude bathers were discovered at John's place by scandalized neighbours who no doubt watched carefully to catalogue any additional, unbecoming behaviour exhibited by the young and the naked.

"Some of the newcomers got interested in island affairs and wanted to join the Community Club but this became quite a burning issue when some members opposed them: 'We don't want hippies; you know they're just troublemakers and they take drugs.' There was quite a to-do about it but we won the vote. Half a dozen or so joined the club and brought their ideas with them—different ideas that enlivened our meetings.

"The North Pender people wanted an RCMP officer and most of us on South Pender didn't. We felt there was no need for resident police. So a motion was passed and a letter was written by Sommerville to the effect that if you have more police, you have more crime. But those who didn't want the hippies involved and who wanted more control for themselves formed a new group, the Property Owners' Association."

John was incensed by the very name of the organization and wouldn't join. But Alan Brookes and Eve joined to find out what was being done. The first new issue was beach access. Some homeowners wanted to discourage people from using the campsites and the public beaches—or from visiting at all. Others wanted to keep the island rural and insisted visitors have access to beaches, campsites and picnic grounds. Eve and John and some of the hippies were thorns in the flesh of the association members.

"People came to the islands for different reasons, of course. Some wished to be very exclusive—and I don't blame them for that. I would love to have had a quieter time. You do come over here partly to avoid the trials of city life—but often the world's trials follow, and you either take part in life or you ignore it and live an isolated life. One friend said to me: 'I suppose it's a perpetual holiday you're on.' And I said, 'I don't know that I've ever worked so hard in my life.' There was the garden, the housework and all sorts of visitors. And we were not so isolated as all that. We had our radio, and later a TV; we learned what was going on outside the islands and we participated in our own way.

"Some people come to retire and play golf and crib and bridge. That's their life and that's O.K. What I quarrel with is that some of them don't want what they call 'riff-raff' on the island. They don't want to share the islands with people who are different, who don't wear the best clothes, or who may not take a bath every day.

"I hate to see beer bottles and junk left on the beach, but you don't teach people by keeping them away. Local owners still take the beach access signs down. Yes, some of the newcomers were draft dodgers and deserters. That was when people like Ken Clarke and Paul Petrie came here, along with many others. They were met with mixed feelings on the islands. One man said, 'All the dregs of society, all the riff-raff, are coming to Canada.' Another person said, 'You know, Eve, some of them don't even have addresses.' I said, 'Instead of criticizing, it seems to me we should sympathise with people who haven't got a home.'

"Our house became more or less a headquarters, a meeting place for those kids, which pleased us very much. There was another property owner who said to me, 'You know, Eve, I think Bill should marry Joan.' I said, 'Why?' and he said, 'Well, he shouldn't do that to her.' And I said, 'Oh? What is he doing to her?' He said, 'Well, you know, he really should marry her.' He wasn't being unpleasant; he was just unhappy about it.

"Then another man on the ferry one day said to me, 'You know, Eve, all these young people with their long hair and beards. They may all be in disguise, you know. You couldn't tell if they'd just committed a murder or some other crime; they're all disguised!' " Some of these 'disguised' young men had taken great pains to opt out of the US military's murderous folly in Vietnam.

One of those who fell in love with the islands and what they had to offer and who returns often to Pender, good naturedly described for me one of the ongoing struggles over beach access:

Eve had persuaded the highways department to erect beach access signs to help visitors find their way to the non-private beaches but nearby property owners would often take the signs down. Eve would then get the highways people to replace them or, failing that, would put up signs of her own.

When one of the access paths became grown over, Eve asked one of her hippy friends to take her rose clippers and reopen the path. When a homeowner complained, she was told, "I'm just restoring the trail." "But you've cut in on our property, " was the objection.

Shortly thereafter a large tree was felled by a determined homeowner with the clear intent of blocking the trail. In the next tit-for-tat move, John Smith and a neighbour waited patiently at the site, chainsaw in hand, for a low-flying airplane to come along and disguise the noise of their cutting thrusts as once again the path to the beach was opened up. A sign was then added: *"Beach Access, Use at Your Own Risk!"*

Then, in a matter of days, a fence was installed in an effort to seal off access and make a final statement about the property owners' rights. An attempt was made to cover it with brambles so it would seem the fence was old and permanent. The beach access sign was sprayed over in a gesture designed, no doubt, to demonstrate the spirit of compromise: the sign could remain but not the message.

Then, "in Eve's honour," several people got busy and built a new trail just past the corner of the new fence, and John wrote a letter to the local paper, *The Driftwood,* suggesting that the fence "wouldn't last." As the war continued, a gate was installed but before long it was quietly detached and thrown into the ocean.

It was now high time, the owners felt, for a final solution. At considerable effort and expense, machinery was brought in to block access with huge boulders. There could now be little doubt about the owners' intent and determination. Such costly and decisive action would end the controversy once and for all. So there! And certainly the boulders remained there, stolidly declaring victory for the owners.

Time passed and tempers subsided. Then it became apparent that the "beach bums" had not acquiesced. The outline of a rocky stairway was gradually taking shape. Soon the more agile and determined of the residents and tourists could carefully pick their way up and over the boulders and once again take to the freedom of the public beaches.

Was this the final episode? There seemed every likelihood that the undeclared battle over beach access would continue.

Gowlland Point and the Smith house became centres for many of the young people's activities. "A lot of grass was smoked here," said John, "but only rarely did people indulge in too much drinking." Some of John's friends would attest, however, that he was one of those who periodically overindulged, both before and after he left Vancouver.

"John was so impossible," said a long-time friend of Eve's. "I'd drive John home from a party and he'd need to be put to bed. He had this thing about needing to be able to see his car in the morning, so he would risk driving it himself or someone would prevail and drive it for him. Sometimes a friend would go over to see him and he would be roaring drunk and, on one such occasion, years later, found that John had fallen and broken his pelvis."

"There certainly was a lot of drug-taking going on," reported Eve. "There was one young fellow who lived down the road with his girlfriend and he was the first person we knew here who took LSD. He talked about it so much we called him 'LSD.' He said taking it gave him 'instant knowledge' and he would wave his hand at our bookshelves, saying, 'You can take in all those books in one night!' Well, the idea was, 'Why study? Just sit home and take LSD and learn everything overnight.' He was a weird sort of person but I don't know it was the LSD necessarily that made him weird.

"I don't think many of them kept up their drug-taking. By not closing the border to US deserters and draft dodgers, Canada provided something of a political safety valve for the United States. There were a lot of young people at that time who definitely felt they were 'dropping out' of society, but most of them found their way into the establishment eventually.

"We thoroughly enjoyed their company and all of us looked for any excuse to have some sort of party. Everyone would bring some food and we would sing or dance or perhaps have a picnic."

John attended a meeting of the Community Club where property owners talked with some urgency about organizing a vigilante group to alert islanders to the expected misdeeds and apprehended dangers (perhaps even an apprehended insurrection?) of the 'disguised ones,' the long-haired, bearded lads and some of their spunky, free-loving partners.

Intervening in that discussion, John announced that he had written down everything that had been said "and if you ever make any trouble, I'll give this information to the police." John felt his warning had a salutary effect on the more excitable of those present. He hadn't, in fact, written anything down.

But at a later meeting the discussion took a dangerous turn

when one resident actually advocated that the property owners burn down the cabins where the hippies were staying as one way of discouraging their obviously irritating presence. On that occasion John *did* phone the police who then warned the residents against any such violence and vigilantism. That seemed to put an end to consideration of direct action aimed at "cleaning out the hippies" before it got seriously started.

Some property owners raised a big stink, so to speak, about visitors relieving themselves on the beach or in the bushes. But that didn't have to be a problem, said Eve. She arranged for some people to dig a hole at the end of Higgs road and provide an appropriate facility for visitors, but some people felt this action merely compounded the problem. It would bring more people, more distractions, more nuisance value if they provided "facilities."

One of the Island Trustees, Bill Norton, wrote to Eve about the offending outhouse he had "noticed" while attending a Property Owners' meeting at the Ted Madeleys. He claimed it was too near the road and "offends by its proximity" to a house. He asked that it be "moved back by at least 15 feet" so it would not be "in view" of the residence.

Undeterred, Eve wrote to the Madeleys referring to the **"View that Offends"** part of Norton's letter:

He claims that it offends by its proximity to a house. I rather doubt this is your opinion, as a nicely-constructed little edifice is surely less 'offending' than the human excrement and toilet paper that you found in your bushes!

We were very careful to place it where it would not be too close to your place and the Roberts'. We hid it in the thick bushes that grow up very quickly and painted it a pretty green to blend with the backdrop.

This was a co-operative enterprise of public-spirited people to benefit visitors and residents. Stephen dug the hole; Ken built the edifice; I paid for the materials; Doug helped put it in place; Sheila and I adorned it with pictures.

This is the result of a long history of non-action on the part of governments and people complaining about the 'public' that uses bushes and beaches lacking any sanitary facilities.

For some years our South Pender Community Club tried to get the highways department or the health department to provide facilities, to no avail. I did contemplate putting a toilet at the foot of my place (Allan provided one for Gowlland) but the need was at the foot of Higgs road where more people 'go'—as you mentioned to me not long ago—in your bushes.

The (property owners) were in complete agreement that it is not fair to the public that there is no facility, and they gave me the go-ahead. I wonder if a pump house would 'offend.' It is so much a matter of opinion isn't it?

Some people criticised the Allens' cabin; others disliked what I considered the beautiful, ecologically-sound teepee; my own place is disliked by some people, and as you know, your place has been criticized for its domination over the public beach—and so it goes.

The Property Owners' Association has taken no action. Perhaps the pioneering blood still flows in my veins!

Sincerely, Eve Smith

Eve snorted her disapproval of the "back-to-the-landers" epithet and what she felt some people who used that well-worn phrase might be implying by it. In any case, she had no intention of sitting back in a bucolic setting and resigning from the world.

Pender Island seemed to provide a peculiarly stimulating atmosphere for Eve. While she loved her home and surroundings and delighted in the peace she found there with John, she used her freedom (from the demands of salaried work required to make a living) to explore her books, to keep abreast of the outside world and to engage her mind actively in every vital issue that came to her attention.

She quite deliberately arranged the constant inflow of magazine articles, government study papers, radio news and lively correspondence which constantly inundated her home so she could keep learning and keep involved.

So, while she thoroughly enjoyed the diversions provided by the hippies, hipsters and perhaps even an occasional druggie, Eve remained primarily a political animal and she would not for long be deterred from using most of her available energy, time and resources trying in her unique way "to make a difference."

Friends of Eve Smith enjoy a swim and potluck picnic at Gowlland Point. Taken in June, 1974, this photo includes **Chuka**, *Allan Bates (long-time owner of the Point), Gertrude Bennett standing in front of the barely identifiable Paul Petrie and her daughter Monica. Eve (in chequered shirt) contemplates Mount Baker in nearby Washington State.*

24 *The Passionate Ecologist*

EVE SMITH SAW ECOLOGY as *the* central issue of the 1960's, 70's and 80's. Even as a socialist proponent in the early days of the CCF she was mindful of the importance of preserving the natural environment.

"In my early days of socialist activity I soon learned that socialist ideology is not something separate and apart from living and life's experiences. I learned to see everything I did, read or wrote from a socialist point of view.

"It is the same with ecology. It is not in any sense a separate part of our lives, something to be pigeon-holed or written about as a separate subject.

"But one of the things I learned in the CCF and the Socialist Party was their preoccupation with the welfare of humans. They didn't really take into consideration the welfare of the world and everything in it. I had many arguments, for example, with people who felt it was far more important for workers to have their wages than it was for them to stop doing things that were environmentally destructive.

"Those discussions and debates led me to think increasingly about the broad ecological picture and I wanted to learn more about what had seemed so obvious to me: the interconnectedness of people's welfare to their environment. So I explored many books on that subject. One of the best is *Road to Survival* by William Voght. *Hurt Not the Earth* also goes into the interrelationship of living things."

In her teen years, Eve was influenced by her attendance at an anti-vivisection meeting, and while some people thought she shouldn't be exposed to those grisly practices at such a young age, Eve was always quite practical about wanting to learn the full reality—the bad with the good.

"You go to school to learn and to be educated and you should learn what doctors and scientists are doing to animals, even if it is brutal and cruel and a great deal of it is totally unnecessary." Eve was then drawn into the SPCA and began to read magazines and books on animal welfare.

She was unable to convince John to support some of the campaign tactics of the anti-vivisectionists, most of whose actions she supported. But that fact did not affect her views one iota.

As John often said, she was clear and hard about where she stood, but John remained appalled that "they would send out these terrible, gruesome descriptions and pictures. Mind you, Eve recognized that she might personally have benefited medically from the knowledge gained from the use of animals in experiments. But her attitude was, 'Society pays a terrible price for the torture of animals, the endlessly repetitious experiments.' Eve was into it in a major way."

Readers interested in this subject would probably enjoy Richard Adams' book, *The Plague Dogs.* Eve recommended it to me and I found it a compelling read, if not nearly so charming as his *Watership Down.*

"When my uncle, Martin Grainger, was an official in the Forestry Service," said Eve, "I learned about the terrible desecration caused by logging methods in the timber industry and I actually went out to look at a number of logging operations myself to see first-hand the clearcuts and the devastated hillsides."

With her political background, Eve readily understood the economics of the forest industry. "It's simply this: if the forest companies can make a greater profit by being wasteful and by not being careful, then they will—if there are no controls. It is the same with overfishing. Certain species obviously will become extinct."

As any review of a representative selection of her countless articles makes clear, Eve never relented in her efforts to influence others to care more and to take direct action to force reluctant governments and corporations to stop destruction of the forests. She was deeply moved about such irresponsible acts and the legacy such greed was leaving to future generations.

Eve was not blinded by her feelings of loyalty to working people. She felt impelled to write a pamphlet called *The Worker and the Environment* which said: "The working class is culpable" to the extent that it has been the agent in so many environmentally destructive jobs in order to make wages. She did not primarily blame workers, however. She pointed to the industries whose machinery enabled them to do so much damage—much of it irreversible.

It was important to Eve to explain that the term "working class" was not a narrow concept in her thinking—and certainly was not limited to male workers. "We are talking about families and communities of people, the unemployed including people on assistance, the disinherited and their families—men and women and children. People who sell their labour for wages. But the ruling class are those who own the natural resources and industries and property of all kinds."

Eve got interested in natural foods in the 1930's. Her personal health status was a strong motivation. "There was one health food shop only in Vancouver. After quite some time they were everywhere, some more reliable than others." Even though she became deeply involved in the CCF, she continued her interest in food and whether it was grown with or without chemical fertilizers, pesticides and herbicides. That interest led her to natural methods of growing foods, organic farming, an interest in animal welfare, anti-trapping and anti-fur campaigns.

Eve's interests spread out through many areas of ecology and gradually knit together. "It's wrong when people assume that if you are interested in one thing, you're not likely to be interested in others. Animals, as a rule, don't destroy their own environment, while people working within the profit system, the private ownership system, become bent on making money and tend to ignore their environment. For me it became an ever-widening circle of learning and activity, as it has been with others."

Eve joined and financially supported many ecology action groups. She learned that some were broadly conservationist and some had a fairly narrow focus of activity, but she considered that generally a good thing, not a criticism. They all had a role to play.

Greenpeace was concerned about whales and seals, but when people learned about them "it was a natural step then to become involved in a whole heap of other things: the ocean, for example."

Discussing the fur issue, Eve pointed out that time and cirumstances and pressures of various kinds influenced the focus of environmental groups. "There was a time when it was fashionable for certain people to wear ostrich and egret feathers as decorations around their necks and in their hats. The beautiful egrets were killed and feathers were pulled out of live ostriches!

Finally, there was a ban on that activity despite the fact that some people earned their living collecting those feathers."

Eve consistently linked ecological degradation to the ruthless push for profits. She couldn't understand why the truth of that message was not well received by many or why they considered it outdated or irrelevant. In each decade she saw unnecessary environmental travesties visited upon the land and wildlife.

She questioned the value of much of what others chose to call "progress." It seemed to Eve that almost all "development" created new problems for people, for wildlife, for what became known as "the environment" and very few such issues escaped her attention. Despite her diminished energy levels, she managed astonishingly well to keep abreast of a rapidly growing list of ecological issues.

For most people, reading the occasional article on current environmental issues was enough to make them feel sufficiently informed. But Eve was driven to "keep on top" of the issues, and that meant working consciously and diligently to expand and improve her sources of information.

At any given point she was more likely than most to have "the latest" available information and research on almost any issue that arose. Others were quite content to accept the predigested, "politically neutral newspaper stories." But Eve had a passion to know the details—*all* the details—and to dig deeply for other, often more reliable, sources on the issues that emerged. That remarkable capacity is what first drew Eve to my attention.

Eve would write, for example, to US national or state-level *Institutes of Environmental Studies* or to university departments to compliment people on their work, to get her name on their mailing lists, to let them know that "people are watching these issues with great interest" and very often refer them to studies undertaken elsewhere of which the particular researcher or official was sometimes unaware.

Often such correspondents would reply with enthusiasm and gratitude. In turn, they would send Eve still more data. Eve's records contain many files of such letters from organizations, agencies, individuals, from far and wide, thanking her profusely for her interest or for her papers, references or the bibliographic lists she would sometimes provide. They, in turn, would send along their latest research papers and informative letters—all of which had to be answered.

Eve's home soon became, willy-nilly, a sort of informal but busy clearing house for environment-oriented data. And Eve's reputation quietly grew as a person likely to be "in the know." If she became interested in a particular topic and wanted to explore it further, off she would go to the bookstores to buy the latest volume on the subject. When *Northern Times* sent books to Eve and published her book reviews, the editors received more review copies "to be passed on, please, to your excellent book reviewer, Ms Eve Smith." But her ecology resource library and information base grew from many sources.

Eve's partner John was, for the most part, supportive, encouraging and approving. Eve claims to have made all the meals while John produced wholesome sustenance from his beloved garden—and periodically adding cabinets and bookshelves to accommodate the growing volume of Eve's files and books which she continued to collect and use to good effect.

When she attended meetings of the *Voice of Women* or any number of groups, she would authoritatively outline her concerns (she had more than most) and pass around copies of relevant papers and copied pages to support her frequent calls for action.

She took great pains to inform groups, visitors and correspondents of the new concepts, ideas or exposés she had received. Ever the educator, she would often pack along to meetings a box of "goodies:" display books, magazines, photocopies of letters, articles and perhaps an attention-getting poster or two.

Seeing Eve in action at a display table, many people would stop to chat, take home some reading material and then, encouraged by Eve, or inspired by her example, they would further inform themselves and perhaps begin an involvement in some new concern about which they had previously known nothing.

Some people were quite astonished by Eve's unusually strong sense of commitment. Others who encountered her through correspondence, found Eve somewhat awesome. Sometimes, in their letters, they even expressed an abiding love for her. For Eve Smith was effectively *networking* and practising the art of "becoming an ally" long before most of us had heard such terms.

Having lived in the natural splendour of BC's Gulf Islands much of her life, Eve took particular interest in the changes happening on the once pristine islands and the adjacent, huge and beautiful Vancouver Island.

Eve's correspondence with forestry, environment or fish and wildlife officials would be supportive and respectful whenever she perceived as positive their proposed changes in policy or practice.

But she also had an acutely sensitive nose for the false and the phoney. She didn't hesitate to chide them or pour scorn on their halting efforts if she felt they were abusing their positions or neglecting their responsibilities to enlighten the public.

She was likely to become particularly incensed where wildlife was involved. She saw, probably with greater foresight than many professional biologists, the trends toward future degradation of wildlife habitat which she felt was "monstrous, criminal" and certainly *not,* as claimed, professional.

Eve would use such strong and, in her view, totally appropriate, language as she demanded of senior officials, "How can you possibly justify your actions?" Often Eve would have bureaucrats feeling their necks as she probed their inaction. Occasionally she would receive in reply a rather pathetic letter blaming everyone but the writer for habitat loss or ineffectual ministry policies.

Behind the bureaucratese that informed the required responses, one could see that there were some, among these officials harassed by Eve, whose consciences had been pricked by her letters. Others even offered her encouragement and quietly and confidentially cheered her on.

Along with their usual, mandatory comments such as "we appreciate your interest and involvement in these matters," they would often include detailed internal studies or analyses. Once in a while a document not available to the public would come from a ministry office. The message implied was: "We don't like the policy either and it will take a public clamour raised by people like you to get it changed!" Eve Smith would do her best to oblige!

In her earlier years on Pender Island, the mail was delivered only twice per week but there was usually lots of "new stuff" to involve Eve's questing mind.

A typical letter arrived in September, 1982 in reply to Eve's expressed concerns about wolves. Note the candid admission of "management" exercised on behalf of private corporations:

"The majority of Vancouver Island is intensively managed for resource extraction, especially by the forest industry. Numbers of most wildlife species will fluctuate drastically in response to rapid changes in habitat condition, negating any type of long-term 'natural balance.'

"Deer populations are managed according to habitat carrying capacity. Herds that are exceeding this capacity are reduced, for the long-term welfare of the species. The same principle should apply when wolf numbers are exceeding prey carrying capacity, again for the long-term welfare of the wolf population. When the habitat base is intensively managed, other components of the eco-system also require active management to sustain viable wildlife populations and associated recreational opportunities.

"We are continuously striving to incorporate wildlife habitat requirements into logging plans. Over the past decade, we have deferred many areas of old-growth timber that are important deer winter range and provide habitat for many wildlife species. Retention of old-growth for wildlife is presently being reviewed (enclosed is a copy of the problem analysis). The final decision on this issue will be at the political level. It is, therefore, very important that the public expresses its views on this issue, such that the decision will be based on economic, biological and social values."

Eve, of course, would grimace at the very language used. She never considered wildlife a "resource" or plaything for self-indulgent humans. She excoriated the very concept that killing off wildlife populations could be in their long-term interest. "Explain that to the dead deer!" She deplored that, in many instances, only verges or fringes of trees at the top of mountains or along roadsides and river edges were left as totally inadequate wildlife habitat. But Eve would study the papers sent to her, mark them, question them, then systematically inform her network of contacts or interested groups about the new government policies-in-the-making.

Such studies did make Eve more aware of sometimes strenuous inter-factional debates within government, between ministry officials of strongly-held opposing views. This sometimes gave her an opening to pursue, or gave her hope that better policies might be adopted. Beneficial compromises would be encouraged, especially if she and her network of wildlife proponents were kept well informed and if someone decided to take it upon herself to lead the prodding. Quite often, that person was Eve.

But even as she encouraged any actions to lessen the impact of outdated logging practices in forested areas, she had no illusions that a provincial government of *any* political stripe would do little more than continue, as she put it, "to bow to the wishes of their corporate sponsors."

In response to our query about her thoughts on the future survival of the Earth's ecosystems given the increasing number of current concerns, Eve provided this personal testimony:

"While I am basically an optimistic person, it's difficult to be optimistic about the future. For one thing, I think we are being slowly poisoned—and I have said this for a number of years.

"There are many thousands of variations of herbicides, fungicides and pesticides used on our food. They are in the soil, the water, the air we breathe. Their harmful effects just keep escalating, month after month, year after year.

"Some of these terrible chemicals slowly dissipate; others linger on for decades. The effects on birds and frogs and other wildlife is most immediately seen. Entire species are disappearing. So why should we humans imagine that we are immune to damage from all these toxic chemicals? We're not.

"There is an enormous increase in the number and variety of cancers. We spend hundreds of millions on research for magical cancer cures. We spend very little on preventive cancer research. Why is that?

"Chemical companies make billions of dollars selling their chemicals that poison our soil, air and water. They don't want research done that will blame them for our deteriorating physical environment and physical health.

"We are really not very healthy people. Just to survive the pollution all around us is a serious challenge. What can be done? On a personal level, either grow your own chemical-free foods or buy organically grown foods. Don't buy foods supposedly 'preserved' by chemicals. They do not 'preserve' our health.

"The patent medicine corporations make enormous profits because we are a fairly sick society. Look how many drug stores there are with people lined up for their prescriptions!

"If we are to make a real difference, we can't just consider ecology questions at a meeting or while reading a newspaper article. We must be much more aware and live with our concerns every day, every hour of our lives. We must practise conservation in everything we do to the best of our ability. Preservation of the human race is linked directly to preservation of all life, animal and vegetable—and that depends on YOU!"

25 *An Eco-Columnist for the* Times

AS PUBLISHERS OF ***Northern Times Newsmagazine*** from 1975 to 1983, my industrious life-partner and co-editor, Pat Cathers, and the writer-editor of this volume succeeded mightily, many felt, in breaking the restrictive bounds of established journalism by publishing a regional, issue-oriented newsmagazine for almost eight years that was unambiguously pro working class.

With no agency advertising to start with (and no government subsidies) we covered the major political, environmental, socio-economic issues as well as women's and aboriginal concerns from our own politically independent standpoint.

Others had tried a similar project elsewhere in the country but none to our knowledge tested the possibility of making such a hard-hitting publication commercially viable.

Since I encouraged and supported Eve Smith in writing her regular column it may be appropriate to say a little more about *Northern Times*. While groups in Northwest BC had talked and passed resolutions about the urgency for such a publication, we started it with personal savings and a few small, non-returnable contributions offered to help with down payments on photo-typesetting and process camera equipment.

We established "supporting subscriptions" at more than double the normal rate and, to our astonishment, they flowed in. Many thought, as we did, that it was time to establish and support a publication concerned with *real* issues, rather than the usual 'who married whom,' 'who went to jail for petty theft' and 'which service club raised $80 for what local charity'—as vital to our survival as these events might be.

Eight of the first ten business people we approached signed on for advertising. Many were fed up with the local, Conrad Black-owned press. Word was soon passed, however, that some "dangerous people—probably Reds" were starting a paper and a boycott was attempted. After our first issue was hand delivered to the mostly Social Credit-supporting businessmen, one frantic fellow actually took a run at me screaming "communist! out! out!" and promised irreparable physical damage to my person if I dared again to enter his furniture store. A year later we were still publishing but my overly exercised verbal assailant (who had subsequently apologized) was bankrupt. Perhaps advertising with the slightly-suspect *Northern Times* might have helped.

We offered free space (and usually nothing more than a subscription as compensation) to any social activist or environmentalist who could write reports or features.

We had a number of such pieces and columns contributed but had to cover most of the meetings, events, protests, conferences, seminars, rallies, etc on our own. There were myriad other chores required to keep our publication earning and I began to wonder why so many working journalists dreamed so passionately of publishing their own (equally exemplary, no doubt) journal.

So—there was the expected opposition from some business quarters. As well, one union porkchopper bellowed his disapproval (for the benefit of his local coterie of buddies) of this editor's "shame in prostituting his talents by selling advertising." He wanted his C.P.-based political tirades faithfully reported but never once subscribed. Successive NDP candidates requested but did not receive free election advertising space and balked at buying subscriptions. But if they had read only Eve Smith's column regularly they would have been better-informed MLAs.

We kept publishing (despite the lack of support by CP-"leftists" and official "social democrats") because the public response was gratifying. Each month, many encouraging letters and supporting subscriptions arrived. A growing number of business people in Terrace, Kitimat and Prince Rupert welcomed our perspective or were conscious of the paper's steady growth as a good investment for advertising dollars.

When two old tires blew apart during a pre-Christmas rush, a garage owner offered brand new rubber in exchange for publication of his Christmas greeting. "And by the way," he said, "I like what you guys are doing. We've got to protect the environment up here because, once it goes, this part of the country won't be worth shit!" Unquote. When our old delivery truck died we negotiated a contra ad contract for a slightly-used $7,000 four-wheel-drive truck to keep our newsmagazines moving out.

One Socred car dealer initially refused to talk to us. When it was jocularly explained to him that his refusal to advertise in *Northern Times* was tantamount to placing a sign over his dealership proclaiming: "No environmentally-concerned person or union member may buy our cars," he suddenly saw that image of people turning away and cheerfully signed a one-year contract.

When we blasted Alcan for its dubious environmental record within its plant and outside, a man from the lower mainland arrived a week later to personally deliver his cheque for $1,000. It was the same fellow, we discovered, who years earlier helped finance a campaign conducted by Eve and John Smith and hundreds of others against fluoridation of municipal water supplies.

Supportive friends delivered papers to several Vancouver outlets. This brought lower mainland subscriptions—and several reporters looking for work. Our supporters saw the newsmagazine through more than one crisis when printers, under whatever pressures, threatened not to extend credit.

On a visit to South Pender I had asked Eve to write a regular column, initially about food, and had whimsically suggested we call it *Beans & Sprouts.* She frowned for several seconds, wondering whether I was perhaps serious when I teased her about a "somewhat obsessive interest in nutrition?"—but brightened, beamed her cheerful-infectious grin at me and agreed.

We both knew, of course, that her column would soon range far and wide—well beyond the dangers of food additives, herbicides and pesticides. I expected it would stimulate and challenge our readers in Northwest BC. It did, and she soon developed a loyal readership and helped extend our subscriber base to other parts of BC and beyond its borders.

As Eve's fan club grew, we changed the heading on her space to simply ***Eve Smith.*** Never a self-promoter, she reluctantly agreed to have a rather stern-looking photo-image adorn her well read and much-respected column.

There were times when the busy editors of *Northern Times* thought we had opened up a Pandora's *Eve-In-A-Box* with our new writer constantly popping up for attention. One scribbled column (on recycled press releases) included a scrap of paper demanding that a "misplaced" column be published and she enclosed an almost invisible (possibly a fourth carbon copy) replacement.

Or Eve might write a strongly worded (if well-reasoned) response to a published letter which had expressed views she deplored. Her probing intellect seemed never at rest. But often, after expressing her "outrage," she would include a note of praise for our "courage and perseverence" or a squiggle and a mini-sketch of personal concern, affection and good humour.

Eve, as a writer of letters, was sometimes pestiferous. We couldn't always publish her missives but we understood and respected her commitment, appreciated her endless industry, and we loved her. It was with great interest many years later that I read Eve's comments in the transcripts of her interviews about her days as a columnist:

"Vic and Pat Cathers gave me this wonderful opportunity. Writing for *Northern Times* was a great godsend for me. It helped keep me researching carefully and on track in many areas because I had regular deadlines, and you don't write a column in five minutes. Before I had finished a piece I would often have half a dozen books open on my bed. You've got to be absolutely correct. I'd try very hard to be accurate. But I had a lot of fun writing and I was very interested in doing that."

Eve wrote her column between the ages of 71 and 78, a remarkable accomplishment in itself. Few people in their seventies have the commitment to undertake so demanding a task. To do it with such consistent competence went beyond even our confident expectations.

This achievement was all the more astonishing when one learned of her illnesses through that period, her breathing difficulties and the loss of part of one lung. She worked hard despite her low energy levels and the need for regular rests throughout her day—all the result of her several bouts with TB.

Efforts were later made to collect and publish Eve's columns in book form but no publisher was interested. An entire book about the vital issues of our times? "Forget it. Too *heavy,* man!"

Northern Times "covered the waterfront" of public concerns and it would fill several pages simply to list the topics we published. This is a partial list of the subjects Eve's columns dealt with:

Radiation hazards, clearcutting forests, world disarmament, healthy food fairs, solar energy, synthetic food engineering by food technologists, lobbying for parks, citizen involvement, moratoriums on uranium mining, a review of a new book on acid rain, vegetarianism's whys and why nots, needless industrial deaths, the link between food and crime, the great nuclear energy brainwash, the People's Food Commission, Eve's brief to same, x-ray hazards, mercury emissions from pulp mills, killing wild animals for fun, aggression and hostility in sports and hunting, corporate control and patenting of seeds, and scores of other timely topics.

Eve's objective—and ours, as editors—was "to make a difference" in people's lives, to heighten awareness. We hosted a meeting to start a group opposed to Alaskan oil tanker traffic that would have destroyed the pristine Douglas Channel and its native fishery en route to a new, non-essential Kitimat oil port and trans-BC pipeline. Eve wrote a blistering attack on the proposal for presentation to an "oil ports enquiry" environmental hearing.

Eve and several of our writers tracked Alcan's proposed Kemano II massive hydro power expansion that would have flooded more lakes and impacted negatively on additional, major fish spawning territories. The Tory cabinet secretly approved it.

Wondrous, isn't it, that governments give away the rights to valuable future assets at enormous cost to the environment only to have the company sell BC the hydro power surplus to their needs—and at an exhorbitant profit! It's gross incompetence.

Many individuals wrote features of personal interest: one woman on learning to be a labour coach, another on a women's developing tree nursery and activities of the Terrace Women's Resource Centre, another on manufacturing 'home-made' solar ovens and northern soil microbiology and on and on. We covered the lively arts and rich aboriginal culture scene. But ecological issues predominated—and environmental groups proliferated.

We were there to encourage people to learn, to care and to get off their couches and help stop environmental degradation of the sensitive northern ecology—and Eve was one of our tribunes.

Professional educators at Northwest Community College considered *Northern Times* "an excellent and continuing source of current information on issues of vital concern to our students and to future researchers and historians." They lobbied the college administration to retain the material but the officials wouldn't listen. Their back copies of the paper were destroyed, although they remain available on microfiche in university archival collections outside the region.

With college officials holding such attitudes, it wasn't surprising their college graduates were reportedly not knowledgeable, articulate about or even interested in political processes. Well, why should they care?

Eve gave them reason enough: "Rain and sun are the givers of life, yet we 'civilized' people, in our rush for growth, development, progress, jobs and profits, are damaging both essential elements. We are paying a price. The sun is almost blotted out in many places by smog when we could and should be using the sun for heating and cooling systems. Sulphur and nitrogen oxides—the primary agents of acid rain—are emitted from ore smelters, coal-fired generating stations, oil and gas refineries."

But *all* precipitation is slightly acidic, so why worry? Relax. Take a break. Head off to a rock concert. It'll all come out in the wash. And it did! Why be concerned about nuclear power plants when there is a certain amount of background radiation all around us? But isn't that one more reason, Eve argued, *not* to add our man-made artificial radiation which causes cancer, birth defects and radiation sickness?

Eve Smith pointed out the connection between industrial profits, industry-controlled governments, and the uphill struggle to achieve positive changes as each "new" environmental issue emerged—and how industry public relations departments often managed to turn truth inside out and blame anyone but the polluters themselves for their deadly activities.

"Some of the most damaging of industries prostitute the words *ecology, pollution*, and *environment* in their advertising. The Inco plant at Sudbury poured out acid rain over the countryside for decades destroying countless lakes and fishery habitat. Inco then mounted a huge ad campaign saying, 'Today's fight against waste and pollution is *your* fight!' The public's, that is, rather than industry's."

Richfield Oil published a beautiful, full-colour photo of Indian weavings and their ads talked of caring for the earth and conservation. One might picture the corporate executives sitting around in their pinstripes at the feet of the elderly Indian weavers learning their lessons as "good corporate citizens responsible to the good earth," but the reality was somewhat at odds: their oil exploration, production and distribution has been a major contributor to land, air and water pollution—and to waste.

I recall Eve being incensed that her BC Hydro bill "contained a wasteful glossy leaflet" telling *her* how to conserve power! So she wrote to corporate officials explaining how *they* could conserve vast amounts of power—by not building the non-essential Cheekye-Dunsmuir transmission lines, by discouraging the use of power-hungry appliances instead of promoting their sale, etcetera.

*

It seemed, however, that even our environmental Cassandra had made compromises when it came to the strictly non-essential use of electricity. Eve Smith was well known on the islands as a conservationist who practised what she preached. She had burned herself using an electric appliance and this news item appeared in the *Pender Post:*

"The many friends of Eve Smith will be glad to hear she is making a good recovery after painful burns from her electric oven.

"She told us that she was getting along well with the aid of her trusty stereo to help her pass the time in bed. 'But I do hope,' she said laughingly, 'that my electric radiator, Electrolux cleaner and rechargeable lantern don't start acting up too!'

"Readers of the *Post* will remember Eve's recent letter of admonition on the necessity of adopting the simple life. She tells me she is getting copies of her letter made on one of those (electric) duplicating machines they have in Vancouver.

"Get well, Eve. The simple life needs you."

Appended to this news item in her files was Eve's handwritten comment: "This was written by my quite humorous husband!" (John had decided to have a little fun at Eve's expense.) "Actually, electrical things *do* hurt my conscience. I think of all those 8,000 moose and other creatures that were displaced by the Bennett Dam built to create Lake Williston (for hydro power).

"I do try to conserve and use as little as possible. And what is the alternative? Coal oil lamps that cause pollution? We burn wood in our heater and have never yet had to cut down a tree just for wood. We did cut some trees (to make space) for a garden. Our fences are mostly post rail cut from logs found on the beach. It's a problem, whatever you do. But *Use Less of Everything* should be our guide."

Eve then added an asterisk beside the words electric radiator, with the note: "Used *only* in case of emergency in my bedroom when I'm sick!"

Although totally supportive of Eve in most of her ecology-conscious campaigns to conserve, John felt little sympathy for

Eve's effort to re-use "every possible scrap of paper." He agreed it tended to provide a good example to some people, perhaps, but beyond that he considered it "a bit nonsensical." He cited the example of the army in wartime re-using second-hand envelopes. "It was just a lot of impractical foolishness."

John would grin and shake his head at the thought of Eve's considerable intensity. He felt Eve "took on far too much," especially considering her health status. John also noted that Eve's commitment to vegetarianism "wasn't total." On a rare occasion he would buy and cook a tasty cut of meat just for a change of diet. Eve would dig right in and enjoy it "if it was there and cooked and in front of her. She was not about to waste a good roast of beef." Thankfully, her sense of humour prevented her from being obsessively absolutist in her vegetarian preference.

Visiting a friend in Vancouver, I was chagrined and amused to discover that one of my letters to Eve had been forwarded (with her scrawled comments filling in the margins and backs of the typewritten pages). I wrote to her cheerily, chiding her about this "ethical lapse" and demanded equal access to all her friends' correspondence. Eve never bothered to obscure her own or others' flaws. It was much more fun to disclose them.

Later, in her eighties, Eve still wrote letters to editors and friends, urging them to action. Asked how she managed to keep so aware, she replied, "It's one of the advantages of aging. In the course of time you have to learn things don't you? I'm not as careful in my filing as I used to be, but I can often remember which book or magazine I've read on a certain issue so I can again turn to it for reference when I'm writing." (Matt Glenday tried with little success to teach Eve proper filing practices.)

"After all, I'm just a lay person who finished only first year high school, so it's been important for me to quote authorities, professionals to back up my arguments so no one can say, 'Oh well, who's she anyway? She has no letters after her name.' "

There was never the slightest doubt in Eve's mind that her efforts were important and worthwhile. She admired enormously the exemplary work of dedicated researchers in many specialized fields of study.

Eve never considered herself an alarmist or anything but a responsible citizen in passing along her concerns about corporate/governmental irresponsibility vis-a-vis the environment.

When we informed Eve that we were soon to cease publication (and I was to work as a native communications education director) she wrote: "My *raison d'etre* has expired with *N.T.!*

"It was my last effort, except for letters-to-editors and politicians. The best things should be the last to go! In these times you'd think there would be enough people who would want to keep *N.T.* going. But capitalism has made us more self-centred and less caring of ethical matters.

"Much love, regrets and sorrow. Eve."

Eve told me in person how much she had "enjoyed being challenged" by her editors. She had a remarkably strong will and convictions and she loved debating the issues. It was fun for her, and I knew she missed the give and take of her earlier years as a political activist. Corresponding, while enjoyable, had been a poor substitute for direct verbal debate, at which she had excelled.

She also said that many of her correspondents claimed they agreed with her probably just to shut her up! But that her *Northern Times* editors "would never be guilty of such a sin."

As publishers we felt no regrets in moving on to other, equally interesting projects. But we knew Eve would miss the work on her column and the broad exposure her ideas were given by our publication. We felt sad about ending that—but it was time for Eve, then nearing eighty, to slow down a little.

Many people who met Eve through her column continued to write to her to exchange views, affectionate greetings—and *news clippings*—for years! Rummaging through her papers I chuckled to find some of my own intense correspondence with Eve. Points of agreement had been checked or marked with approving exclamation marks. My views of apparent dubious quality had been red-circled for later discussion—and debate!

There were also letters from longtime mutual friends and one-time colleagues, some deceased. It was no surprise to see that they had also greatly appreciated and treasured Eve's ability, ideas, lively spirit and affection.

One remarkable friend of mine, Bill Harding of Regina, who had also worked unrelentingly and effectively over the years to focus attention on vital issues, and especially to involve younger people in his generation's political struggles, had written to Eve:

"You continue to amaze me with your determination and productivity! It's cause for celebration for all of our generation!

"But I wish there were more 'mature citizens' who would remain relevant as they grow older and adopt the retirement syndrome. I have just returned from a family visit to Victoria where I met many old friends. But they have all retired in the classic sense—golf, bridge, entertaining—no contact with the younger generation except their own kids and grandkids. Glad to be back with my associates in the struggle—mostly in the 20-45 yr. age group!

"Two things must receive attention here (in Regina) in addition to the ongoing struggle to stop uranium mining, the Cruise, unemployment, women's rights, etc. The first is to fully expose the new P.C. gov't for what it really is. They are financing their drive for 'free' enterprise the same as other gov'ts, by cutting services built up over the years. The other job is to begin building the political alternative by alliances with environmental, farm, labor, women, health groups. We've had an Ecology Alliance but it was narrow, not in policy but in membership. So something has to grow beyond that and, of course, there is no alternative but to work consistently at the grassroots.

"I feel humble using 'new' paper when I write you. Even though they are leftovers from the 1960's.   Best wishes, keep well. Bill."

*

Here were Eve Smith and Bill Harding, two of Canada's lesser-known heroes, respectfully encouraging and saluting each other. (Bill had led the battle against mining uranium in Saskatchewan.) How blessed I felt to have been able to count them, and a few others like them, among my most cherished friends.

There were several emotional retrospective moments as I sat in Eve's old chair on Eve's deck outside her book-lined kitchen-living room-workplace, going through her wealth of correspondence, much of it in similar vein, between seasoned but time-worn activists of struggles, won and lost, for social justice and environmental sanity.

There were letters from many veterans of far too many political wars against the destroyers, the wreckers of nature and of hard-won social services and of caring in our communities. "Those who so struggle, no matter where," (this quote from Camillo Cienfuegos came to mind) "are our true brothers and sisters."

As I said farewell to John Smith and packed to leave South Pender Island—taking Eve's transcripts and some of her papers with me—I wondered about the many gormless, feckless politicians who could not and would *never* understand.

26 *Soc-Dems / Predictable Failures*

TO FIGHT FOR DEMOCRATIC SOCIALISM or submissively to accept a pattern of hesitant gradualism along with the more or less predictable failures of social democratic reformism. That was the choice facing leftists participating in the CCF.

For many BC leftists it was no choice at all. Some, with a solid grounding in socialism, either had to win the CCF to a socialist perspective—over a period of time—or get out. Other leftists were prepared to fight on for years in an admirable effort simply to provide some spine and substance to party policies.

Over time, many found such gradualism both intellectually unacceptable and emotionally intolerable. They left rather than participate in elections to little purpose, i.e. to elect people who obviously didn't know what they were about or who at best were engaged only in mild reformism—or even politics for the fun of it.

Most certainly some of the social democrats, while conscientious reformers, had little interest in or understanding of Democratic Socialism. In that sense, Eve Smith felt, the social worker David Barrett was typical of such would-be reformers. He had run afoul of the Socred administration by becoming a CCF candidate in 1959 while employed by the provincial corrections service.

Barrett's most consistent issue was simply that he had been fired by the Socreds. He was quite delighted they had provided that platform. And no question, he was a fun guy. Whatever else happened, Dave was going to enjoy himself. Clearly, it was a game for him. One wag later said, "Thank heavens he brought a sense of humour to politics with him because he brought little else."

I invited Dave Barrett to my BC Fed office early in 1961 to meet a group of nominally leftist members of the *New Democratic Youth*. He was asked almost immediately whether he was a socialist and to his credit he gave a direct and honest answer:

"When I decided to run for election and won the nomination I was asked by my campaign manager, Laura Albers, whether I wanted to get elected or wanted to be a socialist. I asked if that was my choice, one or the other, and she assured me that it was. So I decided then and there that I wasn't a socialist and that I wanted to get elected."

The central problem with that choice, Eve felt, was that such social democrats generally lacked policy focus. "It became a rather pointless exercise," said Eve, to give so much attention to one's personal electoral prospects and strategies. "Such people failed themselves and their party. They don't concern themselves to learn what democratic socialism means. Rarely do they demonstrate an interest in socialist policies." They might engage, as did Barrett, in strenuous self-promotion for perhaps a dozen years and eventually form a government, and only then begin to ponder what to do.

I saw abundant evidence of that when I represented 'the Fed' at joint labour-CCF meetings to determine policy for the founding convention of the BC NDP. The CCF side had relied on Grace MacInnis to write and present the draft policy. When it became evident that Grace was ailing, the CCF leader, Bob Strachan, was reluctantly dragooned into the role of policy provider.

Strachan's spare few lines on each of several topics were greeted with polite, if not stunned, silence. The witty Alex MacDonald suggested, "We need an attention getter; we need to jazz it up a bit; how about adding something about rapid transit?"

I had been a Fed official for only a few months with my editor's union credential as an *American Newspaper Guild* member (plus my non-acceptable card as a *Teamster*). I had just recently served as *National CCF Youth* organizer. Strachan's papers offered nothing to attract new trade union support or to differentiate the new NDP from the old CCF or, for that matter, from the Socred government in office—and I said so. Bob Strachan good naturedly replied that he wasn't "tied" to his few "introductory lines" and he'd be happy to have me "flesh things out."

I was surprised by the leisurely, non-commital approach of these élite players of the BC CCF. Despite their years of involvement in which to refine CCF policy objectives, they had astonishingly little to offer the new CCF-labour alliance. I wrote the policy papers over two late evenings. I conscripted friend and then *Vancouver Sun* journalist, Bill Deverell, to write a one-page "health plank." The policy committee gratefully accepted this effort and didn't change or add a word. With only minor changes this hastily drafted policy overview was enthusiastically endorsed, by the founding convention. I had expected much more debate.

I had previously expressed surprise at BC Fed meetings that neither the Fed nor the CCF had a clearcut position on hydro policy in opposition to WACky's planned, long-term hydro give-away to the US. The Fed General Secretary, the easy-going but occasionally fiery Pat O'Neill, shrugged and said, "so, write something." My four-page summary presentation of a proposed new water and hydro resources policy, written after a month-long review of available research papers, was passed unanimously by both the Fed and the founding BC NDP conventions.

O'Neill, incidentally, decided personally that the Fed would not pay the proposed increase in the cost of printing the Fed's paper. His quite mad solution was to put a down payment on a monstrous printing press, have it installed at the Fed office, and put a young woman secretary in charge of it.

As then editor of *BC Labour,* I watched with a mixture of alarm, chagrin and amusement as hundreds of sheets billowed out of the press with my brilliant but now ink-smeared and mangled editorial comment filling the room. The husky novice press woman then brutally attacked the sensitive cams on the unco-operative machine with a long, heavy-duty screwdriver and massive mallet. Unwilling to witness the further disfigurement of the beautifully-finished press, I promptly left. After further abortive efforts to "make" the press produce our paper, O'Neill could be heard a block away threatening to throw it piece by piece into the street if it wasn't immediately removed. A strange year, 1961!

For Barrett and perhaps most of his fellow (and instantly "new") Democrat candidates, the goal of the electoral game was merely to replace WACky Bennett. The "ins must be got out, and the outs must get in." But once "in," in 1972, what then?

To wake up one morning and realize one is "the boss of all bosses," the province's premier pol, was probably an enormous personal gratification. Both "WACky" Bennett and "Buffooning" Barrett served lengthy legislative apprenticeships. Some felt their very perseverence and longevity in the legislative precincts was deserving of the reward of the premier's office. The major difference was that W.A.C. *knew* what he wanted to achieve.

Barrett had only the vaguest notion of *social* reform and no serious interest in involving himself in *economic* change. What to do? To feel comfortable in the new role one surrounds oneself with sycophants: uncritical buddies, consultants and communications advisors. But they had precious little to communicate.

So, Dave, now that you're premier, what's the program? Give us time; we'll think of something. Meantime there is role-playing. A person with Barrett's sense of fun and practised ability to articulate was able to baffle 'em with buffoonery. He quickly adopted the old mushroom-growers' technique: "Keep 'em in the dark and feed 'em bullshit!" And, when in doubt, take the boys out for Chinese!

An expensive makeover of the premier's office furnishings including a few tiffany lamps added a touch of innovation to Dave's personal aura but nothing to a distinctive political message. One could try to emulate WACky and take on the finance portfolio. "What's that? We're short of funds? Find me a rich sheik and let's make a deal. What a headline! *'Jewish premier educated by Jesuits borrows Big Bucks from Arabs!'* Who needs those rich bankers in New York?" Fine, Dave, but what's the program?

"Hmmm. I can always pop into a BC Tel office from time to time and let on that I'm taking over!" Can't do that, Dave. They have a federal charter. "Hmmm. Well, what did that Saskatchewan CCF treasurer do? What's his name? Clarence Fines. Government auto insurance! The good old SGIO. Great issue: reduce the outflow of BC cash to US insurers. Cheap car insurance."

Fine! But Dave, you're a social worker. What about poverty? What about reforming the welfare system? And the health business? They say that doctors' incomes are climbing out of sight! "But how? What did the other parties do? A commission, you say? A study? Who've we got? Bring in Dick Foulkes, M.D. He's got ideas. He'll come up with something."

But what about those dozen years in opposition? Wouldn't that have been time better spent developing a program? "Ah, but you don't understand politics! If we'd got specific about what we intended to do, we'd only have created targets for Bennett and the press. Best to wait till you're in office. We just waited till people got really fed up with Bennett—and then we got our chance."

A chance to do what, a study? "Hey, it'll be great, the most comprehensive provincial study of health and social services ever." Except for Quebec's Castonguay Report? "O.K., but we'll spend a million or two and nobody can say we're doing things precipitously. Call us anything, but not precipitous!"

So a potentially useful *Health Security Programme Project* was commissioned. (Nobody will claim responsibility for that name!) "If it's not too precise, all the better. Publish the reports in great, heavy tomes; never mind summaries; baffle 'em with *quantity!* At least it'll show we're doing *something.* Take the heat off! Who else has done such a major review of health and social services?"

Quebec. But will you implement it? "Are you kidding? It's just as well the two irrelevant ministers (Human Resources & Health) don't get along. That's as good an excuse as any for not getting serious about the substance of the report—if any."

In 1973 I was invited to do a study of community health centres across Canada. I asked facetiously whether it was for the *programme* or the *project.* Nobody knew. And nobody thought it amusing. Along with other assignments, I produced a book-length study-report on CHCs from BC to Quebec and some of the more interesting HMO's (Health Maintenance Organizations) in the US Northwest. The *Project* director included fifty-two excerpted pages in one of the aptly-named "tomes" of his *HSPP Report.*

The disinterested health minister, an insurance agent, had no love nor time for Dick Foulkes and dismissed the massive *Project Report* as "a mere green paper." In the jaded minister's view (he didn't have the capacity to study it) it was a mere think-piece. It certainly wasn't considered a blueprint for action. Indeed! It was, therefore, in the main, a waste of time, talent, energy and funds.

Some aide had told the health minister that this socio-economic planner was "a secret red and must be fired." A red what? Foulkes asked. "Well, you know; one of *them!*" The termination was attempted but my salty, hand-delivered note to the premier's office (threatening to behave noisily and publicly) led to a countermand. I later transferred my consultancy to the Human Resources Ministry to head up a Social Policy Secretariat.

But the same, red-baiting treatment was accorded a researcher friend in the ministry of education. Maybe because she stayed temporarily with us, we wondered? No. Could it have been her Porsche? The light dawned. Obviously it was her murderous *Russian* Wolfhound that made off with a few local chickens! She just *had* to be "a red" to harbour a killer dog named *"Che!"*

Where was the social worker-premier in all of this? Too busy, perhaps, being his own finance minister, another failed attempt to emulate the dictatorial, all-powerful WACky Bennett.

The recommended guidelines for CHCs were all but ignored when six "experimental models" were introduced as a tiny, tentative and typically social democratic reformist step. If the government had been any less certain of its plans or more hesitant about them, perhaps nobody would have noticed.

So, instead of a province-wide, region-based plan to co-ordinate and improve health and social services, to lessen the reliance on doctors by training nurse-practitioners, to bring together multi-disciplinary health teams, and (not incidentally) to place a great many more doctors on salary (removing them from the disastrous, open-ended, chargex-like payment system) the NDP ministers remained unfocused and achieved little of great note.

When that happens in any administration, you have to go looking for "the boss." Unlike W.A.C. who watched his ministers closely, Barrett allowed his ministers to wallow in their confusion. Still, the "buck" stopped with the social worker-premier-finance minister who failed to provide leadership. And there was nobody around who dared (like Al Gore speaking to Clinton) to tell Barrett to "get with the program!" Mainly, perhaps, because there was no discernable program.

Eve Smith had been for years in BC one of the serious socialists who tried to educate the public to demand fundamental changes to the health system. She wrote a well-reasoned presentation and submitted it to the *Health Security (Programme) Project.*

I was intrigued and delighted that her paper called for a revamped system of health maintenance and preventive health education. She emphasized the need for *quality* in nutrition! Let's keep people well! It's cheaper and it's smarter! Move away from the medical model (part of which was buying non-essential high-cost, hi-tech diagnostic apparatus for every local hospital).

Push hard, suggested Eve, to promote personal responsibility in health matters. Get *serious* about banning cigarette and alcohol lifestyle advertising. I agreed wholeheartedly. Also, said Eve, it was time to remove the doctors from their pedestals!

I had written earlier that "doctors must be considered merely health workers, not demi-gods; that we should bring them back to reality and prevent them from dictating health and social policy! And only when everyone else has a decent job and nurses are much better paid, should we pay docs more. Meantime, *put them all on salary!* It will be a chastening experience."

Get real, I was told; they'll all head south! Not so. Many physicians who did ship off to the US—also a chastening experience— soon returned, for their sanity! Some whose primary focus was outrageously high incomes, remained (happily for Canadians) far away in some of those doctor-worshipping US states.

Thinking about Eve and her leftist colleagues, one sees that many like her who gave up working within the CCF/NDP, persisted in trying to influence the social democrats through various studies, commissions and publicly through their activities in many issue-oriented groups.

So let's admit that Eve Smith and many others on the Left did, in fact, indulge in much-despised "reformism" in that sense. Readers may find it difficult to see why any leftist working outside the bureaucracy believes his political honour somehow less besmirched than those who struggle for change from within.

Indeed, many CCF/NDP supporters disappointed with the reformist leadership, continued to work within government and outside for stronger policies based on socialist humanism. They would not accept the common currency that idealism and ideology are passé. They believed that incremental improvements made life that much better for some people. That was sufficient.

That, of course, is arguable. People have varying levels of tolerance for what they may consider a major disappointment or even a betrayal. Personally, I was more than keen to move on.

One should remember the physics prof who insists that you can push on something as hard as you like for as long as you like, but if nothing moves you aren't actually doing any work (or having much success). That's precisely how some socio-economic planners felt when working with one or more CCF/NDP régimes.

Did the Barrett ministers make *any* fundamental changes during their brief sojourn in office? Leaving aside my own firmly negative response (which would surely arouse the ire of many fond admirers of Dave, their beloved funnyman) let's turn instead to the view of the late George Woodcock who had a mind of broad compass, certainly one capable of evaluating the bumps and pimples occasionally erupting on the broad face of BC politics and placing them neatly into appropriate historical perspective.

In reflecting on "the continuities that environmental circumstances" dictated to British Columbians, Woodcock generously ventured that even he was hopeful (after twenty years of WACky) "that with the NDP an era of promise seemed about to begin."

Many of those who held even modest expectations of the long-awaited NDP government were disappointed. Woodcock said, "Dave Barrett and his fellow social democrats in fact represented no greater change in the political, social and economic situation than any other exchange of power between parties.

"In terms of real transformation in the state of the province (the Barrett government's) effect was no more than that of an electoral hiccup."

Woodcock identified the "narrow boundaries" of political life in BC and this was illustrated "by the little the social democrats could achieve." They "did no more to shift BC in the direction of a balanced socialist economy than its predecessors had done." And not nearly so much, in my view, as WACky.

The "tough guy" Lands and Forest minister, Bob Williams, took over four failing mills which their owners had proposed in any case to abandon and added a few sundry items to a modest portfolio of government-owned operations. This was all too reminiscent of the Saskatchewan CCF's early shoe and box factory failures. No, fellows, you don't fulfill a socialist mandate to get involved in resource development by bailing out failed businesses!

This was hardly the socialist imperative to "take control of the commanding heights of the economy" advocated by CCF moderates (and even by David Lewis) for many years.

It was left to Bill Bennett, the pale imitation of the main-man Socred, his father WACky, shortly thereafter to make a mockery of Bob Williams' tentative approach to government involvement by giving all British Columbians (including the non-British) five shares each in BRIC, this modest little portfolio of holdings.

These so-called "free shares" in the *BC Resources Investment Corporation* soon plummeted to five cents! Mine are framed as a symbol of joint NDP/Socred economic folly. Where are yours?

The press had speculatively appraised the fuzzy-minded politics of the forests minister as "hard-nosed socialism." Well, hard-nosed, perhaps. Williams "bulldozed" to get his way, in and out of cabinet—but focused his energies on his personal portfolio, including his downtown Vancouver pub. To each his own élixir.

There was still another major opportunity, in the conception of the *Burns Lake Native Development Corporation,* to hammer out a deal with the status and non-status Indians of the BC Northwest's Lakes District, to extend to them the opportunity to work their way into a controlling interest in a huge new regional forestry development—and to provide a renewable economic base.

The majority native ownership opportunity I recommended would have represented a significant breakthrough and a long overdue expression of confidence in groups of aboriginal people in BC to learn to run their own economic and social affairs. But the NDP didn't have the courage to move dramatically and imaginatively forward. It became only a modest change to brag about.

A huge, private forest giant was brought into the deal in still another major forestry resource giveaway by the social democrats. Big business as usual—and not a *sustainable* model! The province took a stake, leaving only 24 percent for the native residents who included skilled forest industry workers, loggers and experienced mill hands who also had by far the most valid claim to ownership of the woods as a resource, and the right to exploit them.

Generally, Barrett's ministers evinced no sustainable drive or clear social goals! The government differed not in any substantive way from either its predecessor or successor Socreds.

What Barrett offered, said George Woodcock, was "a matter of style rather than the substance of radical economic action."

Barrett did not have the political smarts to understand that directly antagonizing the entire labour movement in BC was like chopping off one of the legs of his three-legged stool. He made himself an easy pushover. The NDP "was voted out in 1975," said Woodcock, "largely because it legislated three striking unions back to work." Also, he adopted the favourite posture of social democrat leaders: "We are governing for *all* the people." He would have been better off politically to adopt, candidly, his party's predisposition to improve opportunities, working conditions, wages and welfare. His political friends and longtime backers would have stuck with him. Even his political enemies would have admired and respected that degree of political consistency.

Although the NDP billboards and campaign leaflets proclaimed, *"Vote Barrett for Strong Leadership,"* the government, sadly, had few solid achievements to give substance to the claim.

John chats with an animated Eve in 1986. Her essential oxygen supply, treasured correspondence and incoming (ready-to-recycle) press releases are all close to hand. Said John, "Eve was usually quite cheery, even when she had every right not to be."

27 *What, After All, is "Progress"?*

FOR EVE GREY SMITH, longtime socialist, naturalist, activist, ecologist and writer, two central themes of her life were her challenge to her peers to consider more carefully how they might take much better care of the Earth and what she called "our fellow creatures;" and to constrain (if it was not possible to overthrow) a system whose structure encouraged personal and corporate greed.

Eve finally gave up on direct political party activity, but not before giving all her strength to it for twenty years. Her ecology-related activities soon escalated and consumed most of her life.

In the early 1960's, Eve was asked to contribute to a patchwork of commentaries and reminiscences about the Gulf Islands. It was typical of Eve to select a theme which would remind readers to question the process and the end results of a preoccupation with "development" and so-called "progress."

No person who knew Eve Smith for only a brief period of her long life could make a fully adequate appraisal of her humanity, her politics, her caring, her passions. As in much else in this book, Eve here again speaks best for herself.

Written thirty-six years ago, and looking back some thirty-five years from 1961, Eve Smith remembers her early days on the islands and sounds an urgent alarum for us all:

"PROGRESS"—WHAT IS IT?

By Eve Grey Smith, South Pender Island, BC, 1961

The other day, a newcomer to these islands, who is busy 'developing' a certain area, said to me: "These islands are just coming into their own."

I replied: "I think they are *losing* their own."

"But you can't stop progress," he said.

To those who are engaged in operating marinas, motels,

shopping centres and beer parlours; tearing down trees and tearing up land, progress is represented by financial success and, in fact, this sort of development has come to mean 'progress.'

And in the process, what is happening to the development of our minds? As we become more and more involved in mechanical and scientific progress, what is happening to the human personality and character?

I think of a time thirty-five years ago, while travelling from Victoria to Vancouver on one of the CPR Princesses, gazing with love at the islands, and wishing that I could dive in and swim to them instead of going on to Vancouver. A woman came up to me and said, incredulously: "What can people do on those lonely islands? Do people live on them all year round?"

This thought brought me back to the world around me with a jolt. I took a deep breath and replied: "Yes, people live there all year round, many of them for the express purpose of escaping the stress of modern city life, to find peace and seclusion. What do they do? Well, there isn't enough time for them to do all the things that they want to do; yes, chores take longer without modern mechanical conveniences, but is the development of character and personality, and the ability to live a satisfying life dependent exclusively on electric power, running water and the easy accessibility of a market?"

Are the islands coming into their own? Where are the regattas of 45 years ago? Do you remember when dozens of launches and a few sail boats anchored at Ganges, or Gossip Isle, or Cowichan Bay, and we had splendid swimming, rowing and diving contests? Walking the greasy pole to a laughing, shouting, cheering crowd? Did you ever reach the end and grab the flag before taking a header into the sea? I never did; high diving and swimming were more in my line. The Payne children usually won the rowing races. But now most people have power boats, and few of us know the beautiful feeling of dipping oars into the water, and the thrust forward of the boat, and at night, when phosphoresence marks the oar's downward sweep, and battling a headwind, and learning to feather the oars.

Think of all the people who come to these islands for holidays, to escape the city for a precious few days, just because they are undeveloped. There are fewer and fewer such places for these people to go to; while the need for them increases.

Some of us would rather have trees than bathtubs.

Think of these people, after a few days, looking more relaxed, forgetting their tranquilizers and headache tablets, eating heartily, going for long walks and enjoying the rural scene: sheep, cows, maybe a deer fugitive from the 'sportsman's' gun, investigating the tide pools not yet polluted from industrial waste, as has happened in so many places; or just sitting and thinking—perhaps just sitting.

Certainly clearing land is quicker and easier, with 'cats' and bulldozers, than in the old days when you put a stick of dynamite into a stump and then burnt it out, then plowing the new land with a yoke of oxen or a team of horses. Then your garden had the benefit of their manure and you had the pleasure of their company. There were no great unsightly stacks of rubbish and roots to provide a fire hazard.

To some the sound of bulldozers and power saws is sweet music; to others, music is in the waves and wind in the trees, frogs in the pond, and birds singing.

Those of us who are lucky enough to be able to see trees from every window are, perhaps, the envy of people who live in man-made deserts, where forests have been hacked down and water levels have been lowered, and the balance of nature has been disrupted with devastating results to all and sundry.

To the Mexican who walks three miles for a bucket of water, it's not much consolation to know that the timber magnate has three swimming pools.

Fishing is easier now, though there aren't as many fish; sitting in a swank boat, in a comfortable chair, smelling the poison fumes from the exhaust instead of rowing or, as in times past, when one of the skills of the Indians was raking for herring. The rake was about five feet long, with nails driven through one end, making a comb, similar in appearance to a dog's comb. I remember seeing Indians at the west end of Active Pass, raking in the herring as they passed on a fast tide, or spearing rock cod. Now that is done by skin divers with oxygen tanks!

Raising sheep always has been one of the major industries on these islands. Certainly shipping them in earlier days was a bit of a chore. South Penderites had to row them over to Saturna. My father on Samuel Island would row either to Hope Bay on North Pender or to the Saturna wharf; six miles and 'always a head tide' he used to say.

In those days the land was not overgrazed and stock did not get artificial 'store bought' food supplements, synthetic hormones and antibiotics.

And the folks then had plenty of time for fun, picnics, bathing parties, fishing trips.

There is a far more frequent boat service now, with 'outer islands' ferries that are a great boon in many ways. But they also bring more people with guns to blast away at A.M.O. (any moving object), deer or the odd cow or sheep perhaps.

Forty or forty-five years ago a boat made the round trip out of Victoria only three days a week.

But, perhaps, when there is all this talk of 'progress,' and 'development,' we should bear in mind that where business excess and expansion is achieved at the expense of the beauty of the countryside, *this is in no sense progress.* It represents, rather, *the dissolution of the best values we have.*

There is an urgency in the need for us to recognize the inter-relation of all living things.

28 *Quietus*

EVE INTERRUPTED HER INTERVIEWS frequently to rest or to revive herself with oxygen kept at her bedside. She talked matter of factly about her deteriorating health and with seriousness and good humour about social change and politics.

"I've been asked whether I was scared of dying. Not at all. But being sick for a long period of time? I hated that. I was sick all last winter, feeling just miserable month after month. That's worse than pain.

"A reasonable and intelligent person would be depressed to some extent, but I am blessed with a rather ebullient spirit and it's much easier to take your trials cheerfully if you can. It's easier for yourself and for other people."

How did she keep her spirits strong and sustain her sense of humour in the face of her debilitating illnesses?

"Well, you know, there are an awful lot of things going on that can make you laugh—and there is so much of interest in the world, so much to do. Life just isn't long enough to do a fraction of the things I would want to do. It seems to me so tragic to hear people who have retired say they have nothing to do." She hooted at that ludicrous thought.

"Someone asked me if I was resentful about growing old. No. But I have been so restricted for most of my life by TB. I know I could have done so much more—and perhaps have written better.

"If I hadn't been ill I would have finished my nurse's training. I might have had a completely different life if I had married and moved to Scotland and perhaps never taken to socialism. But long before the days of the CCF I had a certain independence of thought and a perversity of mind that led me to take my own view instead of the conventional line."

No one disputed that. Was she hopeful for positive change?

"There is a tendency away from resistance and rebellion. There aren't so many rebels left, it seems. However, there will always be a revulsion against reaction and accepted orthodoxy.

"I *do* think people have become too *supine*," said Eve. She wondered, at eighty, "whether the young people coming along will have what it takes to carry on with the struggles. They seem not sufficiently radical or militant. They need to be more confrontational. I think people put up with far too much. They should be far more demanding.

"The wealth is there in Canada; it is quite sufficient. There should be no poverty. The food is there; there should be no food banks or malnutrition. There should be much more militancy, more use of sitdown strikes and picketing to close places down if necessary. We've got to take actions that are much more drastic, more provocative—even more outlandish."

Laughing, she said, "I listen to today's politicians of all political stripes as a sort of penance and to keep track of them; not because I have any expectations of most of them.

"People should read Arthur Train's *The Blind Goddess*. She, of course, is justice. Train said that 'the worst criminals are not in jail and the worst crimes are not indictable' and I believe that."

Now that she was approaching the end, perhaps, of her life's work, did she remain hopeful for positive change? Did she expect there would be a resurgence of radicalism?

"Welfare and unemployment insurance have decreased the inspiration, the desire for radical action. In depressions, people developed revolutionary ideas by personally experiencing poverty. But then—there also comes a time when people are so poor they're utterly demoralized and they're beyond taking action.

"And you know, one of the worst crimes of all is *totally needless poverty*. People should read Bernard Shaw's introduction to his play, *Major Barbara.* Shaw said poverty is the worst crime and the cause of most of the distresses and troubles that people have."

Eve was deeply concerned about her generation's irresponsible behaviour—the ecological legacy it was leaving future generations. With finality, Eve said, "Will even poverty matter if the natural world becomes degraded to the point of being unable to sustain itself? Then, no amount of "riches" will help any of us."

She shared the view of Rachel Carson that departments of agriculture and environment were little more than window dressing and mostly public relations efforts. As I write, Agriculture Canada still, in 1997, has no approved biological herbicides, and the hapless Ontario environment ministry is being eviscerated.

Eve remained incensed that we still plunder animals as though they were insensate objects, and that our "people interests" always take precedence over theirs.

In Eve's view, we were not, in fact, engaged in "sustainable" use of the natural world, but rather in its inevitable destruction—unless we experienced major attitudinal changes. She saw little evidence that was happening or would soon happen.

If we were indeed a superior or "chosen" species, as many liked to claim, we would not, with such mindless simplicity, see all of nature as a mere warehouse for human exploitation. Too many still considered old trees "useful" only if they were pillaged and wildlife "useful to us" only if it was "harvested."

She regretted that all of nature had become, in our people-driven world, nothing more than an appendage of "the people economy," to be processed and distributed for humans.

Eve simply never bought into the idea that the massive destruction of natural areas by "developers" was necessary, good or natural or that they had any "right" or "mission" (divinely or selfishly inspired) to "manage" nature. She predicted that our inability to preserve vast natural areas would result in the diminution of the human spirit and personality. That process presented a clear and present threat to humanity's—and the natural world's—continued existence.

*

As for the politics of the 1980's, Eve felt that her democratic socialist colleagues of the 1950's had dealt with political and social realities with a seriousness and thoroughness that reduced, by comparison, the social democratic oratory of the CCF to empty, irrelevant verbosities and the policies of its successor NDP to platitudinous twaddle. A damning indictment.

*

Before I left John's South Pender home he told me it had been Eve's firm wish to be buried in her garden. When interviewed on this subject years earlier Eve had said that if John predeceased her, she would do her best to have his body buried directly in the soil of their beloved home garden. A final, anti-bureaucratic battle? John told me he had confirmed that it would be too difficult to deal with the legalities of a home burial so, when Eve's time had come, her ashes were brought home to enrich the soil of the rose beds she had enjoyed and lovingly tended.

In my thoughts of Eve there stand out her intelligence, infectious good humour and lively spirit, her unusual degree of involvement, her profound caring for all the natural world, and her concern and joyous affection for young people. She delighted in knowing them.

Eve was quite direct. As John said, she did not waste a lot of time wondering where she stood. She worked conscientiously to inform herself—wished, fervently, that all Canadians would do likewise—thus she *knew* what she knew. She reserved special scorn, by the way, for those who refused to care and she had great difficulty understanding them. At best, she considered such attitudes and behaviour to be foolish and reckless.

Eve Grey Smith, through a quite remarkable lifetime of passionate endeavour and exemplary commitment, established a solid standard, a touchstone of personal conduct, for her friends, colleagues, associates and readers—indeed all Canadians.

Eve wanted to urge all Canadians, youthful ones particularly, to have confidence in themselves. But she also wanted them to understand that *the future could not be left to take care of itself.* It needed diligent, disciplined nurturing (like an organic vegetable garden) and intelligent, responsible action on their part.

Only that could secure and assure their future.

In conversation with me years ago, Eve said she longed for the political leadership in Canada of a visionary such as the first leader of the CCF, the gentle J.S. Woodsworth—or a Eugene V. Debs. In 1938, said Eve, Woodsworth had called for . . .

> *"something of the reckless abandon of youth,*
> *a sublime confidence in the future, a faith*
> *that cries . . . it shall be done!"*

Even with the serious health problems that afflicted her, Eve herself, in the minds of many who knew her well, provided much of that "leadership of a visionary" that she longed for in others.

In addressing here Eve's life and times, we can but hope that her spirited example might inspire another generation of similarly committed, provocative—even outlandish—rebels, if that's what it takes to move our world to saner purpose.

Eve Smith delighted, almost to the end of her active and fruitful life, in using her abilities to the fullest in support of the causes she believed in. Her friends and colleagues said she maintained an extraordinary degree of commitment. Many described her as "amazing and unforgettable."